**Juulchin**
TOURISM CORPORATION OF MONGOLIA

# MONGOLIA

WITH JUULCHIN CORPORATION

# NATIONAL UNIVERSITY
# LIBRARY    SAN DIEGO

## JUULCHIN
**Tourism Corporation of Mongolia**
Chinggis Khaan Avenue 5B
Ulaanbaatar 210543
Mongolia
Tel: + 976-11-328428
Fax: + 976-11-320246
E-mail: juulchin@mongol.net
Website: www.mongoljuulchin.mn

## *North America*
**Mongolian Travel USA, Inc.**
707 Alexander Road, Suite 208
Princeton, NJ 08540
USA
Tel: + 1-609-4194416
Fax: + 1-609-2753827
E-mail: mongoltravel@juno.com
Website: www.mongoltravel.mn

## *Europe*
**Mongolei Reisen GmbH**
Chausseestrasse 84
10115 Berlin
Germany
Tel: + 49-30-44057646
Fax: + 49-30-44057645
E-mail: info@mongoliajourneys.com
Website: www.mongoliajourneys.com
www.mongoliasafari.com

*Enjoy and Love* ... *h us!*

Airphoto International Ltd., 1401 Chung Ying Building,
20–20A Connaught Road West, Sheung Wan, Hong Kong
Tel. (852) 2856 3896; Fax. (852) 2565 8004; E-mail: odysseyb@netvigator.com

**Distribution in the United States of America by**
W.W. Norton & Company, Inc.,
500 Fifth Avenue, New York, NY 10110
Tel. 800-233-4830
Web: www.wwnorton.com

**Distributed in the United Kingdom by**
Cordee Ltd.,
3a De Montfort St.,
Leicester LE1 7HD, United Kingdom
Tel. 0116-254-3579
Fax. 0116-247-1176
Web: www.cordee.co.uk

Library of Congress Catalog Card Number has been requested.

ISBN: 962-217-689-5

Edit and design: Michael Kohn
Maps: Tom Le Bas
Cover Concept: Au Yeung Chui Kwai, photo by Etienne Dehau

Photography by Etienne Dehau (pages 10, 16, 18, 19, 44, 51, 68, 72-3, 77, 80, 86-7, 90, 95, 97, 101,
104, 108, 112, 118, 136, 137, 154, 159, 165, 168-9, 172-3, 176, 186, 187, 190-1, 193, 196, 200, 201,
204 top right, 208, 210, 214, 219, 222, 223, 246-7, 250, 265, 268, 272, 273, 284-5, 292, 304), Mick
Ellison (pages 4-5, 251, 254, 255, 257, 260-1, 263), Michael Kohn (pages 9, 27, 33, 69, 76, 91, 109,
119, 122, 125, 140, 146, 158, 211, 228, 233, 241, 242, 243, 269, 294, 296, 297, 301), Sweetwater
Travel (pages 126, 127), Graham Taylor (page 161, 204 bottom, 281, 293), and F. Van Belle (page
204, top left).

Drawings by N. Bat-Erdene (pages 88, 107, 171, 188, 277). Painting, p. 242, by Senge-Tsohio,
compliments Danzan Ravjaa Museum, Sainshand. Archival photo, p. 256, 258, Copyright ©
Museum of Natural History, New York. Copyright © Mongol Empire map p. 58-9 National
Geographic.

Production by Twin Age Ltd, Hong Kong
E-mail: twinage@netvigator.com
Printed in China

# MONGOLIA
## Empire of the Steppes

Text by Claire Sermier
Photography by Etienne Dehau

Translated by Helen Loveday
Additional text and photos by Michael Kohn

# Contents

*Previous pages: a lone palaeontologist searches for dinosaur bones in the Gobi.*

A NOTE ON SPELLING

Several different systems exist for transcribing Mongolian. The one used in this book aims at facilitating the pronunciation for the foreign traveller and may not satisfy all specialists and purists. The spelling of place and proper names follows the system used most consistently in Mongolia. In a few cases, the commonly-accepted English spelling or usage has been replaced by the Mongolian word; specifically Chinggis Khaan rather than Genghis Khan, ger rather than yurt and ovoo rather than cairn.

*Above: the mosaic of Soviet-Mongol friendship at the Zaisan Memorial, Ulaanbaatar.*
*Below: young equestrians in Dornod Aimag.*

# Introduction

Mongolia has become fashionable, and one hears much talk about its beauty and the power that emanates from it.

Yet a journey to Mongolia is a trip like none other. The problem of the language, the difficulties one experiences getting around and finding supplies, and the huge distances to cover are all obstacles to be taken seriously.

But travellers who can drop their usual habits and requirements, and be ready to listen and to learn, will be able to appreciate properly the exceptional discoveries that can be made there. The pastoralists of the steppe have managed to preserve ancestral customs and traditions, which continue to influence their thought and behaviour deeply. What particularly impresses travellers is of course the beauty of the landscape but perhaps even more so the way of being and the values that these nomads have perpetuated in the heart of Central Asia, traditions which predate the existence of the Mongol empire. The attitude of the herders, their sense of hospitality, their great tolerance, their openness, their relationships with one another, with symbolism, with time and space cannot leave one indifferent.

These nomads, profoundly impregnated by the great open spaces across which they move, have always had a profound respect for nature and in general for the elements which surround them. They are proud, but simple and profoundly happy to be alive.

# Facts for the Traveller

## Getting There

Most visitors to Mongolia arrive via air or rail. The following information on plane and train departure times and arrivals is subject to change without notice and must be checked before setting out.

### AIR

**MIAT** (Mongolian International Air Transport, www.miat.mn), Mongolia's national airline, connects Mongolia to Russia, China, Japan, South Korea and Germany. Flights are limited in winter and extra flights are put on at the height of tourist season. The days listed below are normal summer scheduling.

MIAT flies between Ulaanbaatar and Beijing on Monday, Wednesday, Friday, Saturday and Sunday. Flights between Ulaanbaatar and Hohhot in Inner Mongolia (China) travel on Monday and Thursday. **Air China** has flights between Beijing and Ulaanbaatar on Tuesday, Thursday and Friday. It connects Hohhot and Ulaanbaatar on Monday and Thursday.

MIAT flies Ulaanbaatar to and from Moscow and Berlin on Thursday and Sunday. Other MIAT flights go regularly to Irkutsk (Siberia), Osaka, and Seoul. Aeroflot has flights from Moscow to Ulaanbaatar on Tuesday and Friday.

A **Kazakh airline** used to fly between Bayan-Ölgii and Almaty in Kazakhstan. Financial problems forced the suspension of this flight in 2001, but it may resume at any time. Check with the Kazakh Embassy in Ulaanbaatar (Email: kzemby@magicnet.mn, Tel: 312 204) for details.

MIAT also operates internal flights from Ulaanbaatar to most provincial capitals, up to three times a week depending on the destination. Cities on the railway line, including Sainshand and Sükhbaatar, are not serviced by the airline. Domestic fares for foreigners can be two or three times higher compared to the local price; but with a letter from their employer, foreigners working in Mongolia can purchase a card (US$50) allowing them to travel for the local price.

**Hangard Airlines** (Tel: 9911 5735) is a private airline that flies on a regular schedule to Ömnögov and Khövsgöl. Another option for domestic flights is to charter a light aircraft from the reliable **Blue Sky Aviation**. This service is used mainly by aid agencies and mining companies working in Mongolia, but can also be reserved for tour groups. Tel: 312 085 or 9911 2937.

Buyant-Ukhaa airport is 17 kilometres west of downtown. **Departure tax** for international flights is US$13.

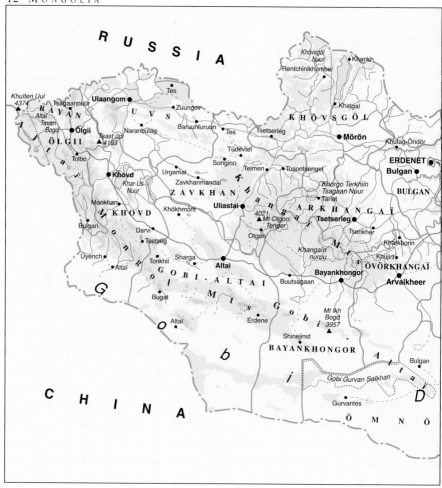

——————— Main Road

——————— Secondary Road

——————— Aimag Border

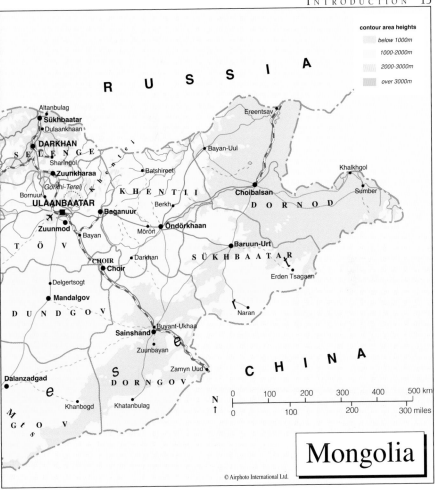

contour area heights

below 1000m

1000-2000m

2000-3000m

over 3000m

R U S S I A

Altanbulag
Sükhbaatar
Dulaankhaan

Ereentsav

DARKHAN
S E L E N G E
Sharingol
Zuunkharaa

Bayan-Uul

Khalkhgol

Batshireet

Khalkhgol

Bornuur
Gorkhi-Terelj
ULAANBAATAR

K H E N T I I

Choibalsan

Sumber

Baganuur

Berkh

D O R N O D

Zuunmod
Bayan

Möron
Öndörkhaan

T Ö V

Baruun-Urt

CHOIR
Choir

Darkhan

S Ü K H B A A T A R

Erden Tsagaan

Delgertsogt

Mandalgov

D U N D G O V

Naran

Buyant-Ukhaa
Sainshand

C H I N A

Zuunbayan

Dalanzadgad

Zamyn Uud

D O R N G O V

Khanbogd
Khatanbulag

N

0    100    200    300    400    500 km

0         100              200         300 miles

Mongolia

© Airphoto International Ltd.

National Park

Principle Monastery

Temple / Monastery

Museum

Airport

For further information, contact:

MIAT, Ulaanbaatar, 8 Little Ring Road. Tel: 325 633, fax: 313 385. Ticketing Office 322 273. Buyant-Ukhaa Airport. Tel: 379 935, 379 519, fax: 379 973, 379 919 Aeroflot, 15 Natsagdorj Street. Tel: 323 321, 320 720.

Air China, Bayanzurkh district, 12th Horoolol two-storey yellow building on the Big Ring Road. Tel: 452 548.

*MIAT representatives abroad:*

Moscow: First location: Sheremetevo Airport, 4th floor, room 635, tel. 7 095 578 27 59, Telex SITA code SVOAPOM. Second location: Spasopeskovslii Pereulok D7/1, Moscow. Tel: 7-095-241 0754, fax: 241 0752, Telex SITA code MOWTOOM.

Irkutsk: Room 04, Ulistsa Lapina 11. Tel: (007) 3952 344530

Beijing: *First location:* Beijing Airport. Tel: (86-10) 64 590 225, Telex SITA code PEKAPOM. *Second location:* Beijing Branch Office, China Golden Bridge Building, East Gate, Ai Jian Guo Men Avenue, 100020 Beijing. Tel: (86-10) 650 79297, fax: (86-10) 650 77397

Hohhot (Inner Mongolia): Xin Cheng Qu Ulan Aiao Qu 5, Hao Lou. Tel: (86-471) 430 3590, fax: (86-471) 430 2015. SITA code: BJSHTOM

New York: 350 Fifth Ave Suite 1421, NY 10118. Tel: (212) 279-6990, Toll free: (800) 642-8768, fax: (212) 279-6602.

Los Angeles: 16250 Ventura Blvd. Suite 115, Encino CA 91436. Tel: (818) 990-7842, Toll free: (800) 642-9768, fax: (818) 501-2098.

Toronto: 1235 Bay Street Suite 801, Toronto Ontario M5R3K4. Tel: (416) 921-3545, Toll free: (800) 642-8768, fax: (416) 972-0185

Vancouver: 1166 Alberni Street Suite 1406, Vancouver BC V6E3Z3. Tel: (604) 684-6428, Toll free: (800) 642-8768, fax: (406) 681-8953.

Berlin: Branch Office, Chaussee Strasse 84, Berlin 10115. Tel: (30) 284 981 42, fax: (30) 284 981 40.

## RAIL

The train from Beijing to Ulaanbaatar takes 30 hours, and the Trans-Siberia express from Moscow lasts four to five days (Ulaanbaatar to Moscow is slower). The train timetable, which is subject to change from season to season, is as follows:

Trains from **Beijing to Ulaanbaatar** leave on Tuesday (no. 23) and Wednesday (no. 3) at 7.40 am. Train 215 from **Hohhot to Ulaanbaatar** departs Sunday and Wednesday at 10.40 pm. Going the other way, trains go from **Ulaanbaatar to Beijing** on Sunday (no. 24) and Thursday (no. 4) at 8.50 am. Because train no. 24 originates in Moscow (and seat availability is unknown), sales start less than 48 hours prior. Train 216 travels **Ulaanbaatar to Hohhot** on Wednesday and Sunday, departing at 9.15 pm.

Train no. 6 from **Moscow to Ulaanbaatar** departs on Wednesday and Thursday at 9 pm. Train no. 4 (Tuesday, 7.55 pm) travels from Moscow to Beijing and stops in Ulaanbaatar. From **Ulaanbaatar to Moscow**, train no. 5 goes on Tuesday and Friday at 1.50 pm. Train no. 3 from Beijing passes through Ulaanbaatar on its way to Moscow on Thursday at 1.30 pm (ticket sales begin less than 48 hours prior). Train no. 263/264 plies between **Ulaanbaatar and Irkutsk** on a daily basis, and takes 36 hours.

## BUYING TICKETS

The International Railway Ticketing Office in Ulaanbaatar is located in a yellow building 200 metres north-west from the station. Tel: 94194 and 94133, fax: 322 994. Open from 9 am to 1 pm and from 2 pm to 5 pm; Saturdays and Sundays from 9 am to 2 pm. The international ticket room is upstairs, book early in summer. In Beijing, tickets can be bought at the station or at the CITS office in the Beijing International Hotel.

# Visas

For most nationalities, a visa is compulsory whether you are staying in Mongolia or just in transit. Thirty-day tourist visas can be obtained at Mongolian embassies and consulates; visitors no longer need invitations. Three-day transit visas are also available for those en route to Russia or China.

A few nationalities are currently allowed visa-free travel in Mongolia; including citizens of Hong Kong, Israel, Malaysia, Poland, Singapore and the USA (90 days). Other nationalities, including UK citizens, pay £25 for a 30-day visa, and £20 for a transit visa. Visas can also be obtained upon arrival at the airport in Ulaanbaatar or at the train border crossings, for US$50 (two passport photos are needed).

The tourist visa can be extended for up to 30 days. Submit fee and application at the rear of the Foreign Ministry in Ulaanbaatar. Overstaying a visa will result in a fine upon exiting the country. Foreigners working in Mongolia on a single entry visa will need an exit visa (US$20) to leave the country.

## REGISTRATION

Visitors staying more than 30 days must register with the police. The Foreign Registration Office is located in the Chingeltei district, Little Ring Road 5A (in a real estate agency building north of the Mobicom building). Tel: 313 259 or 325 796. Registration details are dependent on visa status, and are subject to frequent changes. Call for up to date details.

*The aeroplane 'graveyard' at Buyant Ukhaa airport.*

## PORTS OF ENTRY AND EXIT

International flights arrive and depart from Buyant Ukhaa airport (Ulaanbaatar). The train passes through the frontier posts of Sükhbaatar and Zamyn Uud. The other frontier posts are closed to foreigners, unless they are in possession of a special authorisation from the Border Patrol (*Khiliin Tsergiin udirdakh gazar*). The passport must be valid for six months after the exit date from Mongolia. Newly arrived visitors must fill out a declaration form with the amount of money (unlimited) they are bringing in and declare any objects of value. This form must be kept until departure. Keep all receipts for expensive purchases, especially souvenirs. Antiques and fossils can be taken out of the country with a special certificate and receipt from an officially licensed dealer. Because of increased smuggling, bags are randomly searched at train stations and airports. The export of animal furs is subject to special authorisation.

## MONGOLIAN EMBASSIES & CONSULATES ABROAD:

**Great Britain:** 7 Kensington Court, London W8 5DL. Tel: (171) 937-0150, fax: (171) 937-1117.

**United States:** 2833 M St NW, Washington, DC 20007. Tel: (202) 333 7117, 333 7017, fax: (202) 298 9227.

**Canada:** 151 Slater St, Suite 503, Ottawa, ON K1P583. Tel: (613) 569-3830, fax: (613) 569-3916.

**China:** 2 Xiushui Beilu, Jianguomenwai, Beijing. Tel: (86-10) 6532 1810, fax: (86-10) 6532 5045.

**Russia (two offices):** Ul Borisoglebskaya 11, Moscow 121069. Tel: (7-095) 29 06 792, fax: (7-095) 29 16 171. Ulitsa Lapina 11, Irkutsk. Tel: (7-3952) 42370, 42260.

## FOREIGN EMBASSIES & CONSULATES IN ULAANBAATAR:

**China:** 5 Zaluutchuudyn Örgön Chölöö Avenue. Tel: 320 955, fax: 311 943.
**Canada:** Suite 56. Diplomatic Services Corps, Bldg 95. Tel: 328 281, fax: 328 289
**France:** Apartment 48, Diplomatic Services Corps Bldg. Tel: 324 519, fax: 329 633.
**Germany:** 7 Negdsen Undestnii Gudamj. Tel: 323 325, fax: 323 905.
**Great Britain:** 30 Peace Avenue (eastern section of Peace Avenue), near the Wrestling Palace. Tel: 458 133, fax: 358 036.
**Russia:** A-6 Peace Avenue. Tel: 326 836 or 372 851, fax: 327 018.
**United States:** 59/1 Big Ring Road (west of the Selbe River). Tel: 329 095, fax: 320 776.

# When to Travel

As one of the highest and most landlocked countries in the world, Mongolia is subject to extreme continental climate—with scorching hot summers and long sub-arctic winters. The average temperature in Ulaanbaatar is –25°C (–13 F) in winter and 16°C (60 F) in summer, although the capital can boast 260 sunny days per year. The summer travel season goes from May 15 to October 15. June is usually blistering hot and dry while August is cooler but wet. The rains bring grass and wildflowers, which delight photographers. But the wet conditions make travel difficult in the northern areas. Most travellers come to Mongolia in mid-July for the annual *Naadam* sports festival. Crowds tend to be larger (and prices higher) at this time, so book ahead for hotels, tours and transportation. September and October are very good months to see the Gobi. Spring (March to mid-May) can be unpleasant. Fierce winds and dust storms blow in from Siberia. Snow may still cover the steppes and mountain passes, and where it is melting there is potential for flooding. The lack of rain in spring means that the grasslands will be a grim brown. Mountainous regions, notably Khövsgöl, can receive a snowstorm even in summer. One advantage to spring is that it is relatively 'bug free', with fewer mosquitoes compared to late summer.

## OFF SEASON TRAVEL

Very few travellers visit Mongolia in the off-season, and for good reason—from the middle of October until mid-April, the mercury rarely climbs above 0°C. During the coldest days of winter, the temperature can plummet to –30°C. Further, because of Mongolia's high latitude (Ulaanbaatar is 48° north), the daylight hours are short, with the sun setting around 4 pm in late December. The lone advantage in terms of weather is the clear skies and lack of wind. Weeks at a time can pass in winter without the slightest hint of cloud.

Why would anyone want to holiday in a place where frostbite is a threat outside every doorway? One reason is cost. Hotels in Ulaanbaatar offer good off-season rates, and airfares and tour prices tend to drop as well. Specialised activities such as cross-country skiing, ice skating and ice fishing can be done in winter. The best place to ski is at Khandgait or Terelj, both located near the capital. You can rent equipment here, but selection and quality are poor so bring your own gear if you are serious. There are a few places to ice skate and play ice hockey in Ulaanbaatar, but again, equipment is of poor quality. One place to skate is at the small stadium in the Children's Park. There are hockey rinks in the third micro-district and the eastern end of Peace Avenue. Winter is also the season to join a join a wolf hunting party, or to see the Kazakhs (in Bayan-Ölgii) hunt using their magnificent eagles.

Really the best reason to visit in winter is to see the Mongols in their element (and most photogenic): this is the time when they break out their huge sheepskin cloaks (*del*), fox fur hats, and embroidered boots.

Winter travel requires special planning and equipment. Warm western clothing (hats, jackets, and gloves) can be purchased cheaply in Beijing (the Silk Alley) or in Ulaanbaatar (at the Central Market or the State Department Store). Quality long underwear made from synthetic materials is best purchased abroad, as are heavy boots, which are difficult to find in large sizes. Sheepskin-lined Buryat boots are extremely warm and comfortable, and can be purchased in Ulaanbaatar. Large size traditional boots (size 10 or above) need to be special ordered.

## What to Bring

In most countries, the rule of thumb is to pack light and buy what you need along the way. For Mongolia, consider bringing more than usual for the simple fact that

*Camels are more photogenic in winter when their coats are thick and shaggy.*

*A rare Gobi oasis is a welcome sight for the weary traveller.*

many goods are still scarce. Travellers should bring sturdy hiking boots or walking shoes, and a pair of sandals. A wide brimmed hat will keep the sun off your face. Light clothing—including shorts and t-shirts—are acceptable, although most Mongolians usually wear long pants. A light rain jacket or poncho is a good idea, especially in August. And a poncho can double as a ground mat for your tent. A pair of long underwear (even in summer) is useful if you will be in the mountains, and will not take up much room in your luggage. In general, it is a good idea to dress in thin layers, rather than bringing bulky articles. Sunglasses and sun block are essential, as are airtight plastic bags, which protect your camera and other electronic goods from dust. For your valuables (traveller's cheques, passport, cash etc.) wear a money belt. A handy item is one or two bandanas, which can be worn over the face during a dusty jeep ride, or used as a wash cloth.

Other items to pack include: lip balm, flashlight, notebook and pens, film, spare batteries, a compass, passport photos, multiple forms of identification (keep a photocopy of your passport in a safe place), a small medical kit, and your personal toiletries (including dental floss, which will prove invaluable after a meal of mutton stew). Once you leave the capital city, supplies become more difficult to find. Countryside shops will have little more than basic food, clothing and household items. Some essentials that are very rare or of poor quality in the countryside include: sun block, sunglasses, medicine/medical supplies, flashlight, batteries, spices, maps, camping gear, camera supplies and any electronic equipment.

You may want to consider bringing your own camping gear. A sleeping bag is a good idea even if you plan to only stay in hotels. Countryside hotels don't always have enough warm blankets, and a sleeping bag will come in handy if your jeep breaks down. Down sleeping bags pack smaller and are lighter than synthetic bags, but won't work well if wet. This is usually not a problem in Mongolia as heavy rain is limited to the northern forests. If a sleeping bag seems like too much to carry, a fleece sleep sack is a smaller alternative.

Other gear, including a tent and stove, is purely optional, and probably not needed if you are on an organised tour. Independent travellers wanting to take advantage of Mongolia's limitless camping opportunities will make good use of their gear. If you have your own jeep, it is easy to find a secluded spot on the outskirts of any town to pitch a tent. Other items to consider bringing if you are headed into the wilderness include a foam pad, GPS, cooking pot/utensils, duct tape, Swiss army knife and mosquito repellent. If you do bring a stove, make sure it can burn regular gasoline, which is easily available across the country. Special fuel and gas canisters are difficult to find and not allowed on aeroplanes.

Most travellers use a backpack to carry their gear. 'Travel' style packs with locking zippers offer protection from petty theft, and usually include a convenient small daypack that detaches from the unit. If your bag does not include one, bring a separate daypack that can be used for hikes and trips around town.

## GIFTS

It's important to have gifts on hand for the people who are bound to assist you on your journey in Mongolia. In the countryside, for example, your driver may stop at any random *ger* for lunch, or if its late, to sleep. Such is the way of the steppes and nomads are used to helping travellers. But since these people are unlikely to turn up on your doorstep, it is proper to repay them with a gift while you have the chance. Even the most simple item, a colouring book or a deck of cards for the children perhaps, is appreciated. Bottles of vodka, candy and cigarette packs are customary, but be aware that you will be required to share the gift.

A much better idea is to give useful gifts: pocket knives, duct tape, sewing kits, recent newspapers, books (in Mongolian), flashlights, batteries, toothbrushes, toothpaste and pictures of the Dalai Lama. If your host is preparing a meal, offer to pitch in some ingredients: rice, potatoes, onions or cheese. Clothing is an acceptable gift, but if it is used, make sure it is clean and without holes. Children will appreciate games and toys. You can load up on these items at the State Department Store in Ulaanbaatar or any countryside market.

Mongolians will accept your gift with little fanfare, and will probably slip it into their *del* without much thought. This is considered polite. Likewise, you need not overly-thank a Mongol for his or her hospitality. Helping strangers is a part of everyday life.

# Tour Operators & Travel Agencies

## IN GREAT BRITAIN AND EUROPE

**Mongolei Reisen GmbH** www.mongoliajourneys.com
Chausseestrasse 84, 10115, Berlin, Germany. Tel: 49-30-44057646, fax: 49-30-4405 7645. Email: info@mongoliajourneys.com. Experienced and well organised representatives of Juulchin in Europe. (see advertisement at front of guide)
**BALES WORLDWIDE** www.balesworldwide.com
Bales House, Junction Road, Dorking, Surrey RH4 3HL, UK. Tel: 0870 241 3208, fax: 01306 740048. Email: enquiries@balesworldwide.com.
**Discovery Initiatives**, www.discoveryinitiatives.com
21 The Bakehouse, 119 Altenburg Gardens, London SW11 1JQ, UK. Tel: 01285-643333, fax: 7738 1893. Email: enquiry@discovertyintiatives.com. Trips across the country, notably in Khövsgöl.
**Off the Map Tours**, www.mongolia.co.uk
20 The Meer, Fleckney, Leicester LE8 8UN, UK. Tel/fax: 116-240-2625, Email: offthe.map@virgin.net. Offers cycling, trekking and horse riding tours.
**Regent Holidays** www.regent-holidays.co.uk
15 John Street, Bristol BS1 2HR, UK. Tel: 0117-921 1711, fax: 0117 925 4866. Email: regent@regent-holidays.co.uk. Ten-day tours that take in the Gobi and Kharkhorin.
**Steppes East** www.steppeseast.co.uk
The Travel House, 51 Castle Street, Cirencester, Glos GL7 1QD, UK. Tel: 01285 651010, fax: 01285 885888. Email: sales@steppeseast.co.uk. Offers trips to far flung areas including Bayan-Ölgii and northern Khövsgöl Aimag.

## IN THE USA AND CANADA

**Mongolian Travel USA** www.mongoltravel.mn
707 Alexander Road, Suite 208, Princeton, NJ 08504. Tel: (609) 419-4416, fax: 275-3827 Email: mongol@juno.com. In partnership with Juulchin, Mongolia's oldest tourism company (since 1954), a leading tour operator with excellent, tailor-made journeys, extreme adventure tours and safaris. (See advertisement at front of guide).
**Acacia Travel, Inc.** www.acaciatravel.com
3272 Rosencrans Street, San Diego, CA 92110. Tel: (619) 225-1233 or (800) 243-6996, fax (619) 226-4003. Email: travel@acaciatravel.com
**Academic Travel Abroad** www.academic-travel.com
1920 N Street, NW Suite 200, Washington DC, 20036. Tel: (202)785-9000 or (800) 556-7896, fax: (202) 342-0317. Experts in cultural travel.

**Asia Voyages**, www.asiavoyages.com
1650 Solano Avenue, Suite A, Berkeley, CA 94707 USA. Tel: (510) 559-3388, Toll free: (800) 914-9133, fax: (510) 559-8863, Email: info@asiavoyages.com. Trips to the Gobi Desert and elsewhere.

**Boojum Expeditions**, www.boojum.com
14543 Kelly Canyon Road, Bozeman, MT 59715 USA, Tel: (406) 587-0125, Toll free: 1-800-287-0125, fax: (406) 585-3474 Email: boojum@mcn.net. Wide variety of expedition style trips, mostly in Khövsgöl and Arkhangai. Their cabin in Khövsgöl Aimag is great for fishing trips.

**Eldertreks** www.eldertreks.com
597 Markham St, Toronto, ON M6G2L7, Canada. Tel: (416) 588-5000, toll free: (800) 741-7956, fax: (416) 588-9839. Email: info@eldertreks.com. As the name indicates, they specialise in trips for the over 50 set.

**Fresh Tracks Adventure Travel Centers Inc.**, www.freshtracks.com
1847 W 4th Avenue, Vancouver, B.C., Canada, V6J 1M4, Tel: (604) 737-7880, toll free: 1-800-627-7492, fax: (604) 737-8854. Email: adventure@freshtracks.com. Three-week tours from the Gobi to Khövsgöl Nuur.

**Nomadic Expeditions**, www.nomadicexpeditions.com
1095 Cranbury-South River Road, Suite 20A, Jamesburg NJ 08831. Tel: (609) 860-9008, 1-800-998-6634, fax: (609) 860-9608. Email: info@nomadicexpeditions.com. High-end tour company with solid ties in Mongolia. Offers unique trips including dinosaur digs and visits to the eagle hunters.

**Sweetwater Travel Company**, www.sweetwatertravel.com
411 South 3rd Street, Livingston, Montana 59047 USA. Tel. (406) 896-1902, toll free: (888) 347-4286. Email: info@sweetwatertravel.com. Top quality fishing trips.

**TRAVCOA** www.travcoa.com
2350 SE Bristol, Newport Beach, CA 92660 USA. Tel. (949) 476-2800, toll free: (800) 992-2003, fax: (949) 476-2538. Email: kimberlyw@travcoa.com or request@travcoa.com. high end tours that include other Central Asian countries.

**Travel Concepts International, Inc.** www.travelconceptinternational.com
5500 Bucks Bar Road, Placerville, CA 95667. Tel: (800) 762-4216, fax: (530) 621-3017. Email: info@travelwiththeleague.com. Tours for the famed Naadam festival.

**Uniworld** www.uniworld.com
Uniworld Plaza, 17323 Ventura Blvd. Encino, CA, 91316. Tel: (800) 360-9550. Email: info@uniworld.com. Good sightseeing and train tours.

## IN AUSTRALIA

**Nomads Tours**, www.nomadstours.com.au
PO Box 5755 Wagga Wagga, NSW 2650 Aus. Tel/fax: 61-2-697 18055. Email: kate@nomadstours.com.au. Tours and trekking for the upmarket traveller.

**Sundowners** www.sundowners-travel.com
Suite 15, 600 Lonsdale St, Melbourne 3000. Tel: 61-3-9672 5300, fax: 61-3-9672 5311. Email: mail@sundowners-travel.com. Trips to the main tourist sites, plus good tours connecting China, Russia and Mongolia.

## IN MONGOLIA

Dozens of travel companies have popped up in Ulaanbaatar in recent years. Many are fly-by-night but a few have earned a good reputation for reliable service and 'eco trips'. The following is an abbreviated list of travel agencies based in Mongolia. Further agencies can be found at the following web sites: www.travelmongolia.org and www.asiaco.com (follow links to 'Mongolia/tour operator').

**Juulchin Tourism Corporation of Mongolia,** www.mongoljuulchin.mn
Mongolia's pioneer in travel and tourism, a leading tour operator since 1954 with offices in six countries. This professional operation offers a variety of tours including adventure safaris. The Ulaanbaatar office is located behind the Bayangol Hotel, 5B Chinggis Khaan Avenue. Tel: 976-11-328 428, fax: 320 246. Email: juulchin@mongol.net (see advertisement at front of guide).

**Absolute Mongolia Travel,** www.visitmongolia.com
127 Government Building 5, Barlgachdin Square. Mailing address: PO Box 43, Ulaanbaatar-43. Tel: 9919 3862 or 9911 9949, fax: 352 343. Email: support@visitmongolia.com. A variety of tours including fishing and camel trekking.

**Boojum Expeditions,** www.boojum.com
American travel company (see above) with an office in Ulaanbaatar at Room 16, Bldg 13 (Behind the Drama Theatre). Tel/fax 310 852.

**Gobiin Ogloo,** http://web.mol.mn/~ogloo/
PO Box 1014, Ulaanbaatar. Office: next to the Tuuvshin Hotel. Tel: 323 394 or 459 003. Well-organised tours with a professional, French-speaking staff.

**Karakorum Expeditions,** www.gomongolia.com
PO Box 542, Ulaanbaatar 46. Office: Jiguur Grand Hotel. Tel/fax: 315 655. Mobile: 9911 6729. Email: info@gomongolia.com. Recipient of Pacific Asian Travel Association 2002 Gold Environmental Award. Leaders in active and cultural adventure tours, including mountain treks, cycling and wildlife safaris.

**Nomadic Expeditions,** www.nomadicexpeditions.com
US travel company (see above) has an office in Ulaanbaatar. Tel: 313 396 or 325 786, fax: 320 311. Email: nomadicexp@magicnet.mn.

**Nomadic Journeys,** www.nomadicjourneys.com
PO Box 479. Tel: 328 737, fax: 321 489. Email: mongolia@nomadicjourneys.com. Eco-trips in several regions with good hikes in Terelj.

**Nomads Tours,** www.nomadstours.com.
Well-regarded, German owned travel company (see above) has an office in

Ulaanbaatar. Suite 8-9 Peace and Friendship Building, Peace Avenue. Tel/Fax: 328 146. Email: helge@magicnet.mn.

**Travel Agent**: For purchasing an international airline ticket or make international hotel reservations, try **White Horse Travel**: Peace and Friendship Building, 1st floor. On Peace Avenue, west of State Department Store. Tel: 312 528. Email: jargal@magicnet.mn

## Hotels and Other Accommodation

While accommodation in Ulaanbaatar has improved recently, provincial capitals and resort areas offer only basic hotel accommodation, sometimes without water or electricity or telephones. The pleasant *ger* camps are a better alternative. They can be found in most tourist-orientated regions, including Khövsgöl and Kharkhorin. For hotels, prices vary according to the category of room (and tend to rise a week before the Naadam festival). To call or fax from abroad, use prefix: 976-11

### TOP END HOTELS
*(US$50–100 per single, $80–150 per double)*
**Chinggis Khaan Hotel**, 8 Khökh Tenger Street. Tel: 313 788. The biggest and most luxurious hotel in Ulaanbaatar. The curious exterior design is meant to depict the 'steppes' of Mongolia. It offers a large conference hall, dining hall and supermarket. It once housed a casino until the government outlawed gaming halls in 1999. It is less central than the other large hotels and is often used by visiting diplomats.
**Continental Hotel**, Olympic Street (near the Bulgarian embassy). Tel: 323 829, fax: 329 630. The newest luxury hotel in town. The rooms are spacious and clean, and the gym is attractive.
**Ulaanbaatar Hotel**, 37 Little Ring Road. Tel: 320 237 and 325 368, fax: 324 485. Just a few steps from Sükhbaatar Square, this is the grand old hotel of Ulaanbaatar, used during the socialist era to accommodate visitors from other communist countries. The rooms tend to be small, but well equipped. Breakfast included.
**Bayangol Hotel**, 7 Chinggis Khaan Avenue. Tel: 328 869, fax: 326 880. Conveniently located just south of the Drama Theatre, and offering comfortable rooms, the Bayangol is a traveller's favourite. The Casablanca restaurant on the first floor is a nice addition.
**Palace Hotel**, Chinggis Khaan Avenue, 25A, Khan-Uul district. Tel: 343 565, fax: 343 001. Email: palace@mongol.net. Recently refurbished. Close to the Tank Monument and Naadam Stadium.
**Tuushin Hotel**, Prime Minister Amar Street-2. Tel: 323 162, fax: 325 903. A popular place for consultants and business travellers, the Tuushin is well placed on a quiet street off Sükhbaatar Square.

Edelweiss Hotel, 15A/5 Peace Avenue. Tel: 312 186, fax: 325 252. Email: edelweis@mongol.net. A low-key, but pleasant alternative to the larger hotels. The rooms are clean and comfortable rooms and there is a sauna downstairs.

## MIDDLE RANGE HOTELS
*(US$40–90 per single, $60–120 per double)*
Flower Hotel, 13/3 Khökh Tenger Street. Tel: 458 330, 452 709. This was an older hotel refurbished with Japanese investment in 1995. As such, it offers welcome amenities including a sauna, hot tub, and an excellent Japanese restaurant. Some rooms have communal showers. Located east of the centre in Sansar District.
White House Hotel, Damdinbazar Street. Tel: 367 872. Good rooms and a friendly staff, although the location, west of Gandan Monastery, is inconvenient.
Urge Hotel, in the Montsame building, across from the Central Museum. Tel: 313 772. It is just a stone's throw from Sükhbaatar Square.
Bishreelt Hotel, next to the Lenin Museum and Freedom Square. Tel: 310 063, fax: 313 792 Convenient location and a good restaurant, breakfast included.
Star Hotel, 5 Kinouildveriin Gudamj. Tel: 458 103, 358 137, fax: 358 103. Nice rooms, slightly east of the centre, in the old Russian quarter.
Annujin Hotel, 39 Peace Avenue. Tel: 458 235, fax: 458 281. Located on the eastern side of town close to the UK Embassy. A newly refurbished, three-storey building.

## ACCOMMODATION AWAY FROM THE CENTRE
*(US$25–$100 per room)*
Nairamdal Zulsan. Tel: 332 776. A summer children's camp and hotel, it's located about 30 kilometres north-west of town.
Nüükh't Lodge. Tel: 325 630. Located in a serene valley on the western slopes of the Bogd Uul, this was once reserved as a get-a-way for the cadres. Sauna, billiards and horse riding are available.

## BUDGET HOTELS
*(US$10–$40 per room)*
Mandukhai Hotel, 19/2 Peace Avenue. Tel: 321 578. Located amid the apartment blocks near the State Department Store. A bit run down, but the restaurant offers excellent Chinese food.
Zaluuchuud Hotel, 27 Little Ring Road. Tel: 324 594. A good option for those on a budget, it's located near the University.
Negdeltchin Hotel, 25 A/1 Peace Avenue. Tel: 435 230. A little musty inside, but well placed near the Wrestling Palace.
Narlag Hotel, Sukhbaatar district, sixth horoo. Tel: 350 213.
Ayantchin Hotel, Bayangol district Apt 55A. Tel: 360 443.
Amarbayasgalant Hotel, 15A Peace Avenue. Tel: 312 413

## FOR BACKPACKERS

*(US$4–$10 per person)*

The backpacker hostels are good places to meet other travellers looking to share the cost of a jeep tour. They have good contacts with guides and drivers who can put together a budget camping trip.

**Ganaa's Guesthouse**, in the *ger* districts near Gandan Monastery. Tel: 367 343.

**Nasan's Guesthouse**, near the Central Post Office. Tel: 321 078.

**Idre's Guesthouse**, near the long distance bus station. Tel: 316 749 or 9916 6049.

**Mon-Elch Tour Guesthouse**, near the Tank Monument. Tel: 344 880 or 9914 4407.

## STAYING IN PRIVATE APARTMENTS

Upon arrival at the airport or train station, a local might offer you accommodation in their home for a nominal fee of about Tg5000 per night. If you plan to stay for a while, it might be worth renting out an apartment—check the classified sections of *the Mongol Messenger* or *UB Post* newspapers.

## IN THE COUNTRYSIDE

The best accommodation in the countryside is the simple *ger* camp. These camps are a growing phenomenon in Mongolia, although at the moment they are poorly organised and difficult to find without a tour guide. Catering towards organised tours, the camps offer a private *ger* and meals. The more fancy ones have heated showers and flush toilets, although most are very basic (no shower and pit toilets). Prices tend to be quite high compared to provincial hotels, usually US$20 to $30 per night, but the service is often better and may include horse riding, fishing or other activities. There is no five-star accommodation in the rural areas.

When Mongolians travel in the countryside, they usually camp out by their car or will stay in a friend's *ger* on the way. On the main east-west roads, in a remote area or at a crossroads, travellers may find a string of *gers* that serve as restaurants. These restaurants, which can be used as a 'hotel' at night, are set up for truckers on a long haul.

Tour guides will probably have one or two nights on the itinerary set up for a home stay with a family. Independent travellers should not rely on locals to house them. Carry a tent and be self-sufficient. If you do stay with a family without prior arrangement, remember to always give a small token of your appreciation. If you do not have a gift, give cash to the youngest child or leave it on the 'altar' (dresser), which contains religious objects. Avoid giving it directly to the *ger* owners, as this would imply 'payment', rather than a 'gift'. Do not leave rumpled or dirty money.

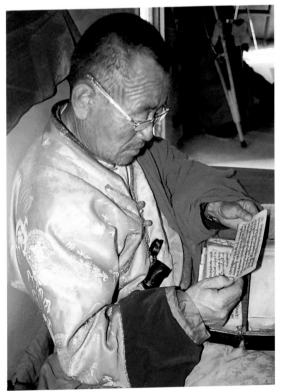

*Above: A stupa at the desert monastery of Khamariin Khiid, Dornogov Aimag. The original monastery was built in 1820 and housed hundreds of monks. Like most of Mongolia's monasteries, it was destroyed in the 1930s during the religious purges. It was rebuilt in 1990 with financial help from local citizens, and is now served by seven monks. Below: Baatar Lam, a monk at Khamariin Khiid, reads a sutra during a prayer service.*

# Time and Electricity

Local time in Ulaanbaatar is GMT + 8 hours. The three western aimags are one hour behind the capital. Mongolia observes daylight savings time in the summer months. Mongolia uses 220 volts 50 Hz. Electrical sockets accept two round prongs, similar to those used in Russia and Europe. Blackouts occur with great regularity in Ulaanbaatar. Some countryside towns, particularly in the west, are left for weeks on end without power, especially in the summer months.

# Currency

The Mongol currency is the **tögrög** (or *tugrik*, shortened to Tg). Until a few years ago the tögrög was divided into 100 *möngke*, but devaluation has caused these to go out of circulation. In April 2002, one American dollar was worth 1,099 tögrög, and one pound sterling was worth 1,540 tögrög. Travellers should carry a supply of US dollars in clean and new notes, as well as traveller's cheques (preferably American Express or Thomas Cook, in US dollars). Credit cards (Visa, American Express, or Mastercard) are only accepted in Ulaanbaatar, and are limited to larger hotels, airlines, tourist agencies, and a few shops. Most Asian and European currencies can be traded in Ulaanbaatar, but the US dollar is the most reliable form of currency.

Traveller's cheques and US dollars can be changed into the local currency, or you can change traveller's cheques into US dollars (for a two per cent commission) at the Trade & Development Bank, at the corner of Trade Street and Little Ring Road, tel: 321 051, fax: 325 449. Cashing a traveller's cheque outside the capital is almost impossible so bring all the cash you need before setting out.

Report lost or stolen traveller's cheques to the Trade & Development Bank, but be aware that replacing lost cheques can take several weeks. This bank also offers money wiring services, a process that takes two or three days. It can also give you a cash advance from your credit card (Visa, Mastercard, American Express).

Moneychangers, who give a slightly better rate than the banks, can be found on the fifth floor of the State Department Store (Ikh Delgüür), and at the Post Office. The moneychangers on the second floor of the Ard Theatre (on the Little Ring Road) are particularly convenient. Moneychangers often congregate in a dirt lot near Betub Danjai Choinkhorlon Monastery, although dealing here may be daunting for the inexperienced. Changing US dollars in the provincial capitals can be challenging, and the rate is not as good as in Ulaanbaatar. Beware of counterfeit US dollars, which have been smuggled into Mongolia from neighbouring countries, notably North Korea. Banks are open Monday to Friday from 10 am to 3 pm.

Moneychangers can be found seven days a week. The Ard Theatre exchange office is open 9 am to 7 pm daily.

# Health and Safety

The average Mongolian lives a long, robust life; often attributed to the dry climate and hearty diet. Similarly, travellers are unlikely to catch anything other than the classic case of 'Sükhbaatar's Revenge', which is due to a change in eating habits and way of life. In particular, fermented mare's milk (*airag*) can take some time for the stomach to adjust to, and should be consumed in small quantities at first. Even the Mongols take small doses of it at the beginning of summer.

No vaccinations are compulsory for Mongolia, but make sure your polio, diphtheria and tetanus shots are up to date. The following vaccinations should be considered before visiting Mongolia: hepatitis A, hepatitis B, meningococcal meningitis, cholera and tuberculosis. A vaccination for rabies is only recommended to people planning on living in the countryside. Consult a health clinic at least six weeks before departure, and carry with you an International Certificate of Vaccination, which is a personal record of your immunizations.

For health care in Ulaanbaatar, contact the following hospitals. In case of emergency, contact your embassy, which can put you in touch with a resident expatriate doctor.

**South Korean Yonsei Friendship Hospital**, on Peace Avenue near the Selbe River Bridge. Tel: 310 945. Open Monday – Wednesday from 9 am to 12.30 pm, and from 1.30 pm to 5.30 pm, and Thursday – Saturday from 9 am to 12.30 pm. A relatively good clinic with English-speaking doctors, and reasonable costs.

**Russian Hospital no. 2**, Peace Avenue, east of the Big Ring Road. Tel: 458 250. The staff here only speak Russian, and costs can be expensive compared to other facilities.

**Municipal ambulance service**, tel: 103.

**Dentist**, at the Yonsei Friendship Hospital. Tel: 310 945. Try also the private dental clinic Evada, tel: 342 609.

**Pharmacies**: Drugstores can be found all over the capital and medication is sold without a prescription. Hospitals, including Yonsei, have in-house pharmacies. Also try Pharmacy Altai (carries Western medicine), 6 Chinguunjav Street, Bayangol district, tel: 360 014 and 361 620.

Pharmacies and hospitals are poorly stocked in Western medicine. Make sure you take with you any prescription drug you know you may need, as well as a broad-spectrum antibiotics, diarrhoea medicine, water purification tablets, an effective mosquito repellent, eye drops and sun block.

**Tap water** in Ulaanbaatar and other urban areas is safe to drink, although some travellers feel more comfortable boiling it first. In the countryside, out on the steppes, boil water for five minutes to kill off bacteria. Mongolians do this too, so it is safe to drink water or tea that has been offered to you. Mongolians also boil their milk, but ask first as fresh milk can be infected with **brucellosis**, the symptoms of which are violent headaches, muscle aches, fever, and sometimes diarrhoea or constipation.

Your chances of getting either **rabies** or **bubonic plague** are slim, but these remain a concern in the countryside. Avoid dogs, even ones that appear tame, and take caution if offered marmot meat.

Mongolian weather is a hazard not to be taken lightly. Warm, felt-lined boots and thick mittens are a necessity for winter travel to fend off **frostnip** and **frostbite**. Drink and eat high protein foods to give your body the fuel it needs to create warmth. Wear loose clothing and dress in layers, to allow body heat to circulate over your skin. Frostbitten toes and fingers should be warmed quickly in 40° C water. Do not massage or rub the affected skin. Despite the sub-arctic winters, hypothermia is unlikely in Mongolia if care is taken to dress warmly. **Hypothermia**, however, can occur to people that have fallen into a cold river or lake. This is largely a concern in autumn and spring when jeeps can fall through thin ice, submerging passengers in freezing water. In summertime, be aware of **sunstroke and sunburn** (especially in the Gobi), by wearing sun block and a hat, and drinking plenty of water.

There are no serious security issues in Mongolia. Nevertheless, keep an eye on your belongings in Ulaanbaatar, especially on the buses and in the crowded flea market. Pickpockets will slash bags with a razor to get their hand inside, so keep your backpack on your chest while in a crowd. Walking on downtown streets at night is safe, but avoid the *ger* districts and back alleyways. Alcoholism is not as bad as it was in the early 1990s, but drunks are still common.

# Communications

THE CHINGGIS KHAAN'S    MILITANT SOLDIERS

MONGOL POST. 100₮

## MAIL

In the 13<sup>th</sup> century, the Mongol khaans developed the world's most extensive postal service—a network that carried messages from the battlefront of Eastern Europe to the emperor's court in China. Relay stations were set along the way and a parcel could move over 100 kilometres per day.

Nowadays, the cost of sending parcels from Mongolia is fairly expensive and notoriously slow. You can send and receive mail at the Central Post Office in Ulaanbaatar (on the south-west corner of Sükhbaatar Square). To receive a letter, have the sender write 'poste restante' on the envelope.

The CPO is open from 8 am to 7 pm in the winter and until 9 pm in the summer.

More reliable and expensive is to ship with DHL, 15A Peace Avenue, 210648 Ulaanbaatar, Tel: 310 919. Allow between one and two weeks for mail to reach its destination. There is a FedEx agent in the Tuuvshin Hotel.

Stamps for a letter cost Tg450 to all destinations abroad, Tg400 for a post card, Tg3,000 for an express letter, and Tg800 for a registered letter or post card. Philatelists delight in Mongolia's eclectic offering of stamps, many of which are worth picking up as souvenirs. Some of the recent personalities featured on Mongolian stamps include Jerry Garcia, Bob Marley, the Flintstones and Princess Diana.

## TELEPHONE

The international code for Mongolia is **976**, and the city code for Ulaanbaatar is **11**. Do not use the city code when ringing a mobile phone (which have eight numbers rather than six). **Telephone cards** for local and international calls are available at the Post Office. A 3,000 unit local card is Tg2,200 and a 3,000 unit card with international access is Tg17,700. A better value for international calls is via Internet phone (Tg400 per minute), a service offered by some downtown Internet cafés.

**Telexes** and **faxes** can be sent from the Central Post Office, and from the business centres of the Bayangol and Ulaanbaatar hotels (cash payment only).

## INTERNET AND EMAIL

Mongolians are **Internet** savvy and a few entrepreneurs are learning the value of e-commerce. Some even use the myriad downtown Internet cafes as their place of work, as the cost of doing business with international contacts by phone is exorbitant. Tune to local radio and you may hear the *Internet Hour*, a programme that fields calls from listeners who have questions about the Net. Foreign aid agencies have helped by getting rural areas on-line and hosting Internet education projects. By 'leapfrogging' technology, the hope is that Internet/satellite communication will replace expensive landline communication.

Internet Cafes are easy to find in Ulaanbaatar and cost about Tg1,000 per hour. Some places have scanners and a few offer snacks. Try the **Internet House Centre** in the MPRP Building (next to the Ulaanbaatar Hotel), which charges Tg900 per hour, or **Micom**, behind the Post Office. The Internet code for Mongolia is **mn**.

Hooking your personal computer up to the Internet is simple, as the Internet

Service Providers (ISP) now offer a sort of 'calling card' for the Internet. The cards are widely available in the up-market hotels, electronics shops, markets, ISP offices, and mobile phone company offices. The cards are good for 15 or 30 hours of use. The ISPs can also set you up with a fixed, month-to-month service plan. Many aimag capitals have Internet access at their Post Office. Service, however, tends to be slow and erratic. For **websites** on Mongolia, check the Recommended Reading in the back of this book.

# Internal Transport

## THE MONGOL ROAD NETWORK

The recently launched 'Millennium Road' project promises give Mongolia a paved highway across the entire width of the country by the year 2015. Until then, travellers must make do with one of the world's most basic road networks.

Metalled roads sprout from the capital north to Russia and as far west as Kharkhorin; a short spur heads east from Ulaanbaatar for about 70 kilometres. (In total, 1,563 km of some 49,000 km of road are metalled). Dirt tracks constitute the remainder of the road system. Some, particularly those in the flat and dry Gobi, are easily navigated. Other roads in rugged or wet terrain can slow vehicles to a crawl. Khövsgöl and Khentii are especially challenging in the wet season.

Mongolia has almost no road signs, and quite often jeep tracks lead off in any number of directions. There are very few people on the roads to ask directions from and certainly no service stations if you have a break down or run out of gas. Renting your own car is therefore not recommended. Always travel with an experienced driver and guide. And if you plan on directing your driver into unfamiliar terrain or want to go mountain trekking, bring a GPS (Global Positioning System) and know how to use it.

Heading west to Bayan-Ölgii, cars usually take the quicker road via Bayankhongor and Gobi-Altai, a route that takes about six days. The northern road, via Mörön and Ulaangom, takes a half a day longer. Dirt roads in the east and south tend to be smoother, allowing easier travel.

## PUBLIC TRANSPORTATION

Mongolia's long distance bus service is limited, slow and unreliable. Buses only depart when all seats (and laps) are paid for so there are no schedules. Mid-journey breakdowns are common, and these days, few buses travel further west than Arkhangai or further east than Öndörkhaan.

Minivans and jeeps are more common forms of public transportation—travelling to all aimag capitals. Similar to the buses, drivers will not depart until all seats are paid for, so waiting for departure can last several hours. Therefore, it is best to join

*Right: 'Roads' in the Gobi Desert are nothing more than rutted jeep tracks, this one is outside Sainshand*

a vehicle that is nearing capacity as the wait will be shorter. Fares for public transportation are reasonable; a 25 hour drive from Ulaanbaatar to Mörön, for example, costs just Tg15,000.

The long distance bus station in Ulaanbaatar is located at the southern end of Constitution Street (Gandan is at the northern end of the same road). Signs (in Cyrillic) detail where the vehicles are headed. Theoretically, you could hire your own jeep and driver here, at a cost of Tg300 per kilometre. Bring a Mongolian friend to guide and translate for the driver.

In the countryside, vans, jeeps and buses wait for passengers at a central location such as a market or gas station. Most vehicles will be travelling back to Ulaanbaatar, so finding transport to destinations further from the capital requires a longer wait.

## GETTING AROUND TOWN

Ulaanbaatar is small for a capital city, but finding specific offices, buildings, restaurants and hotels can be difficult as very few have a proper street address. Places in Ulaanbaatar are usually designated according to their building and district number; so getting a handle on the district names is useful (use the back of the 'Tourist Map of Mongolia', available in Ulaanbaatar shops). Mongolians are instinctively good with compass points and often refer to places as being east, west, north or south of a certain landmark. Remember that Peace Avenue runs east-west and the Bogd Uul Mountain is to the south.

Buses within Ulaanbaatar are a good value—just Tg200 for any distance—but

can be very crowded at peak hours. Bus routes are marked on street maps in Latin letters. Minivans, however, travel on similar routes and are faster.

**Train station:** bus 15 and 20, trolleybus 2, 4 and 7.

**Airport:** bus 11 'Nisekh', bus 22 Nisekh Sonsgolon (express).

**Central market:** bus 21.

**Southern end of town and Zaisen:** bus 7.

**Northern end of town:** bus 6 'Dambadarjaa'.

Below is a listing of bus and minivan routes to areas outside Ulaanbaatar:

**Züünmod:** minivans leave every 45 minutes from the long distance bus station. From the drop off point, hire a taxi for the remaining seven kilometres to the monastery, Manzhir Khiid.

**Nalaikh:** (32 km south-east of Ulaanbaatar) regular minivan service from the long distance bus station, or hire a taxi.

**Sharga Mor't:** a wooded valley good for walking, about 18 kilometres north of Ulaanbaatar. Buses leave from Boombogor Market.

**Khandgait:** a popular area for skiing in winter, 40 kilometres north of Ulaanbaatar. Buses leave from Boombogor Market.

**Gachuurt valley:** north-east of Ulaanbaatar, on a pretty stretch of the Tuul River. Buses leave from the long distance bus station.

**Observatory:** a rarely used, seemingly abandoned, Soviet-era facility set on the slopes of the Bogd Uul Mountain. Take the bus marked 'Khürkheree', which means 'waterfall'. This is a good place to start a trip to **Tsetseeguun** Peak (see p. 154).

## TAXIS

A fleet of little yellow taxis popped up in Ulaanbaatar in 1999, but on the whole there are very few professional taxis in the capital. Try to use the official taxis as they use a meter and will not overcharge. All other private cars are potential cabs. Flag one down and pay the driver Tg300 per kilometre (agree on the fare before setting off). This is a safe mode of transportation, although women should avoid travelling alone at night. The taxi ranks in Ulaanbaatar are located in front of the Ulaanbaatar Hotel, Freedom Square, and the Zanabazar Museum. For pick up service, call Mongol Taxi, Tel: 455 322 or Taxi Ulaanbaatar, Tel: 311 385.

# Shopping

Ulaanbaatar shops—near downtown—offer many curios, antiques, artwork and fine winter clothing. Good leather jackets, cashmere sweaters, camel wool vests and blankets can be found at excellent prices. Traditional embroidered boots with upturned toes, *dels* tied with silk scarves, fox fur hats and stylish Mongol jackets called 'huurum' are mostly home-made but can be found in some shops. Mongol-style paintings, books on Mongolian art, and traditional musical instruments make excellent gifts. Antique shops offer a good range of old kettles, silver bowls, knives and Buddhist artwork. As a word of warning, official opening and closing times in government offices, shops and museums are not held in high regard. Be prepared to alter your schedule and improvise.

Tourist shops are easy to find in the summer months, and one should make an effort to look beyond the pricey gifts shops at the main hotels. The following are worth visiting; note that some are not named, and are only known as 'art shop' or 'souvenir shop':

**State Department Store**, west of the Square on Peace Avenue. Tel: 324 311. Has a large section dedicated to souvenirs, artwork and Mongolian clothes on its fourth floor. The Department Store also has a camping and clothing store for those who have come under-equipped, although selection is slim. Open Sundays from 10 am to 6 pm, and other days from 9 am to 8 pm.

**Gobi Cashmere House**, in the same building as Hanamasa restaurant. Tel: 313 662. Offers a fine selection of products straight from the factory.

**Souvenir shop**, located just before the entrance to the Gandan Monastery, on the right. The back of the shop is given over to Mongol paintings.

**Art shop** on Sükhbaatar Square, with ceramics, Mongol Zurag-style paintings, and water-colours.

**Uran Dösh** (souvenir shop no. 41), 25 Chinggis Avenue. Tel: 324 511. Fair priced items that make good gifts.

**Antique and Art shop**, 21 Peace Avenue. Tel: 321 004. Antiques, jewellery, leather, paintings, and musical instruments.

**Jewellery shop**, 14 Little Ring Road (to the right of the jewellery factory). A selection of gold and silver items in classic Mongolian design. Open weekdays until 8 pm, and Saturday from 9 am to 2.30 pm.

Local artists and students spend the summer wandering about Sükhbaatar Square, the Post Office, and outside the museums, showing off their work to passing tourists. The quality of their work (mostly watercolours) is often very good and certainly well priced.

At the Ulaanbaatar Central Market, towards the back, is a section reserved for antiques and coin sellers (this is the best reason to visit the market). It is, however, illegal to take antiques out of the country unless purchased from an authorised shop (customs agents will ask for a receipt). Some curios at the market are new, including snuff bottles and the famous Mongolian wood saddle. There are many sticky fingers about so leave your valuables in the hotel.

The Central Market (sometimes called Narantuul Market, or simply Market, zakh) is open from 10 am to 6 pm, everyday except Tuesday. Take the no. 21 bus from Peace Avenue, a private mini-van, or a taxi.

## FOOD MARKETS & SHOPPING CENTRES

**Mercury**, west of the circus just off Seoul Street. Offers the best stock of imported goods in the country. **Dalai Eej** market is in the same complex. Open daily.
**Food Land**, near the Wrestling Palace. Rather limited selection.
**State Department Store**, first floor. A convenient location, but the selection is limited.
**Sky Shopping Centre**, in the Chinggis Khaan Hotel. Korean and Western imports, and the chance to ride on the only escalator in the country.
**Sapporo**, in Songino-Khairkhan district. Sells pricey Japanese imports.

## SPECIALTY SHOPS

For **electronics and computers**, try the Anun Shop west of Sükhbaatar Square. Sony and Panasonic have shops on Peace Avenue close to the State Department Store. Nomin Electronics is located in the fourth micro-district.

As for **camping equipment**, the only place to buy quality western-made gear is Ayanchin Outfitters, Tel: 327 172. Located on Trade Street near Golomt Bank. Fishing rods and tackle can be bought at a shop near the Boomboogor Market. Poor quality tents are sold in summertime outside the State Department Store.

# Photography

Unfortunately, there are no quality camera shops in Ulaanbaatar, so bring all your own equipment; including batteries, lenses, filters and other accessories. Point and shoot cameras, and the very rare SLR system, can be purchased in electronics shops and the State Department Store. Print film is widely available in photo studios; but choice is limited. Slide film is sometimes available in hotel gifts shops, but don't count on it. Film can be developed cheaply at one of the photo studios off Sükhbaatar Square, but these are entirely unreliable. Negatives come back in an unprotected roll, pictures are returned with fingerprints, and any film other than 100 or 200 ISO may present a problem for the processor. Avoid risks and develop in your home country.

A fee is usually required to photograph and take videos of museums and monasteries. The fees for video, compared to still photography, are often exorbitant.

It is important to note that while the Mongols are very hospitable, not all like to have their picture taken, always ask first. Most people expect that if you are taking their picture you will give them a copy, so take their address and mail them some prints. Many tourists promise to send pictures but very few follow through. This is sometimes from negligence, but often because matching faces and addresses weeks or months later is difficult. Carry a separate notebook and carefully record the pictures, addresses and people you photograph. An easier alternative, and one that will win you great popularity, is to bring a Polaroid instant camera.

# Food

## RESTAURANTS

A restaurant boom hit Ulaanbaatar in the late 1990s, and travellers now delight in finding a wide range of fine dining establishments. Japanese sushi bars, Italian bistros and German bakeries are a few of the options. While foreigners operate the majority of these, local entrepreneurs have opened Mongolian/Russian restaurants. Traditional Mongolian fare, such as *buuz* and *huushuur*, can be found in the ubiquitous *guanze* (canteens). Many of these, however, are unsanitary, and periodically shut down by health officials. Food outside Ulaanbaatar is basic and repetitive. Meat and dairy products dominate and vegetarians will need to be self-sufficient by bringing their own supplies from Ulaanbaatar.

### TOP END

**El Toro Steakhouse**, south-west of the Peace and Friendship House. Tel: 328 517. Mongolians do not grill their meat, so this is a welcome change if you have been craving a juicy steak.

**Hanamasa**, Near the Gesar Temple. Tel: 327 544. A 'watch em while they cook it' Japanese style restaurant in spotless decor.

**Hazara**, Peace Avenue, behind the Wrestling Palace. Tel: 9515 7604. Sit in a cosy tent and sample some fantastic Indian food.

**Los Bandidos**, off Peace Avenue and close to the Peace and Friendship House. Tel: 9515 6322. The curious combination of Mexican and Indian food under one roof. It is hidden in an apartment courtyard.

**Marco Polo**, Seoul Street near the circus Tel: 318 433. The interior, with its furs and trophies, appears more like a Bavarian hunting lodge. The menu, however, is Italian, and the wood-fired pizzas are excellent.

**Millie's Café**, Seoul Street, 48th building (near the circus). Tel: 325 240. A perennial favourite among the Ulaanbaatar expatriates. The menu includes hamburgers, smoothies, Cuban dishes and huevos rancheros. English-language newspapers and magazines are available to read.

**Palace of Avdai Khaan**, Khöökh Tenger Gudamj, near the Russian Cultural Centre. Tel: 453 118 (book a day in advance). Mongolia's largest *ger*, modelled on the ancient tents used by the khaans. It is generally reserved for parties and tour groups, but worth a look even if you do not eat there.

**Seoul**, In the Children's Park. Tel: 326 554. A cylindrical-shaped building offering Korean food and buffet in a spacious and lively atmosphere, with a bakery on the first floor.

**Victoria's Restaurant**, on the Little Ring Road, across from the Old Children's Palace. Tel: 322 770. A mix of everything: English and German breakfasts to Italian and Mongolian dinners.

BUDGET AND MIDDLE RANGE

**Ankara**, In the Ialalt Cinema building next to Freedom Square. Tel: 322 371. One of the earliest Western restaurants to appear in Ulaanbaatar, this one serves Turkish food and good deserts.

**BMS**, Little Ring Road, near the Ard Theatre. A Mongolian fast food restaurant. The spaghetti and the goulash are passable, the burgers are disappointing.

**Ding Chen**, Little Ring Road, opposite the Ard Theatre. Tel: 9911 5358. Well priced Chinese food. If you have a group, try the Mongolian hotpot (*khaluun togoo*), a speciality from Inner Mongolia.

**Marquis**, 1 Chinggis Avenue, at the corner of Peace Avenue. Tel: 318 285, 9919 0801. Reasonably priced French fare in an elegant décor.

**Palace of Chin Khandorj**, Seoul Street, near the circus. Tel: 320 763. Traditional food served in a government office constructed before the Communist revolution.

**Pizza de la Casa**, two locations: Little Ring Road, near the Ulaanbaatar Hotel. Peace Avenue, near the Peace and Friendship House. Tel: 324 114. A wildly successful pizza chain launched by two Mongolian brothers who learned Italian cooking in Germany. Door-to-door deliveries are available.

**Sacher's Café**, Little Ring Road near the Trade and Development Bank. Tel: 324 734. This small German bakery also serves soups, sandwiches and coffee. Free movies are shown most nights.

# Nightlife

Before 1990, only the hotels had bars, and only foreigners were allowed to go in them. Nowadays, Ulaanbaatar is home to hundreds of bars and discos, of varying degrees of quality. Most are small dive bars but a few around downtown cater to Ulaanbaatar's upper crust. The large dance clubs are scattered about town.

In 2000, the newly installed Mongolian People's Revolutionary Party—the former communists—cracked down on late night partying and enforced a 1 am closure for bars. Discos can stay open an hour or two later. Cover charges of Tg3,000 to Tg5,000 usually apply for the clubs.

## PUBS, BARS AND NIGHT CLUBS

**Chinggis Jazz Bar**, Peace Avenue across from the Russian Embassy. Tel: 9916 8738. Popular local bar with live music, comfy seats and funky interior design.

**Chinggis Club**, on Sükhbaatar Street, west the Old Children's Palace. Tel: 9919 9013. Heavy wood tables and thick jugs of in-house brew. Surprisingly good food.

**Khan Brau**, on Peace Avenue opposite the Drama Theatre. Tel: 326 126 and 326 133. One of the most popular bars in the city, especially in summer when the patio opens. Live music, beer and pub food.

**River Sounds**, south of the Foreign Ministry. Tel: 320 497. Jazz bands and light rock in a central location.

**Hollywood**, Zaluuchuudyn Örgön Chöölöö, Rainbow Club building, near the Chinggis Khaan Hotel. Large disco club with American movie décor.

**Khokh Mongol disco bar**, (formerly Top Ten) close to the train station. Sometimes draws well-known Mongolian rock bands.

**Fire**, located in the Fourth microdistrict. A good-sized club and usually filled with a youthful crowd.

# Entertainment & Activities

Seventy years of Russian domination did a lot to influence Mongolian theatre. The **opera, ballet and dramatic productions** are very good and cost just a few dollars. In the summertime, traditional song and dance routines are put on for tourists. The Mongolian **Circus** is also well known, particularly for its contortionists. As for sport, **wrestling** matches are held periodically in the Wrestling Palace, and there are professional leagues for **soccer** (in summer) and **basketball** (in winter). Tickets can be purchased for a modest sum on the day of the event. Tourist agencies often have the best details on events; listings are also featured in the English weeklies. The following is a list of Ulaanbaatar entertainment venues.

**Tumen Ekh Song and Dance Ensemble**, outdoor theatre in the Children's Park. Tel: 327 916. A show tailored for foreign tourists, this one packs in quality Mongolian dancing and music, performed in summer every Tuesday at 6 pm.

**Ballet and Opera Theatre**, south-east corner of Sükhbaatar Square. Tel: 322 854. Performances in Mongolian include 'Swan Lake' and the 'Barber of Seville'. Two Mongolian operas to see are 'Tears of a Lama' and 'The Three Sad Hills'.

**Drama Theatre**, 2 Seoul Street, south of the Post Office. Tel: 324 236. Enthusiastic crowds come here for drama, both Western and Mongolian.

**State Circus**, the blue-domed building on Seoul Street. Tel: 320 795.

**Cultural Palace**, on the north-east side of Sükhbaatar Square. Tel: 328 486. The stage is generally reserved for the State Philharmonic Orchestra, but other shows may include comedy and musicals. A free Variety Show is performed here during the Naadam festival.

**Puppet Theatre**, the left door of the Drama Theatre. Tel: 321 669. Performances usually made by appointment for group tours.

## CINEMAS

Old Mongolian films produced in the forties and fifties are classics, and are still shown on the national TV station. Since the fall of communism, Mongolian filmmakers have been working on shoestring budgets; and the quality of new movies generally reflects this. Going to the cinema, then, is not a highly regarded activity in Ulaanbaatar. If you are interested in seeing a Mongolian film, call the following cinemas to see what is playing. Ard Kino (Tel: 328 153), Ialalt (Tel: 312 173), Sansar (Tel: 350 544).

A few venues offer movies in English. The Nomin Cinema (Tel: 367 445), located in the 4th microdistrict shows American movies daily. Pizza de la Casa, Peace Avenue (Tel: 324 114) has a big screen TV, VCR and video library.

## HOBBIES

The Hash House Harriers international walking/running club gets together every Tuesday at 6 pm in front of the Bayangol Hotel. The season lasts from the end of March to early October. The Tg3,000 cost includes transportation to the run site (by bus) and drinks and snacks afterwards. The group usually travels out of the city to walk, hike and run in the surrounding hills. It tends to be more a social event than an athletic one.

Other activities among the expatriate set, including chess, soccer, mountain biking, skiing or hiking, are organised on an irregular basis, and will change according to the season, you will need to ask around for details. The board at Millie's Café sometimes carries messages about activities. The expat newsletter, Hello! Sain Bain uu!, contains current details of meetings and events.

Climbing enthusiasts can meet like-minded people at the Ulaanbaatar indoor climbing wall, which was donated by the Alex Lowe Foundation in July 2000. The 30 metre wall is inside the Physical Education Centre, located between OK Centre and the Youth Palace (200 metres south-east of the Chinese Embassy).

Stamp and Coin shows are sometimes held in the city, but you will need some local advice to find them. One place to look is at the First elementary school on Seoul Street (150 metres east of Chinggis Khaan Avenue) which hosts a stamp and coin show on Sunday mornings.

## ADVENTURING

Mongolia is an *Outside* Magazine feature article waiting to happen. You can't go too far out of Ulaanbaatar without coming to some God-forsaken desert, torturous mountain pass, rushing river or dense thicket chock full of wild beasts. Travellers and adrenaline junkies in search of the 'last frontier' often turn up in Mongolia with all sorts of transportation devices that will carry them across this vast territory.

Paddling a kayak around Mongolia's lakes and down its rivers is not a particularly popular activity, though some have tried it. The most likely locations are on the Selenge and Eg rivers in northern Mongolia or the Khovd River in Bayan-Ölgii. A few of the ger camps at Lake Khövsgöl will rent out kayaks and row boats.

Some have tried to **cycle** across the steppes, as is evidenced by the beat-up Western mountain bikes on sale at the Central Market; given up for dead after a few weeks on Mongolia's roads. Because of the lack of pavement, a road bike is useless in Mongolia. Bring a sturdy touring bike with thick tyres or a mountain bike, as well as all the tools and spare inner tubes you might need.

Although you will find long stretches of smooth dirt track to ride on, expect most of your trip to be over poor riding surface. Sand, loose gravel and huge divots will slow you down. Another constant battle is finding the correct route, as many jeep tracks cross each other on their way towards the horizon. A GPS and good maps are essential tools for getting around. As for camping gear, a tent, sleeping bag and foam pad will be useful. Lastly, consider the Mongol dog, which will chase you down upon approaching any *ger*.

More popular than cycling is **horse trekking**, as it should be in this land of equestrians. It is possible to buy a good horse from any herder for about $150. Bring a knowledgeable Mongol friend to help choose the horse or you will be sold an undesirable, half wild beast; or one that won't move at all. If a wooden Mongol saddle is not tempting, you can buy a Russian military saddle at the Central Market (towards the back), or in a shop behind the Central Post Office. Even experienced riders should take a Mongol guide with them to start the journey.

Horse trekking and cycling in the Gobi Desert is rather dangerous and not recommended. Better areas include Terelj National Park near Ulaanbaatar, the Dariganga region in Sükhbaatar Aimag, central Arkhangai Aimag, and around Lake Khövsgöl. In general, travel in areas where there is water, and therefore, people.

Mongolia's mountains—glacier covered and remote, but not particularly high— present a good challenge for medium level **mountaineers**. Some travel agencies in Ulaanbaatar may be able to help with the logistics, but if you are serious, bring all your own equipment.

The highest peak in Mongolia is Khuiten Uul (4374 m) in western Bayan-Ölgii. Special permits are needed to climb it because of its proximity to the Chinese and Russian borders. Peak baggers may also want to consider Kharkhiraa Uul (4052 m) in Uvs Aimag and Monkh Khairkhan Uul (4362 m) in Khovd Aimag.

## FESTIVALS

Compared to neighbouring Asian countries, Mongolia has few festivals. In February (exact date depends on the lunar calendar) Mongolians celebrate **Tsagaan Sar**, the New Year. The largest celebration, and of greater interest to tourists, is **Naadam**, which is held in Ulaanbaatar July 11–12 (see the chapter on festivals for details).

# A brief chronology of Mongol history

**Palaeolithic** – 40,000 BC until about 12,000 BC (domestication of animals occurred around 15,000 BC)

**Mesolithic** – 12,000 BC to 6000 BC

**Neolithic** – 5000 BC to 2000 BC. Metal implements gradually replace stone ones, and agriculture appears. Tamtsagbulag culture. Nomadic pastoralism appears on the steppes around 1500 BC.

**Bronze Age** – 1300 BC to 1000 BC. Metal working now on a large scale. Karasuk culture on the Yenisei (high point of the so-called Animal Style Art). The **deer stele** are thought to date to this time. Period of differentiation between the Mongoloid and Turkish populations. (With Mongoloid elements associated with Caucasian ones).

**Iron Age** – **First millennium BC.** Mounted nomadism is established around 900 BC. The Scythians enjoy their zenith around the fifth century BC. Animal Art develops. Appearance of two distinct cultural zones: one represented by stone cist graves, and the other (north-west Mongolia) by *kurgan* of the Pazyryk type. Iron is commonly used for weapons and tools by 500 BC.

## THE MOST POWERFUL NOMADIC CONFEDERATIONS.

| | |
|---|---|
| Xiongnu | Third and second centuries BC. Princely tombs of Noyon-Uul. |
| Xianbei | 155–400 AD. |
| Ruan-Ruan | 400–552. A vast empire extending from Korea to Russian Turkestan Minusinsk culture. |
| Tujue Turks | First khanate: 552 to 583. Second khanate: 680 to 740. Monuments to Kul-Tegin, Bilge Kaghan, and Tonyuquq. |
| Uighur | 745–840. Conversion to Manichaeism in 762. Creation of Khar Balgas. |
| Kirghiz | 840–924 |
| Qidan | 937–1125. Chinese Liao Dynasty, defeated by the Jurchen (Jin dynasty) |
| Mongols | 13th and 14th centuries: empire founded by Chinggis Khaan. 15th century: first Oirat empire. 17th century: second Oirat empire. |

# History

Most of Mongolia's 'modern' history dates from the time of the 12th century warlord Chinggis Khaan, who Mongols have long considered the father of their nation. Chinggis, however, was just one of many powerful warlords to rise from the steppes. Before his reign, and for several centuries, a long succession of empires etched their place in history; their existence having been preserved in oral epics and the monuments they left behind. Burial mounds, rock engravings, stone figures and the ruins of ancient cities are proof of the highly civilised and cultured peoples who lived here. The majority of the ancient cities listed by the Mongolian Academy of Sciences—27 in all—date to periods before Chinggis Khaan's empire.

The sections in this guidebook describing historical sites will inform on the location and meaning of these remains. Because tourist infrastructure is still rudimentary, these sites are often difficult to find and travelling with an experienced guide is the best way to locate them. Ask your travel company if their guides have background knowledge on archaeological and cultural sites.

Below is a general introduction to the history of Mongolia prior to Chinggis Khaan. For more specific information on his empire, see the Övörkhangai and Khentii aimag chapters.

## The Pre-Mongol Empires

### PALAEOLITHIC (40,000 BC – 12,000 BC)

Beginning in 1949, joint teams of Mongolian and Russian archaeologists started to excavate Palaeolithic settlements across Mongolia. Sites were unearthed around the Bogd-Uul Mountains, the Tuul River, Moïltiin Am, the Orkhon River and Erdene Züü. Palaeolithic remains have also been located in Gobi-Altai, Khovd, Bayan-Ölgii, Dornogobi and Selenge aimags.

One of the most important finds came in 1986, when an expedition in Bayankhongor Aimag discovered stone implements dating from the Lower Palaeolithic era, which confirmed that man was indeed present in Mongolia some 50,000 years ago. The oldest rock carvings in the country date from this part of the Palaeolithic. The most remarkable examples of this art form are the drawings discovered in the **Khoït Tsenkher grotto**, in Khovd Aimag (western Mongolia). They date to the Upper Palaeolithic period (20,000 to 15,000 BC), showing that Stone Age hunters inhabited Western Mongolia. The oldest examples of human art are therefore not to be found solely in Europe, but also in the heart of Asia.

## MESOLITHIC (12,000 – 6000 BC)

Several sites dating from the Mesolithic have been located, notably in Ömnögov, Sükhbaatar, Bayan-Ölgii, Khovd, Gobi-Altai and Dundgov. The most significant finds, however, have been identified in Dornod Aimag, along the Kherlen and Khalkh rivers.

## NEOLITHIC (5000 BC – 2000 BC)

The discovery of the Neolithic site at Tamtsagbulag, in Dornod Aimag, brought proof that an advanced agricultural system was laid down before the age of the nomads. The site demonstrates that the history of relations between nomadic and settled communities is more complex than had been thought previously. Hoes and grain grinding devices were unearthed here, testifying to a developed way of life based on agriculture, combined with hunting and gathering.

The oldest anthropomorphic representation ever found in Mongolia, an amulet representing a carved face, also dates from this period.

## THE BRONZE AGE (1300 BC – 600 BC)

This is the beginning of the 'Horseman Era'. It saw the rapid transformation of a sedentary society into one of nomadic horsemen, the large-scale introduction of metal-working (second half of the second millennium BC), and the appearance of the **Karasuk style art** (carved animal heads on bronze knives).

*A pre-Mongol era rock carving, Museum of National History, Ulaanbaatar.*

The centre of production of the Karasuk bronzes seems to have been Mongolia and the Ordos region. Later, the Karasuk pastoralists seem to have moved towards southern Siberia and from there to the lower Yenisei. Their descendants are probably among the ancestors of the Mongol peoples.

**Deer stele**, monumental standing stones covered in engravings of stylised animals, have been discovered over a widespread area from the Altai to the Trans-Baikal region, passing through Tuva and Lake Baikal to the northern edge of the Gobi. They have been dated to the early Iron Age or the middle Bronze Age. The area from which they spread and their probable place of origin was very likely Mongolia; more than 80 per cent of those found in the Eurasian steppes are concentrated in Mongolia where more than 500 examples are known. This is the oldest form of monumental sculpture known, not only in Mongolia, but in Central Asia in general; it is sometimes considered the only genuine monument produced by nomadic art.

These stone stele, in grey granite or in marble and two metres to five metres tall, can be found in groups or isolated. They are covered in engravings of running deer, with large antlers and a beak-shaped muzzle; their feet are often almost non-existent. These stele may bear drawings of other animals too, including horses, ibex, wild boar, fish, and birds—all characteristic of the **Animal or 'Scytho-Siberian'** style of which the stag is the major element.

Although the exact dating of these monumental sculptures is still unclear, most scholars agree on a period between the seventh and the third centuries BC, the so-called **Scythian period**, characterised by a certain cultural unity across a very extensive territory. The stones were set up at crossroads used by the tribes, on funerary sites, in wide mountain valleys, or in fertile steppes, and they must have marked the site of gatherings linked to ancestor worship, bringing together the various tribes.

The deer stele is thought to represent the stylised picture of a warrior hero whose face is symbolised by a circle, or by two or three oblique lines, perhaps lines which were once drawn on the faces of the deceased and related to ancestor worship. The stylised objects on the stele could be the attributes of the warrior (ornaments, weapons, and shields). This hypothesis has been supported by the discovery in Mongolia of a particular form of deer stones bearing engraved human faces, although of the five to six hundred stele discovered in Mongolia, only three show realistic human faces.

The cervidae family (reindeer, deer, elk, ibex) provide the main decorative motifs of the Animal Style. There may possibly have been a link between the deer stele and some very ancient form of sun worship. Like the horse, the deer is considered an animal that can guide the soul of man and help his passage from this world into the kingdom of the dead.

*Kurgan* is a term of Turkish origin used since the 15th century in Russian chronicles to designate funerary barrows. The Kurgan of Pazyryk were discovered in 1929 in the Eastern Altai, at 1600 metres above sea level.

Inside the barrows were the graves of mountain tribal leaders. Their skeletons, lying on their side, the knees bent, the head facing west or northwest, had been buried with large amounts of grave goods. One of the bodies, mummified, was covered in tattoos. The skulls found belong to Caucasians with a few Mongoloid traits. Other kurgans of the same type—dating from the seventh and sixth centuries BC—have been found near Ulaangom (Uvs Aimag).

## AT THE FRONTIERS OF BRONZE AND IRON

Two distinct anthropological and cultural zones can be distinguished in western Mongolia. The boundary between the two zones passes through the Great Lakes depression (Khovd Aimag), which cuts the territory in two roughly from north to south. In the south, it gives onto the arid expanses of the southern Gobi. The north of Mongolia forms an intermediary zone between these two great cultures that are characterised by two types of burial: **stone cist tombs**, and *kurgan*.

**The eastern zone** includes the Khangai and Khentii mountain chains, and the steppes of eastern Mongolia. It coincides with the cultural zone of stone cist graves. Skulls excavated in these tombs are typical of the northern Mongoloid branch. It is there, according to the Russian researcher V. Volkov, that the primitive stages of the formation of the Mongol tribes occurred.

Just like the deer stele, the stone cist grave culture occupied vast expanses of steppe land in Central Asia, but most of the tombs are to be found within Mongol territory. Cist graves are the oldest type of grave known in Central and Eastern Asia. Built for great families or warriors, they can be found either in groups or isolated; their location is marked by small enclosures of vertical stones laid out in a rectangle. The funerary pit can be up to one metre deep, orientated east-west; the corpse is generally laid on its back, sometimes with the head on a stone 'pillow'. These graves are found throughout Mongolia, except in the north-west. In the south, they extend into the Gobi and to the northern borders of Tibet.

Cist graves are often, but not always, found with deer stele. Although they may be associated at the same site, the stele appear to predate the tombs, and were often re-used in the construction of the walls, roof, or even the floor of the funerary chamber, which explains this apparent connection between them. More often than not, the stele are orientated in the same direction as the body, with the head in the north or north-east.

The western zone includes the western mountains of the Mongol Altai, and the areas neighbouring Mongolia south of Tuva. Cist graves are rare here, and completely absent from those areas of Mongolia that give onto the high Altai and Tuva. Here, on the other hand, the dominant forms of tombs are the *kurgan* of the Pazyryk type, and the *kereksür*. Turkish tribes prevailed here and spread a culture of the Saïan-Tuva type.

In north-west Mongolia, no less than eight different types of burial have been identified. Their external appearance varies from plain, levelled ground, to a simple pile of stones, or a tumulus covering the grave.

The plunder of funerary sites was already widespread by the end of the Bronze Age. Stone cist graves and grandiose monuments to the great nomad warriors of the age were tempting for those in search of easy spoils. None of the measures taken to fight this phenomenon were successful. In the fourth and sixth centuries AD, large *kurgan* appeared with no internal sanctuaries. Nothing, not even a single earthenware pot, is to be found in them. It appears that this deliberate absence of grave goods was the only way to prevent their plunder. Not surprisingly, therefore, the *kurgan* remained inviolate. They can easily be identified—there are no openings and, apart from a few bones, they are empty.

## *Kereksür*

The name given to the tombs dated between the fifth and the tenth centuries AD, that is to the period of the Turkish, Uighur, and Kirghiz khanates. Some may date from earlier empires.

These graves fall into several distinct categories according to their size and shape.

The simplest are a circular stone fill with no enclosure around them. They are often located near more complex *kereksür*, and may, in some cases, be part of the make-up of the latter.

Others have a fill surrounded by one or more circular, square, or rectangular stone enclosures. Their diameter varies between 4.5 metres and 10.2 metres. The circular enclosures may be a closed perimeter or an open-ended spiral shape. These are sometimes difficult to distinguish from *kurgan*. Very often, four large stones are placed around the perimeter, sometimes orientated from the centre of the fill towards the cardinal points.

These tombs are found north of the Gobi and west of the upper Kherlen River, as far as the western frontiers of Mongolia. In the north, they are found as far as the upper course of the Yenisei and the middle reaches of the Selenge. The northernmost groups of *kereksür* are found near Gusinoye Ozero, near Lake Baikal. A large number of them exist in the basin of the upper Selenge, on the southern and northern foothills of the Khangai Mountains.

Some authors seem to use the terms *kurgan* and *kereksür* indifferently to designate old tombs of any period.

## THE IRON AGE: THE PERIOD OF THE HORSEMEN

The early Iron Age is characterised by the adoption of nomadic pastoralism as the dominant way of life, the widespread use of iron for making tools and weapons, and the development of the Animal Style in art.

This key period is conventionally called the **Scythian period**. The practice of riding saddled horses greatly eased widespread contacts between peoples and tribes over vast distances. Powerful groups of nomadic tribes began to form around the middle of the first millennium BC, some of whom became historically and culturally important communities. One of these was the so-called 'Scytho-Siberian group'. The tribes that dominated the steppe were of Indo-Iranian origin, and included the Scythians of the Black Sea as well as the Sakas of Central Asia. Nomadic pastoralism became the prevailing way of life over a vast expanse of steppe land stretching from Hungary to China. Despite this, within a given group, nomadic herders and sedentary agriculturists might coexist. This occurred between the nomads of the Altai and the settled populations of the Tagare civilisation, as well as the Scythian ploughmen and nomads.

Animal Art, a highly expressive nomadic art, developed at this time. It was a testimony to the common cultural traits shared by different peoples living over an immense territory.

Historian V. Volkov explains that economy, art and traits that were developed by earlier settled tribes were adopted by the nomadic peoples of Central Asia. We do not know, however, the exact origin of these peoples—defined either as 'rather more Turkish' or 'rather more Mongol' than one another, as the case may be. The Animal Art of the steppes indicates neither a political community nor an ethnic origin. Researchers note that the many Bronze objects found in Mongolia reflect links with Scythian and Iranian art.

## THE XIONGNU (300 BC – 100 BC)

Chieftains and confederations accompanied the appearance of nomadic herding as the dominant way of life. Horse riding enabled these tribes to control larger herds, leading in turn to a demand for more grazing land. Violent conflicts between tribes over access to this pasture land, and inter-tribal alliances, led to the formation of powerful confederations.

In the second century BC, the Xiongnu crushed the Yuezhi, who had settled on the south-western edge of the Gobi, and drove them west. The Xiongnu soon came to dominate the greater part of Mongolia, founding a powerful empire, and representing a serious threat to China, with which they were to be in constant conflict.

It is interesting to note that the territories later occupied in the Middle Ages by the Mongols correspond exactly to those taken by the Xiongnu.

In 214 BC, the Xiongnu were themselves driven back by the Chinese armies. This event had serious consequences for the other tribes. Each in turn pushed back by the others; the process has been compared to a gigantic billiard game which was to upset the entire human geography of Central Asia and Siberia, resulting in the disappearance of the Indo-Iranian root and its replacement by the 'Turko-Tartars', ancestors of the present inhabitants of Mongolia.

In Mongolia and the Trans-Baikal region, the Xiongnu left 'vallum enclosures', or fortified enclosures, which served as bases for their skirmishes against the forest tribes. The inhabitants of these fortifications were sedentary and engaged mainly in agriculture, as testified by the ploughshares found in excavations. Weapons and decorated pottery were also discovered.

The Xiongnu also built large *kurgan* for burial purposes. Those of Noyon Uul, discovered in the north of Mongolia at 1,500 metres above sea level, have been identified as the tombs of Xiongnu princes. Rich textiles were uncovered here, including a felt carpet with a drawing of a bird of prey attacking a fleeing stag. Horse skulls, saddles bridles and fragments of chariots were also found. Unfortunately, these objects were never properly researched, as the Soviet and Mongol expedition members (1912 and 1924) were subsequently purged.

## AFTER THE XIONGNU COLLAPSE

The Xiongnu Empire (of the north) was dissolved in 155 AD. There followed a period of domination by the **Xianbei** (155–400), and then by the **Ruan-Ruan** (a Chinese term for this group which means 'wriggling insect'). Between 400 and 552, the latter formed a vast empire stretching from Korea to Russian Turkestan, including Mongolia. In 552, they were in turn defeated by the Turks.

The Ruan-Ruan were contemporary with the **culture of the Minusinsk basin**, which was then flourishing along the Yenisei, in Siberia (the Minusinsk depression is located at the confluence of the Yenisei and Abakan rivers). Items found in Ruan-Ruan graves include belt buckles, stirrups, daggers, saddles, and bronze plaques.

## THE TURKISH PERIOD (EARLY MIDDLE AGES)

The Ruan-Ruan khanate was destroyed in 552 by a coalition of Turkish tribes led by the **Tujue** Turks from the Altai. These Turks should be distinguished from the inhabitants of Turkey, who are just one branch of the large Turkish family, the descendants of the Osmanli Turks.

At the beginning of the sixth century, the Tujue lived in the Altai and were the slaves of the Ruan-Ruan. They rebelled in 551, under the leadership of Bumin, and founded a vast empire that spread from the Yenisei to south of the Gobi, and from the Khingan Mountains to Lake Balkash. These Turks represented a serious threat to the Chinese, a threat that forced the second period of construction of the Great Wall of China.

The **first Turkish khanate** was at its peak in the second half of the sixth century, but was later destroyed by the Chinese Tang Empire, which had then reached its greatest territorial expansion. Driven back to near the Great Wall, then under the control of a foreign army, the Tujue rebelled in 679 and 681, and settled once again in Mongolia, establishing the centre of their new empire there.

This new power, the **second Turkish khanate** (680–740) was divided into two independent parts. One included the Eastern Turks, from the Orkhon, who lived in an area that extended from Manchuria to the Great Wall. The second group—the Western Turks of the Altai—had strong links to Central Asia and the Iranian world, and occupied a territory from Chinese Turkestan to the Aral Sea and Persia. While the centre of the empire of the Eastern Turks was the Orkhon basin, they also occupied the Tuul and Selenge river basins.

From ancient times and until the 14th century, the **Orkhon valley** was the political centre of the nomadic tribes: the Turks, the Qidan, the Uighur, and the Mongols all established their capitals there.

The history of the steppe is often seen as a cyclical one, characterised by the emergence and disappearance of confederations of varying importance as more powerful clans developed. The Turks, however, broke this continuity in several ways. By developing an elaborate and dynamic culture, as well as an extensive vision of the world, they provided a solid basis for their policy of expansion of political control beyond the steppe, as far as China and Russian Turkestan.

The spread of this world vision was encouraged when the Tujue developed a writing system and a literature of their own. The 'Paleo-Turkish' script, or **Orkhon**

## THE FOUNDING MYTH OF THE TUJUE

Chinese historical annals record a legend about the origins of the Tujue. It was said that a young boy had been thrown into a marsh by the Huns, his body mutilated. He was the only survivor of the massacre that befell his people, and he was saved by a she-wolf who brought him meat every day. He grew up, and the she-wolf became pregnant by him. Hounded by the young man's enemies, they fled together and found shelter in a cave where the wolf gave birth to ten sons. One of these became the king of the Tujue.

The wolf is considered by the Turks to be an ancestral animal of Heavenly origin. As sons of the she-wolf, the Tujue *khagan* claim this origin for themselves—they are god-kings, 'identical to Heaven'.

script, is a phonetic system using a 'runic' alphabet derived ultimately from the Aramaic, through old Sogdian. It was replaced in the eighth century by the Uighur script. Soviet archaeologists have shown that the Turks of the first khanate founded a number of Buddhist monasteries. But Buddhism was less present in the second khanate, and Turkish texts condemning the construction of Buddhist monasteries are eloquent on the reasons for this: "Because they teach gentleness and humility, qualities which are of no use to a warrior..."

All the ancient Turkish remains in Mongolia date to this second khanate. Over twenty stele, bearing historical, political, and biographical inscriptions, have been found throughout

*Anthropomorphic statues like this one are prevalent in western Mongolia.*

the country. The most famous are those of **Khööshöö-Tsaidam**, carved in honour of Kul-Tegin (685–731) and Bilge Kaghan (716–734, see Arkhangai). These epigraphic monuments are of great importance as testimonials to the Turks' own appreciation of their history.

The Tujue have also left many anthropomorphic and zoomorphic stone statues. The human figures, standing or seated, hold ritual cups against their chests, symbols of their participation in the funerary banquet organised in their honour. Knives, daggers, or swords hang from their belts. These statues, carved in the sixth and seventh centuries, were often placed near the funerary complexes and commemorative monuments of Turkish khanate high dignitaries.

In addition to these human figures, a number of uncarved stone blocks, known as *balbal*, were also placed near the funerary sites. They represent the enemies killed by the deceased during his lifetime. It is thought that these *balbal*, linked to the funerary rites, trapped within them the soul of the enemy who would then serve the person who had killed him.

The zoomorphic statues include stone tortoises, used as bases for the inscribed stele, as well as lions and rams, which symbolise the power of the *khagan* (tribal leader).

Many elements of the Animal Style continued during the Turkish period, and there is a certain continuity, over the centuries, between the deer stele and the Turkish statues. Just like the stele of the Scythian period, these statues were placed in long rows near the tombs, facing east. In support of this, Chinese historical annals often insist on the cultural similarities between the Tujue and the Xiongnu.

The founder of the second khanate (680–744), Qutluq Elterish (ruled 681–691), successfully unified the whole of Mongolia. He was succeeded by his brother, Qapagan (ruled 691–716), who was, it is said, the only figure in the history of Central Asia capable of matching Chinggis Khaan. He conquered the western khanate and formed an empire that stretched from Manchuria to Transoxania; after his death, a serious crisis over his succession weakened the empire.

In 716, Qapagan and his entire family were put to death (the statesman Tonyuquq being the lone exception). Leadership then fell to Bilge Kaghan (ruled 716–734), the son of Qutluq Elterish. Then, within nine years, three *kaghan* succeeded Bilge. The last one died in 744, the year the Uighurs captured the Orkhon valley, bringing to an end the second Turkish khanate.

## THE UIGHUR PERIOD

In the middle of the eighth century, the Turks were weakened by incessant conflict with the Uighur tribes. The latter founded an empire that was to last nearly a century (754–840), and included the vast area between the Altai and Lake Baikal. Its political importance was less than that of the Turkish empire, but Uighur domination led to a period of intense construction. The infrastructure projects left a number of city ruins and defensive fortifications in Mongolia, testifying to a high level of architectural ability.

The Uighur, Turks from a different branch to the Tujue, formed from a fusion of clans and confederations. In the seventh century, they settled their headquarters in northern Mongolia, along the Selenge River, before capturing the Orkhon region. Control of this area was the key to political supremacy—the tribe who held it, held the empire. They set up their capital in the Upper Orkhon, near the old capitals of the Xiongnu and the Turks, and near the future Karakorum of the Mongol empire. The city was named **Ordu-Balyk**, that is, the 'City of the Camp' (*Khar Balgas* in Mongolian).

The Uighur differed from their predecessors in being constant allies of the Chinese Tang dynasty, and in rapidly developing a very high level of civilisation. They easily adopted religions from sedentary cultures, first Buddhism, then Manichaeism; a syncretic religion from Iraq, which they converted to in 762 and which became the state religion. The Buddhist temples were subsequently destroyed. The conversion to Manichaeism was the result of a meeting between the *kaghan* and Manichaeian priests in the Chinese capital, Luoyang. The Uighur had come to the city to help the Tang in putting down a rebellion.

The Uighur abandoned the old runic alphabet of the Turks and adopted a script based on Aramaic or Syriac, used in Manichaeian texts. This alphabet was the forerunner of the Mongol writing system, and allowed them to create and develop an important religious literature, considered the earliest Turkish literature. Later, in order to administer his empire, Chinggis Khaan employed a large number of Uighur, reputed as highly cultured scholars.

Between 790 and 805 the Uighurs had to face several succession crises, punctuated by a series of murders—three *kaghan* followed one another within a single year! In 839, they were further weakened by a harsh winter, which led to a famine and the death of huge numbers of cattle. The Kirghiz, who had been raiding their territory for twenty years, took advantage of their weakness and crushed them. In 840, they burnt Ordu-Balyk, putting the *kaghan* to death and driving the Uighur from their lands. The Uighur fled south, some of them settling in the west of the Chinese province of Gansu until its conquest by the Tangut in 1028, while the majority settled near the oases north of the Tarim River (in present-day Xinjiang province). Here they founded colonies at Gaochang, Khotcho (near Turfan), and Beshbalyk, which remained a centre of Uighur power until the period of Mongol domination.

In Mongolia, the Uighur left city ruins (see under the Arkhangai section), fortified compounds, Buddhist frescoes, and a few inscriptions. The most important Uighur remains are those of Khar Balgas.

## THE KIRGHIZ INTERLUDE

The Kirghiz are Siberian Turks who came from the Yenisei and left only minimal traces of their culture in Mongolia. After 840 they exerted a control more nominal than real over Mongolia. Their interests lay elsewhere, further north, in the forests of the Altai. Beaten by the Qidan, they were driven back to the Yenisei area from whence they had come.

## THE QIDAN PERIOD

The steppes of Central Asia returned to anarchy after the fall of the Uighur khanate and the Kirghiz invasion; no tribal confederation was able to prevent the growth of Qidan power. The Qidan, who spoke a dialect related to Mongol, came from Manchuria where they had been living since the fifth century, around the Shar Mörön River. At the beginning of the tenth century, their leader Abaoji founded the Liao dynasty (937) in Northern China, and conquered a large part of Central Asia. The Qidan were to rule over parts of north and north-east China, Manchuria, and Mongolia until 1125.

To the west, Qidan frontiers extended into eastern Turkestan. To the north, they reached the foothills of the Khingan Mountains. In Mongolia, they took the basins of the Orkhon, Selenge, Tuul, and Kherlen rivers, as well as the region of Lakes Dalai and Buir.

The second Qidan emperor (Deguan, 927–947) continued the territorial conquests of his predecessor and made the Qidan Empire one of the most powerful of the Orient. The Qidan controlled the caravan routes, had a monopoly on the salt and iron trades, and kept up diplomatic and commercial relations with many states, including Song China, Korea, the Arab caliphate, Japan, and Persia.

The Qidan brought a new feature to the Mongolian landscape—urbanisation. They began to build a network of cities (156 of them!), developing an urban architecture that was later taken over by the Jurchen and the Mongols. The remains of dozens of Qidan cities can still be seen today in Mongolia, ten of them between the Onon and Kherlen rivers. These sites, although prized by researchers, are rarely spectacular for the tourist.

Archaeological research on these cities began in the 1950s. The most important sites are those of Khatun Khot, built in 944, which had a garrison of some 20,000 soldiers, and Bars Khot, in the present province of Dornod, which was also the religious centre of the Qidan. Traces of Buddhist temples and frescoes have been found there, testifying to the spread of that religion in Mongolia under the Qidan.

## CHARACTERISTICS OF QIDAN CITIES

In general, several Qidan cities were grouped together, one of them having a purely military function, and the others being economic centres in which traders, craftsmen, and clergy lived. It is interesting to note in the context of the complex relationships between nomadic and sedentary populations, that Qidan lifestyle incorporated elements belonging to both groups.

The cities had a rectangular plan and were surrounded by fortifications with a gate in each side; within the walls, two large avenues, which intersected in the centre of the town, divided the area into four quarters.

Qidan economy was diverse as both commerce and agriculture played a significant role. Farmers grew barley, beans, peas, melons, pears, and mulberry trees (for silk), and the various craftsmen made cloth, ceramics, and jewellery. A large part of the population was sedentary. Around the urban centres, irrigated agriculture was associated with an elaborate form of cattle breeding that was linked to centres of veterinary medicine.

THE QIDAN AND BUDDHISM

The Qidan built their imperial capital in the Orkhon valley, in keeping with the tradition of the Xiongnu, the Turks, and the Uighur. Buddhism, which flourished in the urban centres, had perhaps been inherited from the Uighur, overlords of the Qidan until 840, or from the Wei dynasty in northern China with whom they had been in contact in the second half of the fifth century, at the time of the great flourishing of Wei Buddhism.

The Qidan made Buddhism the state religion, but did not restrict the worship of other sedentary religions, the most important of which were Nestorianism and Manichaeism. Qidan religious policy was characterised by tolerance and ecumenism, as the Mongol empire would be too. Taoism and Confucianism were also present, and all of these would survive the fall of the empire in 1125. They were mainly present among the agricultural populations, although Buddhism and Nestorianism had spread to some extent among the nomads.

To a nomadic people, the need for a state religion only appears once their empire includes sedentary populations different from themselves. Religion, however, did not affect tribal control, unlike what happened in the sedentary populations of Mongolia's neighbours.

The Qidan funerary stele also bears inscriptions, like those of the Uighur, Khirgiz, and Mongols. In some cases, there is a short funerary text, in others only engravings of animals, stylised trees of life, or seals called *tamga*. Mongol culture was influenced by many cultural and spiritual elements of the Qidan, their ethnic predecessors.

## AFTER THE QIDAN

At the beginning of the 12th century, the Qidan-Liao Empire, weakened by internal struggles, was destroyed by the Jurchen, a tribe that originated in Manchuria and spoke a dialect of Tungus. The Jurchen took the dynastic name of Jin (meaning 'gold'), and ruled over a large part of North China from 1125 to 1234.

Part of the Qidan population then emigrated westwards, past the Altai, to found the empire of the Qara-Kitai in Turkestan. It was also known by its dynastic name of Xi Liao, or Western Liao, and lasted from 1124 to 1211—that is, until the Mongol period.

As for Mongolia, its control returned to disorganised and warring tribes. Some of the sedentary religions, such as Nestorianism, were still present, particularly in the old urban areas of the Uighur and Qidan—side by side with the traditional tribal shamanism. The Jin Empire lasted about a century before falling to the Mongols.

# The Mongols

Little is known about the Mongols' past before the first attempts at unification in the 11ᵗʰ and 12ᵗʰ centuries. The Mongol entity as such did not have any real existence before Chinggis Khaan unified of a mosaic of peoples of very diverse origins into a unique nation that took the name of the dominant tribe.

From the 11ᵗʰ to the end of the 12ᵗʰ century, five or six large confederations vied with one another over the territory of present-day Mongolia. At the end of the 12ᵗʰ century, the Mongols had settled in the Kherlen and Onon river basins, forming a small, weakly-structured khanate, a far cry from the great state which Chinggis Khaan would create a few decades later.

Mongol power did not emerge out of nothing. It is part of a historical continuity which had manifested itself centuries before throughout the immense region across which the Central Asian people nomadised, and of which Mongolia is but one part. It is not quite, however, the process so dear to Western imagination which sees the history of these nomads as a repetitive one in which each new "empire of the steppes" simply reproduces what another had done before it.

The empire of Chinggis Khaan is part of a long tradition, but it is also one of the many turning points in this tradition: a key moment which explains the extent of his power, unequalled until then, and also perhaps the successive failures of later attempts at unification. Chinggis Khaan had set up a vast network based on loyalty not to tribal solidarity, but to an inflexible military and feudal organisation.

## THE MONGOL EMPIRE

In 1206, Temujin became Chinggis Khaan, the great khaan of the Mongols, having succeeded in rallying to his person all the dispersed Mongol and Turkish tribes, and having destroyed his powerful enemies, the Tatars, the Kereit, and the Nalman. "And their entire race was scattered like ashes", says the *Secret History of the Mongols* about the fate of the Tai-chiut, Three phases were notable in the years after the 1206 coronation.

The first phase included the **initial invasions** during Chinggis Khaan's lifetime: 1206 to 1227 (one of the assumed dates of his death). In this period, the Mongols swept over north China, taking Dadu (as Beijing was then called), attacking and defeating the sultan of Khwarezm who ruled over a large part of Central Asia (Uzbekistan, Tajikistan, Turkmenistan, Afghanistan, and most of Iran), capturing Samarkand and Bukhara, before crossing the Caucasus and defeating the Russians and the Qipqak Turks in the Crimea.

The second phase, the **period of consolidation**, marked the expansion of the empire under the reign of Ögödei, third son and successor of Chinggis Khaan, from

1229 to 1241. Ögödei finished the conquest of North China (1229–1234) and destroyed the Jin dynasty.

Having brought to an end the conquest of western Iran and occupied the states of Armenia and Georgia in the Caucasus (1230–1231), he launched a series of campaigns in Russia (1237–1240), subjecting the numerous Russian principalities, destroying the Turkish kingdom of Greater Bulgaria, and invading and conquering Korea (1241). His armies then swept into Poland and Hungary to crush the Duke of Silesia at Liegnitz and the Hungarian king at Mohi. In July 1241, the Mongols were at the gates of Vienna when the European campaigns were suddenly brought to an end by the death of the great khaan Ögödei.

After Ögödei, who had been personally named as successor by his father, rivalries and internal dissension between the various pretenders to the throne—descended from the four sons of Chinggis Khaan—threatened the unity of the empire. Regencies, destitutions, fratricidal wars tore up the empire.

What followed was the **period of the *Pax mongolica*** and the 'national' dynasties. The reign of the great khaan Guyuk, from 1246 and 1248, saw the submission of Tibet to the Mongols and was followed by three years of an interregnum before Ögödei's nephew, Möngke (1251–1259), came to the throne. During the reign of Möngke, the last great khaan to rule from Mongolia, the Mongols sacked Baghdad and founded the Ilkhanid dynasty in Persia, which was to dominate the Middle East for almost a century. The Ilkhanids would try, in vain, to form an alliance with Christian Europe in their struggle against the Mamelukes in Egypt. At the same period, the Mongols reached Vietnam, conquered Sichuan in south-west China, and invaded Lithuania and Poland.

The reign of Kubilai, the "most powerful possessor of people, treasures, and lands that has ever been" according to Marco Polo, lasted from 1259 to 1294. Grandson of Chinggis Khaan, he transferred the capital of the empire to Beijing and founded the Mongol Yuan dynasty in China, bringing the conquest of that country to an end in 1279. From then on, the Mongol rulers acquired a reputation for opulence and luxury. When Kubilai came to the throne, his empire extended from the Yellow River to the Danube, and from Siberia to the Persian Gulf.

This period of the 'Pax mongolica', as it is called, was a genuine Golden Age of commercial trade and intellectual exchange between East and West, and the Mongols' contribution to Mediaeval civilisation in general, and to Western chivalry in particular, was considerable. One of the main objectives of Chinggis Khaan's policies had been to make the commercial roads linking the Mediterranean to the China Sea safe. "A young virgin carrying on her head a tray of gold could travel from the Levant to where the sun sets, from the shores of the Pacific to those of the Mediterranean, without suffering the slightest harm", a Turkish historian wrote.

*Baltic Sea*

Legnica, 1241  POLAND  TEUTONIC
KNIGHTS  •Novgorod
E U R O P E
POLISH
AUSTRIA  PRINCIPALITIES
Vienna•  •Kraków  Moscow•
Pannonhalma abbey•  Muhi, 1241  RUSSIAN  •Vladimir
(Budapest) Buda•  PRINCIPALITIES
Pest•  Vassal states  •Ryazan  •(Kazan)
HUNGARY  Sajo  Chernigov
River  Kiev  (Chernihiv)  1237  •Bulgar
Dnieper R.  Volga
UKRAINE  Don  1242

BULGARIA  G O L D E N

Black  Caucasus Mountains  •Sarai
Sea  Golden Horde
TURKEY  capital after 1242
GEORGIA  Caspian Sea  Aral
SELJUK SULTANATE  Sea
OF RUM  1236
Vassal state, 1243  ARMENIA  AZERBAIJAN  UZBEKISTAN
LESSER  1259
ARMENIA  Tabriz  TURKMENISTAN
Aleppo•  (Orumíyeh)•  Ilkhanate capital after 1265
Ain Jalut, 1260  Maragheh  Elburz Mts.
*Mamluks defeat Mongols*  SYRIA  Ilkhanate capital until 1265
PALESTINE•  IRAQ  Tigris R.  1231
Jerusalem•  ABBASID  1257-58
M A M L U K   S U L T A N A T E  Baghdad  I L K H A N A T E
Abbasid capital
EGYPT  falls, 1258  IRAN  1256 •Herat
C A L I P H A T E
Conquered by Mongols, 1258  P E R S I A

A F R I C A

*Mediterranean Sea*
*Adriatic Sea*
*Danube*

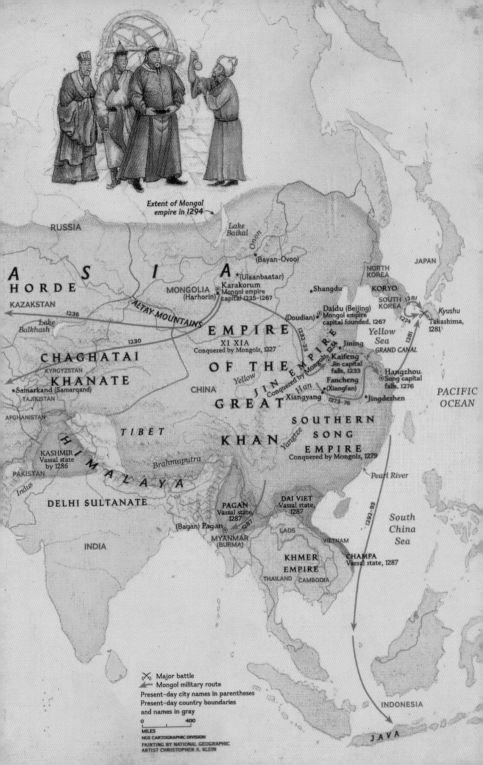

Extent of Mongol
empire in 1294

RUSSIA

*Lake
Baikal*

Onon

(Bayan-Ovoo)

JAPAN

NORTH
KOREA

Shangdu

★(Ulaanbaatar)

A  S  I  A

KAZAKSTAN

HORDE

1236

ALTAY MOUNTAINS

MONGOLIA
(Harhorin)

Karakorum
Mongol empire
capital 1235–1267

KORYO

Daidu (Beijing)
Mongol empire
capital founded, 1267

SOUTH
KOREA

1281

1274

Kyushu
Takashima,
1281

*Lake
Balkhash*

1230

EMPIRE

XI XIA
Conquered by Mongols, 1227

(Doudian)

1232-33

Jining

Yellow
Sea

1281

CHAGHATAI

OF  THE

Yellow

Kaifeng
Jin capital
falls, 1233

GRAND CANAL

KHANATE

•Samarkand (Samarqand)

CHINA

JIN EMPIRE
Conquered by Mongols,

Han

Fancheng
(Xiangfan)

Hangzhou.
Song capital
falls, 1276

PACIFIC
OCEAN

TAJIKISTAN

GREAT

Xiangyang

1273-76

Jingdezhen

AFGHANISTAN

TIBET

KHAN

SOUTHERN

KASHMIR
Vassal state
by 1286

Brahmaputra

Yangtze

SONG

*Pearl River*

PAKISTAN

H  I  M  A  L  A  Y  A

EMPIRE
Conquered by Mongols, 1279

Indus

DELHI SULTANATE

PAGAN
Vassal state
1287

DAI VIET
Vassal state,
1287

1292-93

South
China
Sea

INDIA

(Bagan) Pagan

1287

MYANMAR
(BURMA)

LAOS

VIETNAM

KHMER

CHAMPA
Vassal state, 1287

EMPIRE

THAILAND

CAMBODIA

INDONESIA

⚔  Major battle
➤  Mongol military route
Present-day city names in parentheses
Present-day country boundaries
and names in gray

0                    400

MILES

NGS CARTOGRAPHIC DIVISION
PAINTING BY NATIONAL GEOGRAPHIC
ARTIST CHRISTOPHER A. KLEIN

J  A  V  A

In 1368, the Chinese drove the Mongols from Beijing, marking the end of the Yuan dynasty and the founding of the Ming. This was also the end of the great nomad empires. All attempts at imperial unification thereafter were doomed to fail.

# Mongolia after Chinggis Khaan

In the 17$^{th}$ century, Mongolia was divided into the Western Mongols, or Oirat (also known as Dzungar), and the Eastern Mongols, or Khalkh. The most remarkable figure to emerge from the Oirat was **Galdan Boshigt** who, in the last years of the century, made one last attempt to unify the Mongols before the country came under the complete domination of the Manchus. He succeeded in temporarily unifying the Khalkh and the Oirat. In 1688, after an Oirat attack against the Khalkh, the Khalkh princes called on the Manchu emperor for help. The latter sent his armies against Galdan in exchange for the Khalkh princes' complete submission to Manchu power, a submission made official in 1689 by the Diet of Doloon Nuur.

Despite this, the Oirat were to harass the Manchus for another five years in central Mongolia, until the Manchu emperor Kangxi, at the head of an army of 80,000 men, crossed Mongolia and defeated Galdan near Urga, in 1696.

Twenty years later, the Oirat once again declared war on Kangxi; they captured Lhasa and the Dalai Lama, but were beaten by the Manchu army when it launched a series of punitive expeditions. These ended in 1758 with the massacre of half a million Oirat. Part of the survivors then emigrated to the Volga region where their descendants, the Kalmyk, still live today. The Oirat defeat thus put an end to Mongol independence, and the Manchu occupation of Mongolia was to last for two centuries.

## MANCHU OCCUPATION

Under the Manchu policy of expanding administration, Mongolia was divided into four aimags after it came under their yoke. The khaan of these aimags built palaces for themselves, which were copied by the princes and the high dignitaries in the Lamaist church. The feudal system in Mongolia brought with it an increase in the number of khaans and princes, and consequently in the number of palaces. Today, the only one that can still be visited is the Green Palace at Urga, built between 1893 and 1906 as the winter residence of the eighth Bogd Gegeen.

## THE BOGD GEGEEN LINEAGE IN MONGOLIA

From 1635 on, the line of Bogd Gegeen continued uninterrupted for some three centuries. Of the eight, only the first two were Mongols, all the others being Tibetan. The most well known were the first and the eighth. The first was **Zanabazar**, a name that is the Mongol equivalent of the Sanskrit *Jñanavajra*, or 'Adamantine Knowledge'.

He is better known in Mongolia by his Lamaistic title of Öndör Gegeen ('August Light' or 'Holy'). Zanabazar was the son of the ruler of the most important Khalkh khanate in the 17th century (see the Erdene Züü section), and lived to play an important role in the religious and political life of the Khalkh. He was a great artist (jeweller, bronze caster, and architect), a cleric (compiler of texts, translator, and inventor of the Soyembö alphabet), as well as a politician. He was also credited with the founding of many temples and monastic communities, including the first founding in 1654 of Ikh Khuree, which would later become Urga. By the time of his death in 1724, at almost 90 years of age, his popularity was such that he became the hero of many legends and much hagiography. The search for his reincarnation set off intrigues and rivalries among the Mongol princes as each tried to impose one of his own sons.

The second Bogd Gegeen was the son of an influential Mongol prince, son-in-law of the Manchu emperor. His influence on Khalkh political life was a cause of fear to the Manchus who, after his death in 1757, imposed a rule that from then on all reincarnations of the Bogd Gegeen would be found in Tibet, and no longer in Mongolia. The title would henceforth be given to a Tibetan, born and brought up in Tibet. Having no ties with the Mongol princely families, and uninterested in a people whose language they did not speak, they busied themselves almost exclusively with religious matters, except for the very last one, the eighth.

The eighth Bogd Gegeen was born in 1870 to a family of lesser officials in Tibet. Although debauched and alcoholic—he is said to have become blind from alcohol abuse—he hated the Manchus, and his exhortations helped fuel the increasingly violent movement of revolt against the occupier. In the eyes of many Mongols, he was a symbol of the fight for independence.

Following the collapse of the Manchu Empire, he came to the throne in October 1911, and became the first head of state of an independent Mongolia. His government included five ministers, all princes or high-ranking monks from princely families. He died in 1924, on the eve of the proclamation of the People's Republic of Mongolia. After his death, the monarchy was abolished, and the Great Khural (Assembly) drew up a new Constitution that made the country into a republic. His monastic complex was placed under the jurisdiction of the Mongolian Committee of Sciences, and became a museum.

The Mongolian government forbade the finding of a ninth Bogd on their territory, but this did not prevent Tibet from seeking one on their own soil. Twelve years after the death of the eighth, Reting Rinpoche (the Regent in Lhasa) recognised a four-year old boy from Tromtsikang as the ninth Khalkh Jebtzun Damba (Bogd Gegeen).

When he was seven, the ninth Bogd entered Gomang College at Drepung Monastery and studied philosophy for 14 years, reaching the level of Madhyamika. His primary teacher in those years was a Mongol named Geshe Thupten Nyima.

When he was 21 he left the college to make pilgrimages to different holy sites in Tibet, while practising yoga.

Then came the 1959 Chinese occupation of Tibet. A year later he fled to India where he lived a quiet life as a peasant trader in Darjeeling, Mysore and Madhya Pradesh. He married and gave up his monastic vows, but he served as a lama in the Tibetan communities. His status as the Bogd Gegeen was not publicised, but after Mongolia's 1990 switch to democracy he met with the Dalai Lama, declared his true identity, and was reinstated as the Bogd Gegeen.

The ninth Bogd Gegeen has since travelled around the world to give Buddhist teachings and lectures. He visited Mongolia for two months in 1999 and during his stay was recognised as the head of the Mongolian Buddhist church at a ceremony in Erdene Züü Monastery. Political sensitivities, however, have prevented him from returning. He currently lives in Dharamsala with the Dalai Lama, and heads the Takten Kalachakra Project, which studies Buddhist philosophy, the Kalachakra Tantra and other aspects of the Vajrayana.

## THE PEOPLE'S REPUBLIC AND THE END OF THE MANCHUS

Mongol indignation over Manchu rule periodically flared up, notably in 1905 when the whole of Urga rioted in the streets. In 1911, taking advantage of the Chinese revolution, the Mongols drove the Manchu *amban* from Urga, overthrowing Manchu rule. Mongol princes proclaimed the independence of Mongolia and the formation of a great Mongol state. The Bogd Gegeen came to the throne and Urga was renamed Niisleel Khuree, Capital Camp.

In 1915, Beijing was forced to recognise through a treaty with Russia the autonomy of Outer Mongolia. Inner Mongolia would remain a Chinese province. After the 1917 Russian revolution the Chinese attempted to reclaim the lost province. In 1919, a Chinese general known as 'Little Hsu' set up a military government in Urga with Japanese assistance. Little Hsu was loathed by the Mongols, particularly after he forced the Bogd Gegeen to kowtow in front of a portrait of the leader of China.

This was the period of Sükhbaatar, a figure whose importance has been exaggerated by official history, and Choibalsan. The former, an ex-lorry driver on the caravan route from Urga to Khiakhta (according to some versions of his biography), joined the Communist party at Verkhne-Oudinsk (present-day Ulan-Ude) where he met Choibalsan, an ex-serf on the run from a Lamaist convent.

Between 1919 and 1920, the two of them, in liaison with Russian revolutionaries, set up the first revolutionary groups in Mongolia, and organised a troop of partisans to fight the Chinese and the feudal princes. Suddenly, in 1920, a new character appeared on the scene. Baron von Ungern-Sternberg was the head of a small army of White Russians and Mongols equipped with weapons from Japan. Ungern-

Sternberg—a madman pretending to restore the empire of Chinggis Khaan—drove the Chinese from Urga, and set up a government of Mongol princes. What followed was total confusion and the horror of war.

The 'Mad Baron' benefited from support by the Mongol population for having freed the Bogd Gegeen, who had been held hostage by the Chinese. He won further admiration for driving out the Chinese troops, and putting the hierarch of the Lamaist church back on his throne. Very soon, however, the population loathed him for his excesses. Following Urga's liberation, three days of crisis descended on the streets, as the Baron's troops raped women and pillaged Chinese shops. The attackers, boiling with revenge after the fight, descended on the local populace and massacred anyone who stood in their way of claiming the spoils of war. The Baron ordered all Jews and Bolsheviks, which to him were one in the same, shot.

Sükhbaatar left for Russia to appeal to the Red Army for help and, in 1921, organised a congress of the new Mongol People's Revolutionary Party (MPRP), setting the basis for the People's Revolutionary Army which Choibalsan would use to defeat Ungern-Sternberg. Indeed, the Baron did not last long. He was captured on a campaign in northern Mongolia and put on trial. The Bolsheviks shot the Baron at Novossibirsk on September 15, 1921, and a provisional government was proclaimed at Khiakhta. The USSR, which had been called in by the revolutionary Mongols, sent troops to Mongolia to fight the still active White Russian armies. They took back Urga on July 6, 1921 with the help of Mongol partisans. This victory marks the birth of the People's Republic of Mongolia, although a limited, pseudo-monarchy did last until 1924, as the Bogd Gegeen had nominally kept his throne.

The monarchy was abolished in 1924, the Republic was proclaimed, and Urga was renamed Ulaanbaatar, the 'Red Hero', in homage to Sükhbaatar, who died under suspicious circumstances a year earlier.

## THE PURGES

The Mongol State Security was set up on July 16, 1922 on the model of the Soviet secret services, by bringing together the isolated spying activities of the Bogd Khaan's Ministries of Foreign Affairs, of the Army, and of the Interior. These spies, trained by Soviet experts, succeeded in ridding Mongolia of the last Chinese and White Russians, and were gradually used as pawns by the Comintern, the Soviet Communist Party and by Stalin to launch campaigns of massive purges against members of the MPRP, the country's leaders, and the nationalists.

Towards the end of the 1920s, the Comintern and the Soviet Communist Party created the so-called 'Left Wing' within the Mongol People's Revolutionary Party, and placed it in power, thus imposing the Soviet system on Mongolia. The *de facto* passage of Mongolia to the status of a satellite state of the USSR was a painful one, entailing massacres, torture and summary executions. What had begun as a nationalist movement—which had turned to the Soviets for support against Chinese domination—became a bloody dictatorship, with still untold numbers of victims. Marshal Choibalsan was the master of the country from 1937 to 1952, the year of his death. His name is associated with the period of worst bloodshed in the history of Mongolia since the Revolution.

Choibalsan's foremost goal was the 'liquidation of the enemies of the people'. This entailed political trials, purges and executions in the Mongol leadership that resulted in the deaths of the entire moderate wing of the party. The official figures of the victims of this purge state 30,000 died, although the real figures will probably never be known.

Choibalsan was also responsible for setting up the 'final solution'. This spelled the destruction of almost all the temple complexes in Mongolia during anti-religious campaigns in 1937 and 1938. These years were sufficient to end four centuries of the Lamaist church. This destruction was accompanied by the physical liquidation or the psychological humiliation of the greater part of the country's intelligentsia; there were no intellectual and scientific centres outside of the great Lamaist monasteries. As it is put in the *History of Mongolia*, written in the 1930s by a Hungarian with little sympathy for democracy, "the services of the judicial police, placed directly under the orders of Choibalsan, gradually escaped from the control of the government and the Mongolian People's Revolutionary Party".

At present, the verdict on Choibalsan is still a mixed one. Although accused of creating a personality cult around himself, he is credited for preserving Mongol independence at a time when Stalin planned to turn Mongolia into a Republic of the USSR. Some even feel that the repression of 1937 was the price to pay for maintaining independence.

At the time, the country was operated internally by the so-called 'Left Wing' revolutionaries (associated with the Soviet military penetration of 1921), Buryat Mongols (ethnic Mongols but Soviet nationals), and Soviet diplomats. Key posts within the government were held by Comintern agents directed by the USSR, and by Buryats—the main exporters of the communist revolution to Mongolia. The Comintern forced the expulsion of the old revolutionaries from the government before taking over control of the repression against the Lamaist clergy. The radical pro-Russian Mongols were to eliminate their rivals by using the secret police directed by Russia.

# KEY DATES AFTER THE REVOLUTION

**August 1922**: Prime minister, D. Bodoo, and fourteen other leaders are shot for 'counter-revolutionary' activities. Their crime had in reality been that they were pan-Mongols hoping to reunite the two Mongolias, Inner and Outer. It should be noted that the original ten-point programme of the MPRP, adopted in March 1921 at Khiakhta, called for the unification of all Mongol territories and the formation of a pan-Mongol Republic. (This detail is conveniently absent from the official version of the history of the Mongol Revolution).

**1924**: The commander in chief of the Mongol army, Danzan, is executed. Danzan had stood up against the Russian protectorate and wanted genuine independence for Mongolia. According to a shorthand report of the third Congress of the MPRP, in 1924, the entire moderate wing of the party and its leaders were shot on orders from the Soviet ambassador Vassiliev. At the head of this wing was the 'centrist' Danzan. As first president of the MPRP, he had played a key role at the first Congress, in which Choibalsan was only a secondary figure. From 1926, a 'political tribunal' was created, which lasted until 1930, with Marshal Choibalsan at its head.

**October 1928**: Dambadorj, The president of the Central Committee, is removed from power by the seventh Congress of the Party and exiled in Moscow. The seventh Congress marks a decisive moment against Mongol nationalism. The earlier leaders had been favourable towards Buddhism, but the monastic assets, which accounted for about a fifth of the country's entire national herd, were to be confiscated. The seventh Congress is followed by violent attacks against the members of the Lamaist clergy, by the creation of an anti-religious commission, and the confiscation by the state of the land owned by the monasteries. The monks are forced to return to secular life.

**1928**: The so-called 'Left Wing' of the party launches a violent programme to purge its own ranks and to collectivise the country.

**1931–1932**: A period of massive purges. More than 1,200 people are accused of political crimes, among them are soldiers, aristocrats, and intellectuals.

**1930–1934**: More than 20,000 people, including almost 600 families, flee the country. Several armed uprisings break out, notably in Khösvgöl, Zavkhan, Arkhangai and Övörkhangai aimags, during which thousands lose their lives. These rebellions do not prevent the process of forced collectivisation imposed on the nomadic pastoralists. This however, has disappointing results. Inexperienced livestock breeders fail and the national herds fall from 23 million to 16 million in two years.

**1929:** Choibalsan put in charge of confiscating the possessions of 670 'feudal lords'. He is the only one of the entire first generation of revolutionary leaders to survive the purges of the 1930s within the ranks of the Presidium and of the Secretariat of the Central Committee of the MPRP. Ten of the party leaders at the aimag level are expelled from it, and between 1932 and 1934, the number of party members falls from 42,000 to 7,976. Purges on such a huge scale are organised by the State Security. A large part of the trained officers in the intelligence service are eliminated, and employees who oppose the purges are executed. During these years, more than half of all prime ministers and department heads, all the vice ministers, and more than 20 per cent of officers, are executed. During the third plenary session of the MPRP, some party heads and government leaders severely condemn the actions of the 'Left Wing', removing all their power, and taking a new political stance which has much popular support. By the end of this period, the anti-religious campaigns became—temporarily—less brutal.

**1936:** A number of high-ranking lamas are placed on trial.

**Mid-1937:** A series of purges is launched on an unprecedented scale. In February 1936, the Bureau of Internal Security, enlarges into a ministry, and is handed over to Choibalsan. In the same year, the prime minister, P. Genden (who had condemned the leftist deviations), and the head of the Bureau of Internal Security, D. Namsrai, are both removed from their posts for their lack of support of Stalin's policies. Genden is exiled to the USSR, before being executed in November 1937. The War Minister, Demid, is accused of being a Japanese agent. He dies in August 1937, of 'food poisoning', while travelling to Moscow, although he was almost certainly assassinated.

**October 1937:** High-ranking lamas and members of the military high command are judged and condemned for crimes of high treason during two series of spectacular political trials in which Choibalsan himself reveals the 'conspiracy of the Genden-Demid clique' and the treason of the military commanders. This entirely fabricated conspiracy allows the condemnation of thousands of people, many of whom are executed following a verdict from the Soviet military Supreme Court. Among the victims are 17,000 lamas.

**1937–1938**: The new purge affects the intellectual elite, notably the institution coordinating scientific research throughout the country (the present Mongol Academy of Sciences). Some of the greatest figures of Mongol history are blacklisted and officially condemned: Chinggis Khaan is called a 'strangler' and 'oppressor of the Mongol people'; Tsogt Taij, a highly revered figure in Mongolia and a symbol of the struggle against Manchu oppression in the 17th century, is not spared either. Many historical subjects become taboo. The final solution over the monasteries leaves them in ruins. Nearly all the 767 monastic centres are pillaged.

**March 1939**: Prime Minister Amar, Genden's successor, is executed. From 1939 on, Choibalsan, already Minister of Internal Affairs since 1936, takes over all the key posts. Known as the 'Mongol Stalin', he is head of the Party, Prime Minister, and War Minister. Between 1939 and 1952, the year of his death, only two party congresses are held, as all consultation, even purely formal, is superfluous. By 1940, 35,000 people had become victims of the purges, and 20,000 were executed.

**1950s–1980s**: The State Security keeps up its surveillance. At the beginning of the 1960s, it maintains tight control over more than 60,000 Mongols considered a potential threat to Party ideology.

**1989**: Decision taken to restructure the Ministry of Security.

**1990**: The Ministry of the Interior is dismantled, its personnel reduced by 65 per cent. Thirty-four departments are closed, and Soviet advisers sent home. Like the history of the October Revolution in Russia, the history of Mongolia is officially rewritten during the period of Soviet domination. Existing documents are rare and difficult to acquire. A commission on rehabilitation is set up to do justice to the victims of the political purges and to restore historical truth. More than 20,000 people have been rehabilitated; among these was P. Genden. The epitaph on his tomb could be engraved on those of countless thousands of other victims, "Here lies an innocent person, unjustly accused of political crimes during the years 1930-1942, cruelly tortured and executed."

# The world of the steppes

## Introduction

Mongolia has a surface area six times the size of the United Kingdom, just larger than the state of Alaska. In the north it borders on Russia (central Siberia), with which it shares 3,440 kilometres of frontier, and in the south on China (Inner Mongolia and Xinjiang), along 4,670 kilometres of frontier. It is located on average, 1,580 metres above sea level (80 per cent of its territory is over 1,000 metres), being basically a high plateau inclined from west to east, ringed by mountains on all sides.

The highest part of this mountain system is the **Mongol Altai**, which extends some 1,000 kilometres from the north-west to the south-east. Its highest point is in the Tavan Bogd range, an area of impressive glaciers and peaks over 4,000 metres above sea level. The valleys of the western part of the Altai are themselves at a height of 3,000 metres. East of the Mongol Altai, at the centre of the country, is the **Khangai**. Its permanently snow-capped peaks reach elevations over 3,000 metres, the highest being Otgontenger in Zavkhan Aimag.

The Khangai landscapes bear the marks of ancient volcanic processes: lava flows, conical hills and hot mineral springs. Its rivers form rapids, their waterfalls flowing through deep gorges. The vegetation of the Khangai is richer and more varied than that of the Altai, and the pastureland is considered some of the best in the country. The name 'Khangai' (literally 'that which satisfies a need or a wish') is used in Mongolian to define areas with potential for pastureland and abundant fresh water.

To the north of the Khangai is the mountainous region of **Khövsgöl**, formed by a number of almost inaccessible chains, aligned longitudinally, unlike the latitudinal

*Right: the vast pastures of Dariganga. Opposite: Commemoration of the Communist revolution, Ulaanbaatar 1981.*

ones of the Khangai. The forest zones to the north give way to mountainous wooded steppe, which then becomes semi-arid, and even arid in the extreme south.

To the east of the Khangai are the **Khentii Mountains**; here the main chains extend from south-west to north-east, forming the western curve of the great Khangai-Khentii arc. The Khentii gradually slope down to the steppe in the east, and to the basin of the Orkhon and Selenge rivers to the west. This basin, irrigated by rivers that have their source in the Khangai and Khentii as well as in Khövsgöl, offers favourable conditions for agriculture.

To the east and south of the Khentii Mountains is the great Eastern Mongolian plain (the **Dornod steppe**), at an average height of 700 metres above sea level. Khökh Nuur, at 560 metres, is the lowest point in the country.

Mongolia is situated on a continental watershed and for the most part is orientated from east to west. North of this line, the rivers flow into the Arctic or Pacific oceans, whereas south of it, they flow into the Central Asian depression, which has no access to the sea. The Selenge is the only navigable river in Mongolia. It belongs to the Arctic basin system and is 992 kilometres long, 399 of which are in Mongolia. The Orkhon, the largest of its tributaries, has its source in the Khangai Mountains and flows for some 1,124 kilometres through Mongolia. The Onon, Kherlen, and Khalkhiin rivers all belong to the Pacific basin system, and flow down from the Khentii and Khingan chains.

There are numerous lakes in the north and west of the country. The most important is Lake Khövsgöl, the largest reservoir of fresh water in Mongolia. Similar to Lake Baikal, it has its own endemic fauna and flora. Approximately 80 per cent of Mongolian lakes are saline.

Mongolia also has many hot and cold mineral springs, particularly in the north, in the Khangai and Khentii regions. They have been used for centuries for their undeniable therapeutic merits.

# Flora and fauna of Mongolia

Located at the junction of the Siberian taiga, the Central Asian steppe, the desert zones of the gobi, and the high summits of the Altai and Saïan, Mongolia has a flora and a fauna of great variety, characteristic of these four very different ecological regions. Many specimens of the Mongolian flora have yet to be classified. Of the 150 endemic plants and the hundred or so relic plants in the country, more than 100 are listed as endangered or rare species. The endemic animal species in this Central Asian environment, such as the Saiga antelope, the jerboa, of which Mongolia has four varieties, as well as eight endemic species of reptile, including the **Mongolian agama** (*Stellio stoliczkanus*) and the **toad-headed agama** (*Phrynocephalus versicolor*), live mainly in the desert steppes of the gobi zones.

# THE GOBIS

Contrary to what is generally thought, the Gobi is not a desert in the usual sense, that is, a sandy area completely devoid of vegetation. The Mongols do not talk of a single Gobi but of many *gobis*. They list 33 different *gobis*, according to soil composition and colour. The *gobi* zone represents a third of the total surface area of the country and, within this zone, sandy deserts account for only three per cent of the entire Gobi Desert. This sandy *gobi* is called *tsöl gov.*

When the steppe is saline and semi-arid, when the vegetation thins out and is composed of short, fibrous plants, when there is little or no irrigation, when rainfall is rare and irregular, the Mongols use the word '*gobi*'.

"The term '*gobi*' refers to large enclosed basins, with coarse gravel floors, which are abundant in this region. Their surfaces are generally formed of subhorizontal fill, with little residual relief and frequent small depressions caused by wind action. Dunes and sandy expanses are generally quite limited." (F. Aubin, *Encyclopedia Universalis*)

Areas of *gobi* are not limited to the aimags with the word 'Gobi' in their name. *Gobi* are also found in Sükhbaatar, Dornod, Khovd and other areas. The *gobi* are classified in terms of four main geographic regions.

Pre-Altaic Gobi: this area forms a large basin between the Altai and the Khangai, including the Great Lakes region, and is subdivided into several smaller basins: Uvs Nuur, at 743 metres above sea level, Khiargas Nuur (1,034 metres), and Khar Nuur.

Trans-Altaic Gobi: this stretches from the Altai in the north to the Tianshan Mountains in the south. Part of this *gobi* is therefore located within China (Xinjiang). In Mongolia, it is cut by high mountain chains—the Aj Bogd (3,760 metres) and the Tsagaan (2,380 metres).

East Mongol Gobi: located between the northern steppes and the Khingan chain, this is the largest of the *gobi*.

Gobi-Altai: The eastern part of the Altai Mountains. It is a high rocky area that receives more precipitation than other *gobis*.

Smaller *gobi* are sprinkled across the region and usually familiar to locals, but perhaps not your guide. The **Tsenkher Nom Gobi** (10,000 sq. km) is south of the Aj Bogd Mountains in Gobi-Altai. The **Sharga Gobi** (3,150 sq. km) is found in Gobi-Altai Aimag. The **Khökh Nar Gobi** (4,500 sq. km) is

*See page 74*

*from page 71*

in Bayankhongor. The **Khuis Gobi** (4,000 sq. km) spans Khovd and Gobi-Altai. Lastly, the **Borzon Gobi** (2,100 sq. km) is in Omnogobi.

The Galbaa Gobi, however, is one of the most arid and daunting. After crossing it, the intrepid Russian explorer Nikolai Przevalski wrote in his book *On the Roof of the World*, "This desert and that of the Ala-Chan are so terrible that in comparison those of Thibet can be considered a blessed land... not even an oasis, everywhere is the absence of life, everywhere is absolute silence. It is the land of death in all senses of the word, and its vast wastes extend for hundreds of versts in latitude and longitude."

## THE FLORA OF THE GOBI

The many endemic plants of the gobi zones are characterised by what is called 'high biological activity'. Extremely resistant, they mature more rapidly than other plants, and many have seeds with high protein, vitamin, and fat content. Some of them, having developed great faculties of adaptation to conditions of extreme heat, are almost colourless, swollen, and covered in soft hair, and provide excellent fodder for cattle. Herders sometimes use these seeds, cooked and ground, as a complement for their own diet. The inhabitants of the Gobi have for centuries made flour from high-starch rhubarb roots.

One common Gobi plant is the **Saxaul** (*Haloxylon ammodendron*) which generally grows in the sand as a bush or, more rarely, a leafless tree that can measure up to four metres in height. It is located in the south and south-west, flowers in May, and has a small, yellow blossom. It is adored by camels, but also highly valued as a fuel—the heat it gives out when burnt is three times stronger than that of birch wood. Another Gobi plant is the **Karagana**, or 'false acacia', and the **Golden karagana**. Its roots can dive to 1.5 metres in order to reach the water table. Some shrubs, it is said, manage to send their roots as far as 50 metres under the surface for the slightest trace of humidity! **Camel grass** (*Budurgana*) grows in saline soils in tufts resembling bunches of yellow flowers.

## THE FAUNA

The Mongolian fauna is extraordinarily rich. Birds of prey include **eagles, falcons, goshawks, kites, harriers, lammergeyers, vultures,** and **owls**. One of the most frequently seen in the skies is the **black kite**, larger than a crow, and with a notched tail that distinguishes it from all other raptors. The harrier feeds on steppe mice and can often be seen hunting for prey beside the road.

*Previous pages: Gers on the steppe of the Orkhon Valley.*

Fish are plentiful in the rivers. Among the many species are the *taimen* (*Hucho hucho taimen*), the largest member of the salmon family, which can reach two metres in length and weighs up to 80 kilos. It is a carnivore and hunts grayling, burbot and frogs, and at night preys on the rodents that swim across the rivers. In the north of Mongolia, in Lake Khövsgöl, are *omoul*, another salmonid, which can weigh up to three kilos. It originates from Lake Baikal and was introduced here in 1956. Another interesting specimen is *Brachymistax lenok* (*zeveg* in Mongolian), a member of the trout family. There are nearly sixty other species of fish which are similar to those found in European rivers.

The *yangir* or **ibex** (*Capra sibirica*), a wild mountain goat, lives between 1,000 and 4,000 metres above sea level. Wolves and snow leopards prey on the mountain goat, and the young frequently fall prey to eagles. In Noyon and Sevrei sums (Ömnögov), crossbreeding between ordinary goats and ibex has produced an animal famed for its high quality wool.

The rare **snow leopard** (*Pantera uncia*), with its metre long tail, is found throughout the Khangai and Altai chains, in the Saïan and Tagna mountains, and generally wherever it can feed on *argali* and *yangir*. This nocturnal animal also eats marmot, hare, mice, pheasant, and other birds. In very snowy winters, it may even take cattle from the pastures near the mountains. It bites through the neck or the arteries in the groin, drinks the blood and eats the entrails of its prey.

The illegal trade of snow leopard pelts has grown in recent years and forced conservationists to take action. Although foreign tourists have hunted snow leopards illegally, Mongolian herders also frequently shoot these animals, which threaten their livestock. Recent action to save the snow leopard includes a WWF project called 'Irbis' (the Mongolian word for snow leopard). Under the scheme, designated communities weave winter clothing for the tourist market. The profit from sales go back to the community only if no snow leopards are shot there. Irbis products can be purchased in Ulaanbaatar at Millie's Café and gift shops. For more information on snow leopards, visit: www.halcyon.com/mongolia/snowleopard.html

The **Maral deer** (*khuder* in Mongolian, *Moschus moschiferus*), sometimes called the musk deer, is a small animal, weighing between 10 and 15 kilos. It is recognisable by its white nose and throat. Two vampire-like fangs distinguish the male. This animal is sought after for its musk, a sort of animal ginseng used in traditional medicine and in the making of perfume, lipstick and toothpaste. The Maral deer is found in the steep forests of southern Siberia and Central Asia and sometimes found grazing in mountain prairie or near glaciers. In Mongolia, it is found in the Khövsgöl, Saïan, Khingan, and Tagna mountains.

The **Sable**, a small furry animal resembling a marten, has long been prized for its pelts. They were hunted nearly to extinction in the early 20<sup>th</sup> century and have been

*An owl chick, still groggy after a nap. Dornod Aimag.*

protected since 1930. There are a few on the Bogd Uul Mountain near Ulaanbaatar, but sables of Khentii are said to rear the finest pelt. Sables are also found around Lake Khövsgöl, and in the Delger-Mörön, Tenggis, Tsagaannuur, and Shishged river basins, in the Altai, and at the mouth of the Bulgan and Khovd rivers.

Along with the sable, the **marten**, the **otter**, the **beaver**, the **Altai pheasant**, and the wild **reindeer**, are also protected animals.

The **lammergeyer**, a large vulture, is often found in the Gobi. This scavenger has a tremendous wingspan that can reach three metres. It is known to inhabit the Noyon Bogd and Gurvansaikhan (Ömnögov) mountains where it has given its name to the Yoliin valley, one of the biggest tourist sites in Mongolia.

## RARE ANIMAL SPECIES IN THE GOBI

Very few travellers actually spot Mongolia's rare animals in the wild. Stuffed versions of these creatures, however, are invariably on display in the provincial museums and the Museum of Natural History in Ulaanbaatar.

The **wild camel** (*khavtgai* in Mongolian, *Camelus bactrianus ferus*), is found only in Central Asia and in very small numbers. It is thought that there are just a few hundred individuals left, wandering between western Mongolia and China. In comparison to the domesticated Bactrian camel, the khavtgai has smaller humps and lacks pads on the knees. It is quick, has excellent eyesight and hearing, and when afraid can run without stopping for some 50 or 60 kilometres. It prefers areas of deep sand, and grazes in herds of 50 or 60 animals. The **Golden Camel Museum**,

*Above: Herders of reindeer, the Tsaatan, in Khövsgöl Aimag.*
*Below: The sand dunes converge with the steppe in Gobi-Altai Aimag.*

inside the Ulaanbaatar Natural History Museum, is a good place to learn more on this species.

The **wild ass** (*khulan* in Mongolian, *Equus hermionus pallas*) is also extremely rare. It is close to the ordinary horse in size and shape, but has a longer and more powerful head, and ears like a donkey's. It lives in arid deserts, without water or vegetation, and grazes in herds of 200 to 300 beasts—likely for protection against wolves. A wolf cannot match the khulan in speed and must rely on a herding technique in order to hunt them. The pack divides into two groups, the first waiting in ambush, and the second herding the khulan towards it (the same tactics are used for hunting gazelle). The khulan can only escape by cutting across the direction of movement of the wolf pack. The largest populations of khulan are in eastern-most edge of Ömnögov Aimag, and the eastern Gobi, as well as in the Galbaa, Zeemeg, Borzon, and Khovd *gobi*.

It sometimes happens that khulan get mixed in with herds of domestic horses. This is not discouraged because the Gobi Mongols believe that an ordinary horse will become a racehorse if it passes through the dust kicked up by a khulan. The khulan are also known to graze with camels (as do the zeeren and the *argali*). The Mongol hunter will therefore train one camel especially for the purpose of approaching this animal. They hide behind the camel and drive it forward with a stick fixed to a ring in the camel's nose.

Until a few years ago, the only specimens of the **Przevalski's horse** (*takhi* in Mongolian, *Equus prjevalskii*) were found in Western zoos. They suffered habitat loss during the 20th century and by the late 1960s, had completely disappeared from the wild. Attempts, however, are now under way to reintroduce this horse gradually to its native land.

The **Gobi bear** (*mazaalai* in Mongolian) is the world's only desert bear. Listless and shy in appearance, it has a large head and chest, a short tail and small eyes. It is not much taller than an ordinary one year-old bear cub. The Gobi bear is extremely rare, but still found in scattered parts of Gobi-Altai, Ömnögov and other southern regions.

The **Gobi lynx**, like the *mazaalai*, is about half the size of the ordinary lynx.

There are three sorts of Gobi antelope and gazelle: the *zeeren* gazelle (*Procapra gutturosa*), the **black-tailed gazelle** (*Gazella subgutturosa*), and the **Saiga antelope** (*Saiga tatarica mongolica*). The black-tailed has yellow-grey fur that blends into the light colour of the sand and the sun-burnt grasses. These are protected species. The zeeren weighs between 25 and 35 kilos, and bounds along with its tail straight up; it can run at a speed of 60 to 70 kilometres per hour, keeping up this up for about 15 kilometres. Once very abundant, its numbers have been drastically reduced through intensive hunting. It is found in the Gobi, as well as in Sükhbaatar and Gobi-Altai.

Captured zeeren young can sometimes be seen accompanying nomadic families in the region, and they soon learn to feed from the goats.

Native territory for the Saiga has been dramatically reduced in recent years, and its' numbers have consequently fallen. It has long been hunted for its horns, a valuable ingredient in traditional medicine. There were literally millions of Saiga before the second World War, but they were massacred on a huge scale to feed the troops of the Soviet Red Army. Also damaging was the construction of the Trans-Mongolia railway, which cut off key migration routes (this likewise reduced numbers of other gazelle species). They are still seen around the Sharga Gobi and south of Khar Us Nuur (Uvs Aimag). For several years now, Saiga have been bred in Khalium sum (Gobi-Altai Aimag).

The **Gobi lizard** is the only protected species of the 34 types of reptile that live in Mongolia. Some lizards have transparent eyelids that protect them during sand storms while still allowing them to see.

The fat-tailed **jerboa**, or 'kangaroo-rat', is a small, relatively common Gobi rodent that resembles a miniature kangaroo, moving about in the same manner. It digs its burrow between the roots of the saxaul and eats its branches. Like many other small desert animals, when faced with a prolonged period of drought, it goes into 'estivation': having stored up sufficient fat like the camel, it buries itself in the ground and goes into a state of lethargy by slowing its basic metabolic rate. It can survive for months like this. To stay alive in the heat of summer and the cold of winter, birds, who cannot bury themselves, nest in the tunnels vacated by these rodents. For some of the birds of the Gobi, the periods of egg-laying are triggered off only by the sporadic arrival of rain, independently of the natural rhythm of the seasons as is the case for other birds.

The *argali* (*Ovis argali*), sometimes called 'Marco Polo's sheep,' is a large wild sheep with horns can measure nearly two metres in length, and weigh 30 to 40 kilos. It lives in bands of five to 15 animals and is found in the mountains of the Gobi-Altai, the South Gobi and the Eastern Gobi. One of the most sought-after animals by foreign hunters, the sale of argali hunting permits is an important source of revenue for the government.

# Mongolian Culture
## World vision and Shamanism

*"If I were given the task of defining Culture, not that of the great schools and of theses, I would define it as the propensity to respect. The propensity to respect the other, the propensity to respect that which you do not know, the propensity to respect bread, earth, nature, history, and culture, and as a consequence of this, the propensity to respect the self, to dignity."*

Andreï Bitov, *A Russian in Armenia*

At the heart of this way of life and of thought is a cosmic vision of the world. In this world, that which 'lives' is not simply that which can be 'seen'. There is no irreducible difference between the mineral, vegetable, human, and animal worlds, any more than there is any break between the world of the dead and that of the living, the visible universe and that of the spirits. Man is part of the cosmos and his human nature does not give him any particular right over living beings or the dead. The entire universe is living and everything that is, lives according to a force that inhabits it. But this force exists in limited quantity, just as what is given by nature—health, animals, rain, fecundity—is also limited. Any imbalance in nature brings with it an imbalance in man.

## Mongolian symbolism

A symbol is an object which allows one to recognise not the identity or the function of something, but its relation to other things. Through the permanent consciousness, in Mongol culture, of peoples' place in the cosmos, through the powerful desire to be in harmony with the universe, the nomad lives in a highly symbolic world in which objects are not defined according to their identity or their use, but are seen and categorised according to the relationship they have with Heaven and the spirits.

The hearth is at the centre of the *ger*, and the *ger* is a microcosm in itself. The hierarchy that underlies the spatial organisation of the *ger*, with the hearth as the main point of reference, clearly reveals the *ger*'s sacred aspects. The central pillar—the smoke hole at the top of the tent—is directly related to the cosmic axis, and as J.P. Roux puts it, represents a 'highway' for the spirits. The many prohibitions and taboos—including magical ones—relative to the behaviour of each person within the *ger*, as well as the spatial divisions of the *ger*, should all be understood through their relationship to objects made sacred through their heavenly characteristics.

*An ovoo, the residence of ancestral spirits.*

Any act that threatens their sacred character threatens the balance and happiness of the family. These fastidious rules continue to be scrupulously respected today by the majority of steppe pastoralists.

A large number of prohibitions, still in force in present-day nomadic society, are also precautions meant to avoid harming the master-spirits of nature, who provide the vital forces. They encourage people not to take more than they need, and to give back to the spirits what is owed them in a relationship based on exchange. The universe is full of invisible and omnipresent spirits. Humans have to develop good working relationships with them, and act to win them over without offending them. The numerous codified precautions and rites of appeasement all stem from this.

The *ger* is a microcosm, and the human universe is always perceived in relation to the cosmos. In the same way, the cosmos are humanised. The mountain, for example, is the personification of all cosmic forces and appears as an anthropomorphic figure with a spinal column, a back and a neck on its northern flank, cheeks, cheekbones, sides, ribs, and shoulders on its east and west flanks, a forehead, eyebrows, a knee and even a liver on its south side. These are still the terms used today in Mongolian to name the different parts of a mountain.

The spirits (of the dead, of nature, etc.) are not deified but instead are humanised. The nomad does not have a relationship of 'veneration' with them but one of partnership. Nor are they all-powerful. People can interact with the spirits and even trick them.

Prohibitions and taboos are not simply a codified and exotic classification of more or less automatic, superstitious actions. They form a coherent system, integrated into an imagined universe and a concept of 'reality' that belongs to a nomadic society.

Traditional popular belief explains that many of the misfortunes that befall people and their livestock are the result of evil actions by the spirits, and in particular by the souls of the dead. Obtaining and maintaining good health, fertility, and fortune depend on their relationships with these invisible beings.

Many visitors to Mongolia complain of the difficulty in dealing with locals. Westerners are often baffled by Mongol 'superstition' and unwillingness to 'break these rules', in order to serve their guest more faithfully. Yet, many of these difficulties can be smoothed over through understanding and respect towards this centuries-old culture, which holds an infinite number of riches, ready to be shared with those who are willing to make the effort to listen to this old wisdom. The steppe pastoralist, but also some of the Mongol city-dwellers, continue to respect the traditions of their country, and would rather risk contradicting a tourist than offending the spirits.

*Ovoo* worship is one common custom that foreigners quickly experience. However quickly a traveller might want to reach his destination, he must take into account the need for the Mongols accompanying him to stop at the first important *ovoo* (cairn, the abode of a spirit) on the outskirts of town, and respect their custom of circumambulating it three times, adding a stone on each pass. In this way, the journey will have every chance of starting off well.

Do not be surprised if, having asked to stop at the top of a pass to admire the superb countryside spreading out before you, the Mongols with you are eager to get going again as fast as possible if sunset is approaching. Dusk is dangerous, for this is when humans are most vulnerable to evil spirits, which are more daring with the onset of night.

Urinating in water (such as a stream) is sacrilegious. Do not do this. At the time of Chinggis Khaan, only death could repay such an offence.

If someone saddles a horse for you to ride, do not refuse the offer. Unsaddling a horse that has not been ridden is bad luck. If you do not want to ride, have the courtesy to trot about for a bit (a test drive, if you will), and then dismount.

When arriving in sight of a *ger*, it is absolutely vital to bring your horse to a walking pace. Arriving at a gallop would be taken as an aggressive act. Stepping on the doorstep of a *ger* is an offence to the spirit of the door frame, tantamount to stamping symbolically on the neck of the master of the house. When seated in a *ger*, never stretch out your legs with the heels of your shoes pointing towards the central hearth. This shows disrespect to the spirit of the fire.

# Fire symbolism

Fire has been an object of veneration to the Mongols since ancient times and its cult grew under the influence of Uighur Manichaeism. Traces of this cult, which existed long before the clan system, can still be seen today, for example in the domestic hearth, which is considered sacred, and in a number of prohibitions and precautions still observed by the nomadic herders.

When a *ger* is set up on a new site, the nomad family starts by placing the metal stove in the centre, and only then are the trellis walls unrolled. In the old days, the three stones that held the hearth symbolised the father, the mother, and the daughter-in-law, who will be the mother of the descendants.

Fire, the god of life, represents the link between the ancestors and their descendants, and symbolises the succession of generations. Dancing in the flames of the hearth are the souls of the children yet to be born. If offended, these souls will leave, resulting in the disappearance of the family.

The legal codes of Chinggis Khaan, the *Yassa* (*yas* meaning 'bone' or 'clan'), fixed people's behaviour with regard to fire, and established a system of prohibitions that were observed long before their codification.

To direct pointed or metallic objects towards the fire is to risk ripping its head off or putting out its eyes. It is forbidden to spit on it, to pour water or milk on it, as that would blind it—this is a serious act which heralds the family's ruin. If some urgent reason should arise which necessitates that the fire be put out, one must first say, "God of the Fire, pull your feet away", which lifts the prohibition.

A further offence would be to throw garbage on the fire. It is also forbidden to dry boots by pointing the heels towards it or to stretch the legs out with the soles pointing towards the hearth.

Chopping wood or bones with an axe near the hearth disturbs the god of the fire. The tongs (used for the fire) must not be left open, as this is a presage of a quarrel. Lighting a fire with birds' feathers, or the dried shards of garlic and onions can cause illness or blindness in cattle.

There are also prohibitions linked to ashes. The ashes from the hearth must not be stirred or mixed, lest the cattle will disperse and the minds and thoughts of men may go astray.

One must not walk on the hearth ashes left by a family that has moved camp elsewhere, nor let ones horses' hooves trample them.

The container for fuel (*argol* or wood) is the container for offerings meant for the fire. It must never be sat on. Because it is an offering for the fire, *argol* (animal dung) is much more than just a fuel. It is charged with ritual significance and has a protective function much like magic, enabling a family to prevent misfortunes it may have attracted by violating a prohibition and stirring up the spirits' anger. If one trips over the doorstep upon the entering the *ger*, place a piece of *argol* in the fire to avert misfortune and secure happiness within the family.

Fire is lastly considered a messenger from heaven. The most frequent method of divination in ancient times, which goes back at least to the Xiongnu, is scapulomancy, or divination by reading the cracks on the burnt shoulder blades of sheep. Like the shaman, fire is an intermediary that allows communication with Heaven. It can reveal omens through the cracks it makes in the bones, as well as in logs, or in the colour and regularity, or irregularity, of its flames. It also carries to the spirits the offerings that they are most fond of: butter, sheep's sternum, and alcohol.

## The *ovoo*, abode of the local spirits

The *ovoo* is the ubiquitous pile of stones found atop hills and passes. In forested areas they are sometimes made from branches into the shape of a domed hut. The building of an *ovoo* is an old and widespread custom among all the peoples of Central Asia, which existed long before the spread of Buddhism there and even before shamanism. These cairns were most likely designed as tombstones, and later became shamanistic altars. Their construction seems to have been related to archaic funerary cults and cremation rituals.

Consequently, they are closely related to the cult of ancestral spirits. Commemorative rites were held near them in springtime, bringing together various members of the clan. Sacrificial rites were carried out to the souls of the dead to whom food was offered, and a horse sacrificed – its skin tied to a pole near the place where the ancestors were buried. Thus the living, having invited the spirits of the dead, shared out their food with them and informed them of the events which had occurred in the past year.

A *naadam* (sport event) usually followed the *ovoo* ceremony, and included the 'three manly games': a horse race, archery, and wrestling. This ritual ended with a large collective feast prepared by the women of the clan, who were kept apart from the most important elements of the ritual, just as they were kept apart from the burial rites of the tribal elders.

In post communist Mongolia, the food offerings to feed the souls of the dead, and the *naadam* organised near the *ovoo*, are held openly. The Mongols' relationship with the spirits never broke, but under the socialist regime all exterior manifestations of it was condemned as suspicious and backward. *Ovoo* ceremonies are not held regularly, so travellers must inquire with local authorities for details.

Each clan has its particular *ovoo*. Geographically and spatially, the *ovoo* marked the symbolic limits of the clan's territory. On a sacred level, the rituals held at the *ovoo* guaranteed the protection of the spirits on whom that territory depended. This included spirits of the ancestors, spirits of nature, earth and water.

## THE *OVOO* AND LAMAIST COSMOLOGY

The spread of Lamaism brought great changes to the cult of the *ovoo*. The Lamaised *ovoo* became a sort of temple built in honour of the protector of the nearest monastery and displaced the ancestral spirit that had been there before. Henceforth, it was built in accordance with Buddhist cosmology. A very elaborate ritual appeared which governed the construction, consecration, and benediction of an *ovoo*, the presentation of offerings, and the carrying out of prayers. The consecration and acceptance of the *ovoo* made the spirit cooperative and kindly.

The consecration ritual of the *ovoo* complete, travellers can cross the pass in less fear, assuming that they treat the spirits with due respect. But a spirit can be easily disturbed if the rocks or items on the *ovoo* are haphazardly moved, or if people fish and hunt nearby without bowing to the spirit. Another way to incur a spirits' wrath is to lay out a dead body near the *ovoo*.

Regardless of past political and religious changes, the *ovoo* has maintained its importance. The names of the spirits and the details of the ritual may vary, the cult of the *ovoo* may have lost its original meaning, and many traditional *ovoo* may have been destroyed during the years of repression; but the deep motivations that lay behind their emergence have not disappeared.

*Following pages: Jockeys race towards the finish in the annual Naadam race in Ulaanbaatar.*

When visiting an *ovoo*, the circumambulations are made in a clockwise direction. By following the path of the stars and the sun, the Mongolian hopes to imitate the constellations, and join the cosmic process. But perhaps not so cosmic, are the items heaped onto *ovoos*, including beer cans, vodka bottles, car parts and crutches. To the Mongol, however, these items are not junk—each was left with some purpose or meaning.

## THE GRAND MASTER

The Grand Master of the spirits on Earth and of all that exists—mountains, space, deserts, rivers, forests—is represented as an old man with white hair, dressed in white, and leaning on a stick with a dragon's head. He is the synthesis of all the spirits of nature—the protector of the herds, and the dispenser of fertility and longevity. Among his special symbols are a pear—symbol of the woman's reproductive organs, and a long skull—symbol (researchers say) of the male organs.

Some places in Mongolia, including one of the mountains near the capital, are known for their strong ties to this quintessential figure. He can be seen represented on a *thanka* and on monastery walls (at Bulgan City, for example), on a rock carving outside the monastery of Manzhir in Töv Aimag, and among the masked figures that take part in Lamaist Tsam dancing. The retrieval and canonisation of this important figure by Lamaism in the 18th century symbolises the allegiance of all the spirits of shamanism and the 'Yellow Religion'.

*The shaman's dance.*

# The Mongols and their horses

*"They gallop like the wind and their power is that of a mountain avalanche."*
Song dynasty annals

The history of the 'empire of the steppes', like that of nomadic pastoralism, is indissolubly linked to horses. According to a Mongol saying, "a Mongol without a horse is like a bird without wings".

'Mobility' was the key concept and the most important strategic doctrine of the Turko-Mongol tribes—the tactics and logistics of their armies were entirely determined by the horse. Horses were broken in through long hunts organised since the time of the Xiongnu in which up to 10,000 horsemen took part. In the Mongol period, each autumn, the khaan organised large hunts to help train his cavalry.

Centuries of tight relations between the nomads and their horses, along an accumulation of attitudes and traits of character inherited from the oldest periods of horse riding, have created a very specific psychology and vision of the world.

The Mongolian language, first of all, is imbued with the omnipresence of the horse culture. As an example, the word for 'riding a horse' (*nisast*) developed long ago as a generic term for expressing the idea of 'behaviour'. Horse references are also found in the terms of respect for welcoming someone ('have you ridden well?' or 'ride in peace'), or expressions in current usage such as 'to go to see one's horse' (for a man) or 'to go to see one's mare' (for a woman), which are euphemisms for going to the bathroom. Certain concepts, such as the word for 'poor' in Mongolian (*iaduu*), formed from the verb *iadakh*, which means 'to go on foot'.

The Mongolian word *mergen*, which means 'wise', also has the sense of 'skilful archer'. In the old days, the best horseman could time the launch his arrow so that it did not deviate when the horse's hoofs struck the ground at full gallop.

The Mongol horse is small, being about the height of a double pony (1.3 metres at the shoulder) and relatively light (between 300 and 350 kilos on average). Unlike Westerners, Mongols do not give their horses names. It is enough to designate them by the colour of their coat. Yet, however many horses are around, there is never ambiguity. The Mongolian vocabulary is rich in precise terms for the nuances of a horse's coat. When the inexperienced eye sees only a 'white' horse, the herder will see a 'snow white' or an 'ash white' one.

Some nomads believe that the environment affects the colour of a horse. Large quantities of snow falling on a certain region will explain the great number of snow-white horses in that area, while bay or red-brown horses will be more common in areas where the earth is of a warm colour.

Men are generally reticent to ride a mare or stallion, preferring geldings. Many horses are trained to amble—walking by lifting two feet on the same side together—a much appreciated pace in the steppes nowadays but once considered undesirable in for horses used in military campaigns.

The young, one or two-year old horse is examined at the end of summer or in early autumn. It is broken at the age of two. In the springtime, the herds are inspected and young males are castrated.

Catching an untamed horse is a difficult art but one which the *malchin* (cowboys) have long mastered. Instead of a rope lasso, the Mongol uses a long pole called an *uurga*, formed of three willow or birch branches, each about a metre long, and placed end to end. At the tip of the pole is a leather strap with a slipknot in it.

This is also the time when the horse's mane is cut. Only the stallions keep a long mane. Until the early 20th century, the Chinese were major importers of horse mane, which is used to make rope. The Chinese also imported a large number of Mongol horses which they used, among other things, to breed mules.

Livestock are branded and the mark is called a *tamga*. There are several hundred

## THE MAKING OF AIRAG

The leather bag on the right of this photo is filled with *airag*—fermented mare's milk, Mongolia's drink of choice. A plunger is used to stir the *airag* as it ferments, and it's customary for guests to give it a few 'plunges' upon entering the *ger*.

*Right: A young jockey heads for the starting line at a Naadam horse race, Ulaanbaatar.*

shapes of *tamga*, distinguished from one another by small additions above, below, or within the sign. They used to be common to an entire clan. Among the marks still used today are the characteristic signs of the runic script of the Orkhon Turks, and the square letters of the 13th century. Others are said to represent old totems or magical symbols. In the shamanistic vision of the world, the *tamga* give off a secret power that can bring success to some and misfortune to others. *Tamga* appear sometimes among old rock engravings, in particular those of the Turkish period.

# Horse selection

Mongolians have traditionally grouped their horses into four categories: horses used to shepherd sheep, horses to ride when rounding up the herd, 'postal' horses (weapons horses) that were used in military campaigns and for postal relay, and finally the race horses, which are chosen with great care.

The Mongols are particularly fond of their race horses and believe that their qualities are handed down through the maternal side, by the mares that gave birth to them.

The Mongols are experts at detecting future racehorses by observing various external and internal signs that characterise the promising horse. The signs to look for when choosing a good horse have been documented and passed down through the centuries, so that racehorses of the 17th century are little different from their modern counterparts.

According to old chronicles, "a good horse must have a narrow forehead, thin mane and tail, a wide chest, a horizontal back and steady back legs. The pelvic bone must be near the floating ribs. Being constantly at the front of the herd is a sign of valour. Small and straight white teeth show a saddle animal, but one who would be ill-suited to long distances."

# The *naadam* races

The training of race horses—the result of centuries of experience—is meticulously carried out in stages, taking into account the age and characteristics of each animal. The aim of each of the three stages is first to ensure weight loss, then the acquisition of a minimal speed, and finally progression on to the maximum speed.

The determining factors that indicate whether a horse is ready for the race or instead needs to continue training are the consistency and colour of the sweat and droppings, as well as the regularity of breathing.

## WEIGHT LOSS

The training begins two or three months before the *naadam*. The horse is left out to graze on the best pastureland but must not put on any weight. For two days it remains tethered. From the third day it is covered with a felt blanket and, at the hottest time of the day, led up a slope. Proper training regularly alternates with periods of scraping off the sweat with a *khusuur*, a sort of long wooden pallet often carved with the twelve animals of the zodiac. This is the main method used to eliminate the excess food and increase blood circulation and muscular activity. The sweat wiped off is called 'frothy sweat'. As its excretion continues, the animal's food intake is gradually reduced. The droppings then become firm and brittle. After this, the animal has to lose his 'watery sweat', which is colourless and salted.

## THE 'TAR'

The *tar* is a race run as fast as possible over a distance of about one kilometre, used to train the horse to develop regular breathing and the fastest rhythm when running. The distance run is gradually increased. When the horse's breathing becomes stable again after these races, the time has come for the next stage, called *sungaa*—training over a medium distance.

## THE 'SUNGAA'

Ten days before the competition the horse must run a distance of 10 to 13 kilometres. Four or five days before the race it runs 15 kilometres. This race is meant to develop the horse's regular breathing pattern and to determine the results of the training. If the breathing is not satisfactory, it will be necessary to turn to a particular, rather delicate exercise that requires much attention and experience: the horse must run at full gallop two or three days before the competition.

The animal is primed when several signs are observed. It will stand in a balanced manner, its droppings will be compact and dry, no sweat will form under the saddle after a race, the blood vessels under the skin and near his nostrils will be visible.

The national Naadam, held every July 11–12 in Ulaanbaatar, is a showcase for the country's best racehorses. The exact date of the regional *naadams* changes by the year; and travellers should inquire with local authorities about the dates. In addition, travellers should look out for a special, nationally organised horse race that, in recent years, has been held in the first week of August.

# The horse in Mongol symbolism

One of the oldest Mongol ornamental motifs is the heavenly horse or 'wind horse' (*Khii mor*), which is seen on ritual cloth flags or on simple pieces of paper attached to a particularly venerated *ovoo*. This horse is the symbol of the energy of life, of the sacred fire, of enthusiasm, the intermediary force between the world of humans and that of spirits. Before the 20th century, it symbolised the spirit of the ancestors. On the *ovoo*, the ritual flags bearing its effigy are reminders of the important role that the horse—in flesh and blood rather than in its symbolic form—played during funerary rites from the days of the Xiongnu until the 13th century at least. This was the most frequent animal to be presented as an offering to *Tengri* (Heaven), impaled on a mast. As a totem—or even an ancestor in some tribes—the horse's role was to lead the dead to the place where the ancestors dwelled.

For a warrior, to die while fighting on horseback was an act of heroism. He would be buried with his stirrup on his left.

In Mongol culture, the horse is also a symbol of healing. When a community endures a period of hardship, monks will climb a mountain and, whilst chanting, throw 'paper horses' to the winds so that their spirits may come to the aid of those in distress.

# Nomad architecture

The old conceptions about Turko-Mongol architecture and, what was once seen as a radical and irreconcilable opposition between the sedentary and nomadic ways of life, have become obsolete since the discovery of a number of ancient city sites in Mongolia. The importance of the cultural heritage transmitted by the nomads since ancient times can no longer be put in doubt. The terms 'architecture' and 'sedentary' are no longer indissociable. The need for mobility does not prevent palaces and temples—which could accommodate up to 10,000 people—from being spacious, and architecturally complex.

The specificity of nomad architecture led to the appearance of a particular style in Mongolia, which makes ingenious use of millennia of experience in mobility and 'demobility'.

## From hut to *ger*

The primitive hut, architecturally very simple, gave way on the one hand to the *ger* with a conical roof—widespread among the Turkish peoples—and on the other hand to the black *ger* with a round roof, dominant among the Mongol peoples.

### CAMPS AND NOMAD TOWNS

The terms *ordoo* and *örgöö* designated both temporary military camps and the places of residence of the khaan. Later, by extension, they were also used for the centres of population that developed around the khaan's residence.

There were two types of *ordoo*. One was the temporary nomad *ordoo* camp, which appeared during military campaigns or during the seasonal migrations to other pasture lands. The second was the semi-sedentary camp (*khot*, a term which was to be used later for towns), which served as capital, monastery, fortress and market all in one, bringing together artisans, merchants, families of soldiers, and prisoners. Next to the nomad *ordoo*-towns were fixed, permanent towns such as Karakorum, Bars-Khot, and sedentary monasteries, such as Uliastai, Khovd, and others.

### THE GREAT CIRCLE

The old Urga was also known as the 'Great Circle' (*Ikh Khuree*). The word *khuree* also served to designate monasteries because, originally, any complex formed of religious buildings was built around a main temple, following the same plan as nomad camps, in which the *gers* were laid out in a circle around those of the chiefs and the elders.

## FROM *GER* TO MONASTERY

Religious buildings developed from the *ger*. The first monasteries were, from the 13th century, *ger*-temples that could be dismantled and transported. The canopy tent and the *ger* gave rise to different types of architecture. The original light-weight materials (felt, wood, cloth) gave way to more lasting ones (stone, metal, wood) sometimes used for the construction of the khaans' gigantic palaces and sedentary temples. The cupola-shaped roof was inspired by the *toono* (crown) of the *ger*.

The assembly hall of the first monasteries adopted the shape of a canopy tent. Their plan developed gradually from a circle to a rectangle. The monks' quarters surrounded the temple halls on three sides, except for the main entrance in the south. The main axis of the monastic complex was always orientated north-south. The monastery as a whole faced south, or very rarely south-east when the lay of the land made it necessary. Within the monastery, the location of each hall in relation to the main hall depended on its relative importance, but in no case could it ever be placed south of the main hall.

An important monastery included, apart from the temple halls, the palaces of the high lamas and princes, the monks' quarters and also, later on, a commercial zone. According to the original monastic rules, these *maimatchen* were to be set up at some distance from the monastery, but the rules were only applied early on, and at the end of the 19th century, the commercial outskirts extended onto the land of the main Mongol monasteries themselves.

*The Mongol ger serves as sleeping, eating and social space for the entire family.*

# Mongolian art

Mongolian art is the product of a rich cultural heritage: Hun, Ruan-Ruan, Yenisei Kirghiz, Jurchen, Turkish, and Uighur, but it has also benefited from a synthesis of influences from India and Tibet. From all of these sources, a specific Mongolian art style developed.

Mongol art did not appear as a passive absorption of various cultural influences, but as an active process of adaptation of these elements into a separate style. Furthermore, this art exerted a deep influence on other cultures, such as on Persian art of the 13ᵗʰ and 14ᵗʰ centuries, leading to the formation of a Mongolo-Persian style and affecting the development of the Persian miniature by the integration of new elements into it. The Mongolo-Persian style in turn exerted a great influence on modern Mongolian art, as can be seen for example in the paintings of the famed artist Sharav.

## Religious art

Leather, silk, cotton, and linen cloth were traditionally all used as backings for paintings (*thanka*). The artist himself prepared the colours with mineral pigments (made from precious stones, turquoise, coral, pearls, mother-of-pearl, or metals such as gold, silver, copper and iron). The pigments were blended into a mixture of leather, horn, and animal bones boiled up with a sweet syrup. To this they also added a little earth or water collected by pilgrims in holy sites, or blood from the artist's nose, mixed in with gold powder, silver, precious stones, sap or resin of medicinal plants.

Mongolian paintings done in the traditional Mongol *Zurag* style for the nomad monasteries were first of all small in size so that they could be easily transported. Later on, larger canvases were used, and the art of appliqué was developed, which finally took over from painting. Appliqué embroidery has existed in Mongolia since ancient times, as testified by a carpet found in a second century Xiongnu tomb. From the 18ᵗʰ century on, however, monks turned the appliqué technique into a veritable national speciality, particularly at Urga, which began to export its appliqués throughout the Tibetan world. Some of these works can reach 16 metres in height. They are composed of a mosaic of cloth and are made according to a technique that is both time-consuming and costly. This procedure was mainly used for making very large *thanka* that were publicly unveiled during ceremonies such as the *Tsam*.

*Right: detail of bas relief Buddhist art at Gandan Monastery.*

# Popular art

Popular art is characterised by the widespread use of extremely old decorative motifs with highly symbolic contents. These motifs are reproduced on many everyday objects such as saddles, stirrups, belts, boots, hats, *ger* furniture, carpets, doors, knife cases and tobacco pouches.

The construction of a Mongol *ger* brings together many craftsmen: blacksmiths, carpenters, joiners, tailors, embroiderers and metal-workers. Each region of Mongolia has developed its own specialised craft, according to local preferences. The Dariganga, inhabitants of Sükhbaatar Aimag, are renowned gold and silversmiths, making decorations for domestic objects and horse harnesses. In the west, the Oirat and the Torguut have historically been known for their furs. Inhabitants of the north-west aimags specialised in making the metal and wood structural elements for the *ger*. And in its day, Urga was the centre of the appliqué technique.

Animal art, although its day has long since passed, is still reflected in the art of the present-day pastoralists of Khovd, Gobi-Altai, and Khövsgöl, particularly in the decoration of saddles with motifs of animal combat, still seen in the central Gobi.

A renaissance of traditional art has exploded since the fall of communism in 1990. Artists no longer paint the classic scenes of Soviet grandeur so prevalent just a few years ago. Lenin, Stalin and Choibalsan are no longer the inspiration of artists, as most cultural workers have turned to a historical figure that was prohibited for seventy years—Chinggis Khaan.

# Ornamental design

Mongolian ornamental design is a veritable alphabet expressing the nomad's conception of the world and philosophy. It is composed of a few basic motifs from which a large number of variations are derived. Many are auspicious ornaments— talismans charged with beneficial qualities, intended to attract good luck and prosperity. For a nomadic herder, this means long life, good health, many children, and strong herds. An auspicious ornamental motif on a saddle or a stirrup brings good luck to the rider and increases the speed and endurance of his horse.

The use of ornamentation did not disappear during the socialist period, it went underground. All outward signs of wealth were forbidden, yet ornamental designs could still be found in *gers* and the silver studs on Mongol saddles.

There are three main categories of ornamental motifs: geometric, zoomorphic, and plant motifs. Each element of the design is painted in one or more colours. The harmony between the composition of the motifs on the one hand, and the background and the main colours on the other hand, produce an effect that is both aesthetically-pleasing and has semantic significance. The particular use of certain precious stones and metals in itself bears a message: turquoise is the symbol of fidelity, gold and amber of love, silver and pearls of purity and nobility of soul.

The *ölzii*, or 'never-ending knot' is at the centre of Mongol symbolism. It is a variant of the ancient labyrinth motif, and is an auspicious sign shaped as a plaited, squared interlace symbolising the universe and eternal movement. The spiral symbolises the dynamic expanse of the universe. It also has a beneficial power attached to it. It is thought to bring long life and happiness to its bearer, driving away evil spirits, and protecting men and cattle from dangerous enemies, wolves, and other wild animals.

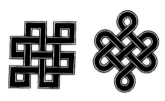

*the ölzii design*

Lamaism took over this motif as symbol of the endless cycle of rebirths. Religious art has reused motifs from popular decorative art and has been influenced by the latter.

The name of the esoteric symbol, the **swastika** (*khus* in Mongolian), well known to us, comes from the Sanskrit svasti, 'salvation'. It is a sign of good luck and happiness, and is known to the Mongols as the 'sign of 10,000 years'. It is thought to have appeared in Mongolia in the Bronze Age, perhaps even earlier. After the collapse of the Mongol empire, Altan Khan tried to assemble the dispersed tribes by bearing a swastika on his banner. The swastika was forbidden from 1938 on, by edict from Choibalsan, and is little seen in Mongolia today, although it appears to be slowly coming back. The swastika is said to have arrived in Medieval Europe, in Scandinavia and in Eastern Europe with the Huns.

The motif of the **Khaan's bracelet**—the double circle—symbolises the endless eddy into which the organic and inorganic universes are dragged. This motif represents the concepts of faithfulness, friendship, strength, and stability. The motif of the **Princess' earrings** is a variant expressing strength and endurance.

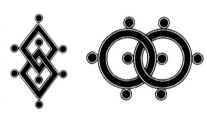

*The Princess' earings and the Khaan's bracelet.*

The **T-shaped arabesques** (including different varieties and combinations of the T-shape) express eternal movement, the eternity of life, the absence of beginning and end. Some of them are strongly reminiscent of the fret motifs of the ancient Greeks. In Mongolian design, they are found only on very important objects, for example festive tents, sacred containers or the most precious clothing, and are always placed in the centre of the object.

Carpet motifs are the most characteristic creations of late steppe art, using earlier motifs, pre-dating the Animal Style. Carpet motifs can be geometric, zoomorphic, or more often, horn-shaped, representing the stylised horns of animals. Felt carpets decorated with these horn motifs are still made today by the Kazakhs in Mongolia. The motifs on Turkmen carpets represent the animal totems of the clans of the women who made them.

Among other **zoomorphic motifs**, mention must be made of camels' humps, animals' hoofs, stylised muzzles, peacocks, stylised dragons and eagles. The eagle motif—representing a sun god and the ancestor of the shaman—can be found from the Bronze Age until today. It is often seen in the decoration of the Buryat in the 19th century, and of the Kirghiz. It may be the representation in animal form of individual protective tutelary spirits. The auxiliary spirits of the shaman also have a zoomorphic appearance.

Plant motifs are the most common in Mongolian decorative art. They can be seen on clothing, on everyday objects, in the homes, and on embroidery where they are often done in gold or silver thread, or in a light colour. They are also used in architecture. They are never found on felt objects, but on metal (engraving, chasing) or wood (painted on chests and small, low tables in the *ger*). They are also found on ritual bowls and on statues of the Lamaist pantheon. Among the Kazakh in Mongolia, these motifs are found on carpets, hats, costumes and drums.

The interlace of flowers, leaves, and petals symbolises origin and growth. The leaves represent the source of life on Earth, the flower and the bud the concept of unity and eternity of being. It is possible that plant motifs were little used by the ancient Mongols and that they spread only later as a result of contact with their southern neighbours. **Motifs linked to the cosmos** express an archaic symbolism that represents respect and fear for the powerful forces of nature. Fire, thunder, mountains, sun, moon, clouds, water, animals, plants have all inspired these motifs.

# Mongolian music

## Traditional Songs

Traditional Mongolian music follows the pentatonic scale and can be rhythmic, with a regular structure, or free, varying according to the mood and personality of the singer. The **long song** is the oldest form of melody. Its origins can be traced back to ancient poetry and it still retains an epic aspect. It is always sung in solo, and is characterised by a melodically unrestricted vocal production, with a particularly wide range of tones and voices that require great breath control from the singer who must vocalise as long as possible while modulating the vowels. This type of song, often melancholic, recalls the solitude of the nomad and the immensity of the steppe. It is an art in itself, which does not require an instrument although it is often accompanied by a fiddle or a lute.

The **short song**, a more recent form, is quick and lively, often humorous in character. Its themes are love, the home country, horses, and women. Technically less trying than the long song, it is still very much part of everyday Mongol life. No social event or gathering can fail to end in songs and it would be rude to refuse to sing along if one is invited to.

*The musician on the right plays the moriin khuur.*

The **diphonic song** (overtone singing) is the most spectacular and probably the oldest form. Known as *khöömii* in Mongolian (literally 'pharynx'), it is a vocal technique by which a single performer can produce two or even three separate lines simultaneously. The notes are continuous and low, made by forcing air through a constricted throat, and a series of harmonies made by the tongue which, rolled under the palate, gauges the breath, producing sounds remarkably similar to those of a flute. The vocal imitation of the flute and the Jew's harp was traditionally the exclusive province of men.

The diphonic song is linked to shamanism and is characterised by the production of sounds imitating those of nature: the soft noise of the wind, cascades and rivers and birds' songs are just a few. Apart from Mongolia, diphonic singing is also traditional in Tuva and the Gorno-Altai, and among the Oïrat, Khakhass, and Bashkir.

The Mongols have an ancient and rich tradition of **epic songs**. Their most remarkable epics are those of Geser and Jangar which are transmitted by bards in a sung versified form, sometimes accompanied by a moriin khuur or a tovshuur (pinched string instruments), and by khöömii throat singing.

The horse, the main subject of Mongol poems and songs, is also the main theme of the epic, and there are close links among Turko-Mongol peoples between the epic and shamanism. Epics are full of shamanistic themes, formulae and images, and the actual performance of an epic was thought to possess magical powers.

The *magtaal* is another form of song that continues to play an important role in Mongol life. It is a poetic praise, an epic-like hymn with its origins in shamanistic poetry. Dedicated to the sacred mountains, to a powerful wrestler, or to a victorious horse, it is performed at all the important events of nomadic life. No *naadam* worthy of its name would be without a *magtaal*.

## Musical instruments

The *moriin khuur*, or 'horsehead fiddle', has ancient origins and is a purely Mongolian instrument. This fiddle with a trapezoidal sound box, has two strings of horsehair, most often accorded to a fifth, and is played with a bow made from horsehair. Its scroll head generally ends in a carved horse's head, symbol of the racehorse ridden by the poet-musician on his mystic travels. In older times, every family had a *moriin khuur* that was played during the *naadam* to the archery songs and to the *magtaal*, the songs of praise dedicated to the victorious horse. Played solely by men, it was above all an instrument intended as an accompaniment to a vocal performance.

The *moriin khuur* originated from the banks of the Onon, where, it is said, the most famous fiddle players come from. An old legend, of which there are many versions, tells of its invention.

"Once upon a time, there was a poor herder whose only possession was a thin, russet horse who was his greatest friend. One day, he found him lying on the ground, dead, near his *ger*. Heartbroken, he began to make a fiddle from his friend's bones, tendons, and hair. Then he fixed the horse's head to the handle, and overcome with grief, lay his own head on it to unite himself spiritually to his dead friend. As the bow began to move and brushed gently across the strings; the horse's head shivered and gave off nervous neighs... Thus the melody was born which spread throughout the steppe across the autumn grasses, softly caressing the young man and his horse..."

The **Jew's harp** (*aman khuur* in Mongolian, literally 'mouth fiddle'), made of stone, leather, bamboo, or iron, is an instrument much used in Mongol traditional music. To the Turks, the Jew's harp, made by the blacksmith, belonged exclusively to the shaman who played it when predicting the future or driving away evil spirits. Before giving it to him, it had to be consecrated to make it infallible and to ensure that the gods could hear it. Recently, an entire orchestra of Jew's harps brought together some 412 players.

Among the other instruments used in popular music are the **limbe**, a bamboo or metal wind instrument resembling a flute in shape and sound, but more powerful in tone. The **khutchir** is a fiddle with a long handle and four silk strings. Its oval sound box is covered in snakeskin.

Visitors may also see the **shanz** (or *shudarga*), a three-stringed lute, or the *yootchin*, a table zither with fourteen strings that are struck and played with two bows. The *yataga* is a table zither with ten to fourteen pinched silk strings.

The musical themes of popular songs are rich indeed and many of them echo the symbiosis between man and nature and the animal kingdom, modulating sounds imitating the songs of birds or other sounds from nature. Itinerant musicians, storytellers and improvisers were forbidden in Ulaanbaatar from 1930 but their musical traditions have remained alive.

# Festivals

## *Tsagaan Sar*, the Mongolian New Year

This important traditional festival has deep popular roots and was at one time completely unrelated to Buddhism. *Tsagaan Sar* means 'white month' or 'white moon'. The colour white is the symbol of all that is beneficial, of happiness, purity, and frankness, but also of milk products, which represent the basic foodstuffs of the nomadic pastoralist. The beginning of the Mongolian year once coincided with the autumn equinox, before the onset of winter. In this season, when the cattle begin to give less milk, the nomads start to eat curds; thus the 'white month' should be understood as the 'month of the curds'. Later, the great khaan Kubilai moved the beginning of the year to the first new moon of spring so that the New Year was no longer celebrated in autumn, but in February, the exact date being calculated according to the lunar calendar.

The Mongols use three calendars—the seasonal calendar popular among the old pastoralists, the solar calendar, and the Buddhist lunar calendar.

The **Mongolian lunar year** is divided into twelve months of thirty days each, to which an extra thirteenth month was added every four years. With the coming of a new annual cycle, the nomads added one year to their age and to that of their cattle, without taking into account their actual date of birth.

The festival of *Tsagaan Sar* was very popular among the nomads, and the Lamaist church had little choice but to integrate it into its own system. After the installation of the government in 1924, its celebration was temporarily forbidden, but it reappeared under a new name, the 'day of the cooperative herders', in an attempt to

*Passing the snuff bottle— a greeting important to the Tsagaan Sar tradition.*

rid it of its religious content and to limit its celebration among the nomads. Despite this, the tradition was kept up even among the city-dwellers, who made a point on this day to attend the Buddhist services held in Gandan, the only official monastery in Ulaanbaatar.

This celebration has two distinct forms. The popular one reflects very old traditions, and the religious form dates back to the arrival of Buddhism in Mongolia in the 16th century.

The popular form of this festival includes a series of deeply symbolic rituals that must be carried out in strict observance of the rules to ensure a happy and favourable year. To the nomad, this means the well-being of his family, his clan, and his cattle. Each gesture that is made and each word that is said at this crucial time are fraught with prophetic consequences for the year that has just begun.

The preparations begin a month before the festival. The *ger* has to be thoroughly cleaned before the New Year, but never on the first day of the year. The last day of the ending year is an important day called *bituun*, 'conclusive'. New Year's Eve, *bituun oroi*, is spent saying farewell to the old year and ushering it out. *Bituuleg* is the name of the festival held on the night of the last day. A huge meal is prepared and all the guests eat large meat dumplings cooked in stock (*bansh*), milk products (*tsagaan idee*) and milk tea (*suutei tsai*).

Before the feast, it used to be the custom to split open a boiled mutton or cow bone to symbolise the opening of the *bituun*. During this meal, each person ate as much as possible as a guarantee of abundance in the new year.

Before sunrise on the first day of the New Year, everyone leaves the *ger* and bows in the direction of each of the cardinal points, starting in the east where the sun rises. Each person then makes offerings by sprinkling mare's milk (*airag* which has been kept frozen since autumn for this day) or cow's milk in honour of *Tengri*, Heaven. The family then returns to the tent and gathers around a great fire, which must on no account be lit from the previous day's embers. The eldest son presents a bowl of *airag* or milk to his parents on a *khadag*, a ceremonial silk scarf, symbolising the bestowal of blessings and good-luck wishes on those who receive the scarf. Each child in turn presents a *khadag* to his parents, after which the family members pass round the snuffbox.

The first greeting of the year is expressed through very specific ritual gestures and mutual salutations. Under this ritual, called *zolgokh*, the oldest person places his or her arms out straight, with the palms turned down, on the outstretched arms of the youngest person, and both pronounce traditional formulae of good wishes while gently touching cheeks. This gesture indicates that the elder can count on the support and respect of the younger. If the two people doing this are of the same age, one of their outstretched arms is placed under that of the other person. In this greeting, it is necessary to take the utmost care in one's dress. The hat (obligatory for men) must be straight on the head, the *del* (traditional cloak) must be buttoned up to the neck, the belt adjusted, the sleeves pulled right down and the cuffs turned back.

Even after the end of the celebrations, relatives or friends meeting for the first time since the New Year, whatever the month, greet each other in this way. This greeting, however, is not to be used between husband and wife during Tsagaan Sar. If they disregard this prohibition, it is said that their marriage will break up and that they will become enemies. Once the ritual greetings are done, the parents say a blessing (*yerööl*) and express good wishes to all the members of the family.

After sunrise, everyone gathers around the hearth to share the New Year tea. At sunrise, ritual fumigation (*san*) used to be carried out near at a small *ovoo* set up by the *ger*, around which, one did a circumambulation. Food and other offerings were placed near the *ovoo*, and the eldest and most respected person expressed words of gratitude and prayed to the spirit of the mountain and the area.

All through the day, care must be taken that no disrespectful word is uttered and that all quarrelling is avoided. Crying or arguing on that day is a sign of unhappiness and disputes to come throughout the year.

On that night, no one should sleep in a *ger* that is not their own, lest they should become disorganised and lazy in the coming year.

Each person is meant to celebrate the first day of the 'white month' and not become absorbed by any other activity on that day. Only on the following day is it possible to return to the usual tasks.

When all the members of the family have finished the ritual greeting, the men, dressed in their best clothes, set off for the *ger* of the oldest relative of their generation, or of the most important figure in the area. They bring with them a kettle of tea and platters of cheese, *aaruul* and *ööröm*. After more ritual greetings, handing over of presents, and a short conversation, they prepare a sort of milk porridge. All the dishes have to be tasted three times. Each guest drinking *airag* must make a wish of good luck to the master of the house. Then the remaining porridge is divided and each person receives a portion to take home to offer his own guests. It is said that the more people that share the dish prepared in the *ger* of the eldest herder, the happier and more prosperous will be the coming year.

Afterwards, the men saddle their horses and the visits continue, in principle according to hierarchical order, from the closest relatives to the furthest removed. There are exchanges of greetings, tobacco pouches, food, and presents with the master of the house. The oldest guests or particularly dear ones receive *khadag*. The children are given sweets or a little money. The value of a gift is unimportant. What counts is the token of consideration shown. No formal invitations are sent out and guests can arrive at any time of the day.

During the feasts, the master of the home presents all his guests in turn with a bowl of *airag*. Mongol etiquette demands that the men always be served before the women. The person who receives the bowl must stand up and sing, usually accompanied by the rest of the party. Refusal to sing is considered impolite.

The traditional 'white food' is laid out on a low table, with an entire boiled saddle of mutton. The cooked head and the feet of the animal are also served. According to custom, the master of the house starts the mutton, cutting a few pieces from it, which he passes to his guests according to age and gender.

Various games are played on the evening of the first day of the year. Dozens, if not hundreds, of games can be played using the anklebones of livestock as dice or building blocks. *Khorol*, another popular toy, is a game of wooden dominoes with drawings on them related to the twelve animals of the zodiac. Horse racing and wrestling competitions were once organised on a wide scale. This tradition is slowly returning in both Ulaanbaatar and the countryside.

These games and rituals are important from a symbolic point of view, and have kept a quasi-ritual function. Just as the stories told on the eve of a hunt were indispensable for success, so the games and the laughter please the spirits and are an auspicious sign for a good year.

In the city, the 'white month' is celebrated for only a single day, but in the steppes the visits and greetings can go on for up to a month.

# Naadam

Naadam is Mongolia's most well-known festival, and the one that most tourists see as it occurs at the height of summer. Horse racing (see page 92), is one of the three 'manly sports' on show. The other two are archery and wrestling. This ancient festival dates back many centuries and was originally created as a celebration during weddings or spiritual gatherings. It later served as a way to train soldiers for battle.

In Ulaanbaatar, the festival occurs annually on July 11–12. The main arena is the Naadam Stadium, located south of the

*Wrestlers perform the eagle dance.*

*Wrestling at the Naadam Stadium, Ulaanbaatar.*

Children's Park and near the Tank Monument. The festival begins before 9 am with a ceremony at Sukhbaatar Square, complete with lavishly dressed soldiers astride horses. Yak-tail banners are paraded from the Square to the Naadam Stadium where the opening ceremony includes a show and speech by the President. An all access pass to the stadium costs Tg16,000 and can be purchased at the stadium or from tour operators. If you only plan to see the opening ceremony, you can buy a one time entry pass for Tg8000.

The wrestling starts immediately, although the action does not get intense until the final rounds on the second day. The wrestling costume includes boots (*gutul*) the tight fitting briefs (*shuudag*) and a curious jacket (*umsgul*) with no chest. According to lore, the jackets used to cover the chest until a disguised woman entered the competition and won. The jackets were then redesigned to prevent any females from entering the competition again.

Outside the stadium is the archery field, where the *del*-clad contestants take aim at a target of fist-sized baskets. 'Bone shooting' is sometimes added to the venue. In this game, the participants flick sheep anklebones at a target of stacked bones. Years ago, another competition existed whereby the participants had to break the backbone of a cow with a single blow from the hand. Sometimes, the bone, polished by all the hands that had tried but failed to break it, would be passed from one nomad camp to the next until, finally, someone succeeded.

*Naadam* festivals occur during the month of July across the countryside. But with no regular schedule, finding one can be difficult, so ask for details at travel agencies. An excellent resource for Naadam facts and history is the World Party website (www.world-party.com). Type 'Naadam' in the 'Go' box to find the link.

# Maidar Ergekh

This great ceremony is held at various times in Mongol monasteries: in the first fifteen days of the 'white month', for the last summer moon or the last autumn

*Right: Young lamas parade at Gandan Monastery for the Maidar Ergekh ceremony.*

moon. The aim of the ceremony is to present the coming of the Fifth Buddha (the Buddha of the Future), Maitreya (Maidar), and to pray for rebirth in Heaven.

The statue of Maitreya is carried triumphantly out of the monastery and set up on a four-wheeled cart drawn by a green wooden horse or a white elephant, symbols of the speed of the spread of Buddhism and the victory of the faith with the coming of the Fifth Buddha.

The monks, the orchestra, and the cart leave the monastery in procession, passing under the great triumphal arc, and set off on a circumambulation of the sanctuary. The procession stops at each of the cardinal points to bless the orients, read and recite the *Rabsal* (texts dedicated to Maitreya), make sacrifices to Maitreya and the spirits of the earth, and attract by their blessings good will and fecundity. In some monasteries, Tsam dancing accompanied the circumambulation of Maitreya. In it, the dancers act out a theatrical performance showing the repression of the enemies of the faith. The form this procession has taken is specific to Mongolia and to the Buryat, and does not exist in Tibet.

When the ceremony is complete, the statue is returned to its sanctuary where it will remain until the following year. Only some of the monasteries dedicated to Maitreya organise this great festivity. Most of the other 'specialised' monasteries are dedicated to Ayush (Amitayus), the Buddha of Long Life, to whom numerous rituals were addressed for a peaceful and long life and good future reincarnations. The ceremony of the circumambulation of Maidar (Maitreya), banned by the communists, has been given new life since 1990. Most provincial capitals now host a ceremony of some form, but the largest are at Erdene Züü, Amarbayasgalant and Ulaanbaatar.

# Mongolia today

## Population

Mongolia has a population of 2.65 million (2000), nearly a third of whom live in the capital, Ulaanbaatar. The next largest cities are Darkhan (95,000), Erdenet (75,000), Choibalsan (45,000) and Baganuur (25,000). About half the population live in rural areas.

Mongolia is a young country. About 70 per cent of the nation is under the age of 35—thanks to a 1960s baby boom when families were encouraged, and rewarded, by the government to have children. While 44 per cent are under 16, just four per cent are over 65. Population growth, however, has slowed significantly over the past ten years and now stands at 1.5 per cent. The life expectancy is just over 67 years.

## Ethnic and linguistic groups

The Mongol language belongs to the Altaic family, which includes Turkish, Tungus and Manchu. It is an agglutinative language (like Finnish and Basque), which means that it uses the juxtaposition of particles to express syntax and morphological nuances, and works on the principle of vocal harmony. Its grammatical structure and its syntax are close to that of Turkish. The two main groups of dialects in Mongolia are the eastern dialects (Oïrat), and the western ones (Khalkh and Barga).

The Mongol Academy of Sciences has recorded about twenty ethnic groups of either Mongol or Turkish origin. About 82 per cent of the population, however, are of the Khalkh ethnic group. In the western part of the country, a significant slice of the population speaks a dialect of Turkish. The largest of these ethnic groups are the **Kazakh** (five per cent), the **Uriankhai-Tuva**, the **Tsaatan**, and the **Khoton**.

Descendants of the **Oirat** speak a slightly different variation of Mongolian. They are subdivided into several ethnic groups: the **Bayat** (2.1 per cent), the **Dörvöt** (2.8 per cent), the **Zakhtchin, Miangat, Ölöt**, and the **Torguut**.

The **Buryat** represent 1.7 per cent of the population. They form an enclave near the northern frontier with Russia but they can also be found in the large towns. Among the other groups are the **Dariganga** (1.3 per cent) in the south-east of the country, as well as the **Utzemtchin** and **Barga** in the west. In addition, there are some 3.5 million Mongols in China (Inner Mongolia, Qinghai, Xinjiang), and about 500,000 in Russia, mainly Buryat from Siberia, but also some Kalmuk.

# The Mongolian script

When Chinggis Khaan built his empire, Mongolian became the imperial language as well as the common one. Turks, Iranians, Chinese, and Russians were among those who used it. The use of a script soon became indispensable, and the Uighur alphabet was chosen. This is formed in part by borrowings from Sogdian, whose roots are to be found in the Syriac script of the Nestorian missionaries. The ancient Mongolian script, also known as Uighur Mongolian, therefore has an Aramaic origin.

The Mongolian script is read vertically from left to right. At the beginning of the 20th century, just before the 1921 Revolution, an attempt was made to reform the written language. Some wanted to adapt Mongolian to the Latin alphabet. This failed, notably because the USSR saw this as a reflection of an undesirable pan-Mongolism. In the 1930s and 1940s, Stalin began to unify the alphabets of the different Republics of the USSR, as well as that of Mongolia. In 1946, Cyrillic was imposed as the official script in Mongolia. The old Mongolian script was henceforth read by only a small minority of specialists. This prevented the great majority of Mongols having any access to an important part of their cultural heritage, notably to the historical chronicles written in old Mongolian.

When reform came in the late 1980s, a group of intellectuals, scientists, and publishers asked the Grand Khural (parliament) to authorise once again the use of the old Mongolian script. In 1995, the government decreed that all teaching would be done in this script in the lower grades, and it would be used for subjects such as history and social sciences in the higher grades. Financial difficulties are not the only obstacle in this project. A mountainous problem has been the rift between the classical written language and the spoken one. This script does, however, have one great advantage as it can be adapted without any difficulty to the different Mongolian dialects because of its system of notation of sounds. It also has special signs that allow it to transcribe very easily foreign languages such as Chinese, Sanskrit, or Tibetan.

# The economy

For centuries, Mongolia's economy was based on nomadic pastoralism. Under communism, Mongolia attempted a shift towards agriculture and industry with a centralised and planned economy. Collectivisation carried out at the end of the 1950s drew the former nomads into structured cooperatives in order to breed livestock. Emphasis was placed on developing the livestock breeding programmes and the raw material processors—including meat packing plants, leather and wool factories. State farms were developed and arable land extended. Mining, processing

*The interior of a Mongol ger. The 'male side' is to the left and the 'female side' is to the right.*

and energy were built up in the industrial complexes of Ulaanbaatar, Darkhan, Erdenet, Choibalsan, and Baganuur.

The stability and growth that Mongolia had been witnessing for decades came to an abrupt end in 1990 when the Soviet Union abandoned subsidies to the country. The USSR had previously accounted for 30 per cent of the GDP and massive debts started piling up. (Still today Mongolia is billions of dollars in debt, including an estimated $10.5 billion to Russia alone).

Factories shut down and exports fell by two thirds between 1990 and 1992. Inflation skyrocketed and a system of ration tickets was introduced for people to buy meat, milk, flour and bread. International aid, mostly from Japan, arrived to keep the power stations operating through the harsh winters.

The situation improved somewhat by the mid-1990s. The ration system was no longer needed, but still about 35 per cent of the country was earning under US$18 per month. Then in 1996 the newly elected democratic Coalition embarked on a series of bold moves known as the 'shock treatment'. Pensions and other social services were cut and import taxes were eliminated. Unstable banks were closed and a number of state run businesses were privatised. The American economist Jeffrey Sachs was the inspiration for this plan, which the government hoped would allow for more reform in infrastructure and banking.

The programme did very little to eliminate poverty, but it did create a greater business atmosphere in the capital. Foreign investment in particular was encouraged and two large seminars for mining and tourism were staged in 1997 and 1998. Businesses and shops opened up in Ulaanbaatar and by the late 1990s, the capital was no longer a quiet, colourless city. Billboards and pastel painted shops lined the sidewalks and the streets were filled with cars imported from Korea.

The privatisation plan was made on a vast scale. This is on-going and a recent project has readied some of the biggest companies for sale, including MIAT airlines and Gobi cashmere. The herds have also been privatised and thousands of former city dwellers have taken to the steppes to reclaim the nomadic ways. For the moment, pastureland cannot be privatised, ensuring maximum freedom for the nomads. Land privatisation, however, has become a hot topic amongst politicians and the debate is expected to last for years to come.

Apart from its herds of livestock, Mongolia has rich mining potential: copper, coal, silver, iron, lead, zinc, tungsten, oil (notably at Zuun Bayan and Tsagaan Els) and gold. There are over 100 gold mining companies in Mongolia and production stands at 10 to 12 tonnes per annum. This figure is steadily rising—in 1992 there were just eight mining companies that extracted a mere 775 kilograms of gold.

## INDUSTRY AND AGRICULTURE

This sector accounts for about 34 per cent of the GDP, and employs 12 per cent of the work force. Mongolia's major export items are copper and raw animal products (hides, cashmere and wool). In 1999 China received 30.1 per cent of Mongolia's exports, followed by Switzerland (21.5 per cent), and Russia (12.1 per cent).

In 1999, exports totalled US$454 million while imports equalled US$512 million, giving Mongolia a trade deficit of US$56 million. In 2001, the trade deficit jumped to US$169 million (exports: US$385.2 million, imports: US$554.8 million). On a positive note, the Gross Industrial output in 2001 reached Tg272.5 billion, an 11.8 per cent increase compared to 2000.

Prospects for business in the countryside have been poor, although mining operations are underway in several areas. The city of Erdenet grew on copper and Zaamar sum of Töv Aimag is the centre for gold mining. Tourism is staking its claim as well, especially around Lake Khövsgöl, where locals are profiting from tourist camps and the sale of souvenirs.

The Mongol territory is composed of about 80 per cent pastureland and eight per cent forest. Desertification and deforestation, however, have taken their toll in recent years. Crops are limited to wheat, barley, and potatoes, most of which are farmed in Selenge Aimag. Arable land represents only 0.7 per cent of the total surface area.

## BUSINESS OPPORTUNITIES FOR FOREIGNERS

"Come one, come all" is Mongolia's attitude towards foreign investment. Indeed, since 1990 the doors have swung wide open for the world business community and while a handful of Westerners have jumped in, most of the money comes from Mongolia's neighbours China, Korea and Russia. From 1990 to 2001, foreign companies had invested US$470 million in Mongolia and created some 50,000 new jobs. In 2000, foreign companies paid US$10.4 million in taxes, and accounted for 27 per cent of total exports.

Western companies have taken an interest in cashmere and mining, while on the ground in Ulaanbaatar, there are a few foreign owned tourist companies and some upscale restaurants, which largely cater to expatriates and tourists. Mongolia's small market has prevented the big chain companies, i.e. McDonalds and Starbucks, from setting up shop.

On the one hand, the government has put incentives in place to lure foreign money into the country, including big tax breaks to major investors in construction, mining and energy. Wholly-owned foreign companies are permitted, minimum investment (registered capital) is $10,000, and tax breaks lasting 5 to 10 years are offered depending on investment sector. Sole ownership of buildings by foreigners is permitted under Mongolian law, and under law reforms being proposed in 2002, ownership of land may become a reality. Mongolia bills itself as a 'gateway' to the large markets of Russia and China, and promotes its work force as young and well-educated. In their own words, many investors say they have stayed on through the lean years simply because Mongolia offers a more friendly and relaxed living atmosphere compared to its larger neighbours.

On the other hand, many businesses, particularly restaurants and tour companies, have experienced snags, and often complain of grinding through red tape that lingers from the bureaucracy of old. Paying out of bribes has become a concern, as one businessman put it: lock the doors when the taxman comes around. And in the late 1990s, the fall of multiple governments held up important laws on foreign investment. Observers hope these are issues of Mongolia's 'transition period', and will be resolved in time.

Investors should first contact the Foreign Investment and Foreign Trade Agency of Mongolia (FIFTA), a government agency that offers a 'one stop' service centre providing information, business applications and support for visas and residency permits. Write to: FIFTA, Sambuu Street 11, Ulaanbaatar 38. Tel: (976 11) 320871 or 326040. Fax: (976 11) 324076. Email: investboard@magicnet.mn. or click on: http://web.mol.mn/~invest//english.htm

For more information on starting a business in Mongolia, see the United Nations Mongolia Mission website at: www.un.int/Mongolia/busin.htm. There is extensive information on the US Embassy in Mongolia website: www.us-mongolia.com. The Mongolia Development Gateway website (www.mongolia-gateway.mn) offers good articles on the economy and development. The Mongolian Business Development Agency offers quality consultation, Tel: (976–11) 311706. Fax: (976–11) 311 092. Email: mbda@mongol.net. Website: http://www.mbda-mongolia.org

## THE GREAT ZUD

As the tsunami is to the Japanese, the tornado to Oklahomans and the hurricane to Floridians, so the 'zud' is to the Mongols.

Like the wrath of God, a zud, severe winter, will descend on Mongolia every few decades and wipe families clean of their herds of livestock. A zud can last several winters, as it did from 1999-2001, and can include different disasters. A black zud means drought; a white zud means heavy snow; and an iron zud occurs in the spring when snow melts and freezes again, creating sheets of ice. All three prevent the livestock from being able to dig to the earth for grass. In 1999, Dundgobi province suffered a different kind of zud after its grasslands were devastated by a plague of field mice. The effects of the recent zud were still being felt in 2002—each year the herds grow smaller and weaker, and the prospects for Mongolia's centuries-old livelihood grow ever the more grim.

Mongolia suffered zud in 1944 and again in the early 1960s, but those who can remember say nothing was as bad as the 'Millennium Zud'. In 1998, Mongolia was home to some 32.8 million sheep, goat, horses, camels and cattle (including yaks). Three years later that figure had dipped to 26.1 million.

A livestock census taken in 2001 counted 285,200 camels, 2,200,000 horses, 2,100,000 cattle, 11,900,000 sheep and 9,600,000 goats. Despite the vast number of livestock deaths since 1998, the number of animals is still up compared to the days of communism, with the exception of camels—there were 800,000 in 1960.

The livestock famine has drawn international attention and Mongolia has received large aid packages from international donors. A restocking programme funded by the World Bank promises to help some families, although massive reform in this area is sure to be developed in the coming years. Recent surveys show that herders favour cooperative action, whereby some of the profits would go back into the development of veterinary, fodder and credit services. Herders also realise that it was not merely the combination of summer drought and winter snow that did in their grasslands, but also overgrazing. There were simply too many herders clustered too close to towns, while pastures far from market went unattended. Therefore, the conundrum facing decision-makers is how to get herders to occupy these lands.

In total, Mongolia is home to 180,000 herding families. Many of those that lost their herds during the zud have been forced to the cities where they join the armies of urban poor in search of basic labouring or trading jobs.

# Politics

From 1924 to 1989, the Mongol political system functioned practically on the same model as the Soviet one. Mongolia was a republic with a unitary state structure and a legislative body, the People's Grand Khural. Political power was entirely concentrated within the structure of a single party, the MPRP (the Mongolian People's Revolutionary Party), which had an absolute monopoly over the daily operations of political life. According to the principle of 'democratic centralism', all power (political, legislative, and executive), was concentrated in the hands of a single political leader who was also the government prime minister, first secretary of the Party, and head of the Politburo (the executive body of the Party which in practise controlled the Central Committee of the Party). At the local level, government was in the hands of the small khural of the People's deputies. They controlled aimags and sums, the latter were formed from subdivisions of the agricultural collectives.

The deputies of the small khural, elected locally for a period of two years, had to apply the decisions taken by the higher government bodies. Although they were in theory entitled to debate political problems and take their own decisions, in reality, all the decisions taken by the small khural could be amended or annulled by the larger government bodies.

In the late 1980s, Mongolia marched with the USSR when liberal reforms came under the leadership of Mikhail Gorbachev. The central system of governing and managing relaxed, and more freedoms were allowed in economic and social development. Massive changes came, however, in 1990, when a group of young democracy advocates took to the streets of Ulaanbaatar and led huge protests.

The government bowed to their pressure. Thus the MPRP's monopoly on power ended in the spring of 1990 when revisions to the constitutions allowed other parties to participate in elections. The office of president was formed, and was meant to coordinate the action of the legislative and the executive chambers. He or she is elected by a direct vote for a period of four years.

Legislative power now belongs to the Grand Khural (Parliament), executive power is shared between the president and the government, while judicial power is becoming more autonomous. These new democratic aspirations have become more concrete with the adoption, on January 13, 1992, of a new Constitution.

## THE CONSTITUTION OF 1992

The first Constitution of the Republic was adopted in 1924. The second, very close to Stalin's version of 1936, appeared in 1940. The third was adopted in the 1960s.

The 1992 Constitution brought in a parliamentary form of government, with representatives elected by direct universal suffrage for four years. The Grand Khural, composed of 76 members, can oppose the president's veto by a vote with a two-thirds quorum. In agreement with the democratic principle of the separation of powers, the Constitution stipulates the (theoretical) independence of judicial power.

On an administrative level, Mongolia is divided into *aimag, sum,* and *bag* (provinces or regions, districts or prefectures, and sub-districts). The capital is divided into districts and *khoroo*.

The new Constitution was adopted in February 1992. What had previously been known as Outer Mongolia, Autonomous Mongolia (after 1911), and the People's Republic of Mongolia, was henceforth called simply Mongolia.

The MPRP remained in power until the June 1996 elections. The public, eager for change to their battered economy, voted in the Democratic Coalition—formed by the National Democratic Party, the Social Democratic Party, the Green Party, and the Believers (Buddhist) Party. The party leaders were mostly the same men who led the street protests of 1990. The new prime minister, an economist named M. Enkhsaikhan, implemented a large scale reform package that included a zero-import tax and a cut back in pensions—a scheme applauded by western donors, welcomed by the business community, and loathed by people seeking social services.

Inexperience and greed, however, tore the Coalition apart. In four years they went through four prime ministers and saw three of their MPs jailed for taking bribes during a casino tender. Even more shocking was the October 1998 murder of S. Zorig, the leader of the 1990 protests. A massive manhunt was conducted but the murder remains unsolved.

By 2000 the Coalition had broken apart into several parties and were ultimately disgraced in the Parliamentary elections when the revamped MPRP came roaring back to win 72 of the 76 seats in the Ikh Hural. It selected for a prime minister Nambariin Enkhbayar, a former student of English Literature at Leeds University and one time translator of Western novels and Mongolian epics. Pacifying Western fears that the MPRP would revert to its communist past, Enkhbayar labelled the party 'centre-left' and condemned the purges his party committed years ago.

One year later, the incumbent President N. Bagabandi (MPRP) was re-elected in his presidential bid. He ran his campaign on promises to raise pensions and government salaries, and boost national production of key exports of cashmere, wool and leather. Most of all, he said since his policy was closely aligned with Enkhbayar's, there would be less conflict in the Government House, compared to the previous term when he was constantly at odds with the Democrats.

With both national and local government seats firmly in the hands of the MPRP, opposition parties can only play a minor role in the operations of the country. The Democrats remained silent for nearly two years. In April 2002 they crept back into the public eye by organising anti-government street protests—condemning the MPRP for failed campaign promises, and accussing the government of media censorship and corruption—thus setting the stage for a comeback bid in the 2004 elections.

# Religion

As of 2001, there were 186 religious centres operating in Mongolia. Of this total, 112 are Buddhist monasteries and 65 are Christian. These numbers, however, are disproportionate to the actual practitioners of Christianity and Buddhism—more

*Temple offerings include money and silk scarves.*

than 90 per cent of Mongolians are Buddhists.

Christianity has gained strength in Mongolia since 1990, backed by financially endowed and motivated Western missionaries. Young people and the needy are drawn to the faith by humanitarian support and opportunities to practice English or study abroad. It is illegal in Mongolia to openly proselytise one's faith, so Christian organisations advertise on television and through personal contacts. Some missionary groups have gone to great lengths to support social problems, including care for street children, and distribution of medicine to hospitals. Buddhist groups, while offering spiritual solace, have little funds for such projects, and require donations to remain active.

Despite this, Buddhism has undergone a revival since 1990, resulting in the construction of dozens of new monasteries, and the restoration of temples destroyed in the 1930s. The Buddhist art school at Gandan Monastery is thriving and high lamas from Tibet, Nepal and India have made trips to Mongolia. The Dalai Lama has visited several times, most recently in 1995 in the company of Richard Gere. The restoration of Buddhism, however, is hampered by the lack of experienced monks; nearly all of Mongolia's great Buddhist lamas, artists and philosophers were massacred in the 1930s. Curiously, because of this lack of trained monks, Mongolia has had to look abroad for Buddhist teachers—Buddhists from Australia, Europe and North America have gone to Mongolia to teach the faith that Mongolians practiced for several hundreds of years.

There are surprisingly few places in Mongolia where foreign visitors can study Buddhism. The best place to start is the Foundation for the Preservation of the Mahayana Tradition (FPMT), which has its main building on Trade Street (the pink building close the Zanabazar Museum, tel: 9911 9765 or 321 580, Email: fpmt-mongolia@magicnet.mn). Lecture and meditation classes (in English) are held every week at the building; they are free and all are welcome.

## Restored Culture

Soviet culture and history was brushed aside after 1990 when Mongolians were given the opportunity to rediscover their ancient roots. Old festivals resumed, traditional script was taught again in schools, Buddhist temples opened, and modern

# Faith Surfing

Thubten Gyatso is probably the only Buddhist monk to have surfed hurricane waves off the coast of Florida. He has also practised medicine in London, trekked in the Himalaya Mountains, and sailed down the Indus River on a boat. What is his next challenge? Restore the Buddhist heritage to Mongolia. This is no small task, but Gyatso is well prepared for the unmarked path that lies ahead.

*Thubten Gyatso*

His interest in Oriental cultures was sparked in the 1970s when Gyatso (then Adrian Feldmann) enrolled in a Buddhist meditation course in Nepal. He admits now that he never intended on becoming a monk, and for a long time was sceptical of his teachers. He spent long hours debating the principles of Buddhism, but at last recognised it as truth—the ultimate test being a three-month silent retreat to a log cabin that he built near Coff's Harbour north of Sydney, Australia. He was finally ordained in 1975. This change in lifestyle, which included donning crimson and gold robes, did not mean an end to his past. He still enjoyed his lifelong activities of bodysurfing and hiking.

Between catching waves, Gyatso has spent the years educating other Westerners in Buddhist thought and meditation; but new goals were set in 1999 when his Nepali teacher, Lama Zopa Rimpoche, asked if would go to Mongolia to represent the Foundation for the Preservation of the Mahayana Tradition (FPMT). Lama Zopa set up a Buddhist centre in Ulaanbaatar with the goal of educating the Mongols on their faith, and rightly guessed Gyatso was the person to conduct the lectures.

Mongolians respect foreigners and doctors, and since Gyatso was both, he won instant popularity. His students now cram into lecture halls to hear him describe the faith, and ask for his blessing afterwards. Rebuilding the Buddhist culture that was lost for most of the 20th century is no easy task, Gyatso thinks in terms of generations rather than years. But he is quick to point out that Mongolia was once one of the great intellectual centres of Buddhism and monks from there were highly regarded in Tibet, Nepal and India. While much work needs to be done, it is a reputation many Mongolians hope will one day be restored.

variations on traditional clothing became fashionable. The restoration of the Chinggis Khaan cult was at the forefront of these changes and his image appeared on everything from vodka bottles and lapel pins to banknotes and wall hangings. The Soviets had tried to portray Chinggis as a barbarian, but his immediate popularity showed that few had bought into that notion.

## CLAN NAMES

Another curious change in recent years has been the rediscovery of clan names. The use of clan names dates back to the eighth century. In those days, the tribes chose the name of an animal, heroic warrior, a nearby mountain or a certain occupation. Family trees—written into books or sewn on tapestries—were guarded by the family and passed through the generations. One reason for accurate note taking was to avoid inbreeding—it was forbidden to marry within the clan for nine generations, until the blood was clean.

All this ended in the 1920s when the communists banned the names and confiscated or burned the family books. The Soviets feared the clan alliances might supersede loyalty to the new government. Under their system, the father's name was to be used in place of the clan name, and by the next generation the clan names were lost under the rug of communism. This allegedly led to birth defects due to accidental incest.

In 1990, the new freedoms allowed for the study of the names, and researchers travelled about the countryside to document them. By the end of the decade they had published a book with 1,200 names divided by region. Mongolians are now required by law to register a clan name for a new identification card system. Because so many forgot (particularly people in Ulaanbaatar), families have travelled to their ancestral homelands or phoned relatives to search for answers.

Those who cannot find a name are encouraged to devise a new one. (Gurragcha, Mongolia's only spaceman, chose 'Cosmos'). One problem, however, has been an over-request for the name 'Borjigan', the clan name of Chinggis Khaan. To encourage research, In October 2000, a competition was held in Ulaanbaatar to determine which family could best trace their roots. The winner, a man from Dornod Aimag, traced his lineage back 13 generations, and was awarded Tg1.5 million in cash.

# Health

The most widespread diseases among the Mongols are pulmonary and bronchial infections, hepatitis A and B, bacterial dysentery and amoebiasis, enteritis, trachoma, cerebral-spinal meningitis, and brucellosis. The bubonic plague is endemic in Mongolia, and its main vectors are rodents, notably the marmot. There have been two known cases of HIV and AIDS, although the true number is suspected to be in the hundreds.

A 1994–98 study showed infant mortality at 65 deaths per 1,000 live births, and child (under 5) morality at 81 deaths per 1,000 live births. This is a significant improvement over the 1984-88 levels, which were 83.5 and 125.3 respectively. The top three causes of under five deaths are respiratory infections, pre-natal disorders and diarrhoeal disease. In 2001, the infant mortality rate fell to 30 infants per 1,000. Maternal mortality is also down, from 240 per 100,000 live births in 1993, to 160 in 1999.

The application of a pharmacology policy on a national scale through the creation of an Essential drugs programme, with technical support from the World Health Organisation and financial support from Holland, has greatly improved supplies of vaccines and basic drugs. Nevertheless, many Mongols have little or no access to drugs and medication.

# Hunting and fishing

The Mongolian term *mergen* means both 'wise' and 'skilled archer', a reflection of the importance given to hunting skills in traditional nomadic Mongol society. In the great nomadic confederations, there was no difference in status between the hunter and the soldier. The same rules governing hunting applied in military campaigns, and a spirit of cooperation reigned which made for formidably efficient coordination.

Laws on hunting were installed in 1927 to reflect more socialist attitudes. During the period of collectivisation, a few cooperatives specialised solely in hunting were created, and compelled to enforce very constraining plans. The strict laws and special training developed an elite class of hunters, which still exists today. The socialists also instilled the idea that all resources should be used to their greatest potential, and moved away from traditional ideas on sacred sites and Buddhist law. At the same time, foreigners were allowed into the country to take part in expensive hunting trips, a practice that continues today.

Starting in the 1990s, The World Wide Fund for Nature (WWF) teamed up with the Mongolian Buddhists to re-instate the ancient laws on hunting and protection of sacred sites. More than 600 sacred sites across the country were identified, and the monks have been charged with educating local people not to hunt in these areas. This project was considered "Mongolia's Gift to the World," and announced at the 'Sacred Gift for a Living Planet Conference,' held in November 2000 in Kathmandu, Nepal.

## WOLF HUNTING

This form of hunting demands a particular skill on the part of the hunter; and good wolf hunters enjoy prominent reputation in Mongol society. The wolf's great intelligence and his exceptional sense of hearing arouse admiration and respect, and it has always been a matter of honour to kill one. Unlike the hunting of other game, wolf hunting is authorised year round, although the main season for taking pelts is in winter.

During communism, great collective shooting-parties were regularly organised to contain the wolf population to a reasonable level, as overpopulation of wolves constitute a threat to livestock. The wolf (Latin *canis lupus*) generally attacks young, weak or sick animals separated from the herd, which is why he is known as the 'health police of the steppes'. However, contrary to general belief, the wolf's main diet is not large game but various small rodents: mice, marmots, squirrels, and small birds. Wolves also eat fish, particularly when the graylings are spawning in shallow water. The wolf never hunts near his lair. It will instinctively keep this place well hidden in order to protect its young.

The state funded collective shooting-parties ended in 1990, and subsequently the wolf population boomed. By the late 1990s, newspaper reports of wolves attacking livestock had become common. In response, a private organisation called the Union for Protecting Livestock from Wolves (UPLAW) was formed in an effort to cull the numbers to a manageable level. UPLAW is a small organisation, but manages to set up a few wolf hunting parties each year. Successful hunters are rewarded with a sheep, and the wolf parts (organs and pelts) are sold in shops. UPLAW also supports 'clubbing', which involves pulling newly born wolves out of their den and killing them with a club.

*Wolf hunting is still a popular pastime in Mongolia.*

The best season for wolf hunting is winter when the great packs gather, and spring when they reproduce. The Mongols hunt wolves collectively or alone. Many hunters try to coax a wolf within gun range by imitating its howling. Traditionally, the hunters travel by horseback. When the rider is level with the wolf, the cornered animal will suddenly turn and face his pursuer, ready to give a last fatal assault. Then the hunter hits him with a precise blow on the muzzle, using a heavy club with small pieces of lead on the end, thus knocking him out. More commonly, children will be sent to one end of a glen, and make noise as they walk through it, thus sending the wolves ahead of them and towards the awaiting hunters.

During the breeding season, when the hunter is in sight of a pack of males following a female, he must begin by attacking the last in the line, then the next one, and so on until he reaches the female. If he kills the female first, the males will turn against him.

In the far west of Mongolia, the Kazakhs still hunt wolves with trained Golden eagles. Much skill is required to capture and train an eagle, and watching this sport is on the main itinerary of some tours.

In the Khangai and Khentii mountains, the **collared brown bear** is hunted, while in the Altai, the prey is the Altai bear, slightly smaller in size, and much sought-after for its fur at the end of the long period of hibernation.

In the north of Mongolia, in the area around Lake Khövsgöl, the Tsaatan, who herd reindeer, also hunt wild **reindeer** using among other techniques, a trap with a crossbow. Also hunted is the **Altai deer**; the Chinese prize its antlers for their medicinal value. Between mid-May and the beginning of June, the antlers are full of hormone-rich blood. The most appreciated are those of males between 6 and 7 years old—animals in the prime of their life. The Chinese value other parts of the deer, including the testicles, penis, and tail.

## MARMOT HUNTING

Hunting marmots is a favourite pastime amongst rural Mongols. There are literally millions of these furry creatures on the steppes and each is valued for its pelt and meat. With the coming of the first frost, they block up the entrance to their winter quarters with a mixture of earth and excrement. Sealed off about three or four meters below the ground, they cover themselves in dry grasses, and begin their hibernation. By the spring, they have lost much of their fat, but as soon as the greenery reappears, they quickly put on weight again. It is then that the hunting season begins.

The Mongols have various methods of hunting marmots. They place traps and nooses in their burrows, they smoke them out of their holes, and they track them with dogs. The most traditional method is for the hunter to dress in white with a white headdress with small ears. He then hops around, all the while shaking a stick with white horse hair on its end. The marmot at first feigns to be uninterested, but gradually its curiosity, heightened by the behaviour of this strange creature, gets the better of its vigilance, and it allows the hunter to get closer and closer. When the animal is finally within gun range, the hunter aims for the head, so as not to damage the fur. The marmot is one of the main vectors of transmission of the bubonic plague, an endemic disease in Mongolia, and there are regular prohibitions on its hunting.

## PROTECTION OF RARE AND ENDANGERED SPECIES

The snow leopard, Saiga antelope, *argali*, wild camel, Gobi bear, wild ass, and certain cranes are all endangered species in Mongolia. A wide range of laws control or prohibit the hunting of these species, but weak enforcement continues to threaten wildlife. One problem has been the authorisation of hunting without sufficient data on animal populations. In the eastern aimags, for example, thousands of gazelle are shot every November, despite the lack of an accurate count of their numbers. The gazelle population is reportedly five times smaller than its total in 1950. Poaching is another matter for concern. Herders shoot snow leopards to protect their livestock; hunters poach deer to feed their families; and marmots are illegally shot for their skins.

## FOREIGN HUNTERS

Tariffs charged to foreign hunters are often exorbitant, sometimes reaching US$30,000. The government earns about US$700,000 per year on foreign hunting licences, and the tourist companies that support hunting trips also succeed financially. Such hunting is overseen by the Ministry of Nature, which has a programme to ensure that wild animal numbers do not decline. In addition, projects set up by conservation organisations like the WWF are encouraging local people to be more vigilant in protecting rare animals.

Foreigners are allowed to hunt in Mongolia from mid-April to mid-November. Theoretically, a wounded animal must be retrieved and paid for. One of the most sought-after animals is the wild *argali* sheep, a 180 kg animal with horns that can approach two metres in length over their curvature. The *argali*, one of the world's largest sheep, are found in Gobi areas and the western provinces. Males and females live in separate herds except during breeding seasons (October to December). Also popular with foreign hunters are wild goat (ibex), gazelle and antelope. Maral deer and wild pigs are hunted in the northern aimags.

## FISHING

Although there are some 58 species of fish in the Mongolian water basins, including sturgeon, salmon, loach, pike, and perch, fishing is much less developed than hunting. Traditionally, the Mongols did very little if any fishing, except in a few areas such as Tsagaannuur in Khövsgöl Aimag. Fish have become more popular in recent years, and can be purchased in Ulaanbaatar markets.

The most renowned fish in Mongolia is the *taimen* (see special topic page 126). The Lenok trout (*zeveg* in Mongolian) is another popular fish. Both it and the taimen migrate with the seasons and locals will have the best knowledge of fishing grounds, and are usually happy to reveal the best fishing holes. Generally, these fish migrate upstream in the summertime. Fishing in spring is said to be the best season, but winter fishing through the ice is possible if you are properly equipped. Foreigners must purchase a fishing permit, which can be bought in the national parks and protected areas, or directly from the Ministry of Nature. A permit for a taimen is US$50 and all other fish are US$2. To export a fishing trophy, anglers must pay a tax of US$100 for a fish up to one metre. For any fish longer than one metre, the tax is a minimum US$200. Exact price depends on the species.

## ENVIRONMENTAL ORGANISATIONS
To learn more about fishing, hunting and the biodiversity project of Mongolia, contact the following organisations.
**Ministry for Nature,** Tel: 326 595. Trade St 5, Ulaanbaatar 11.
**Mongolian Association for the Conservation of Nature and Environment (MACNE),** Tel: 328 002. Ulaanbaatar PO Box 1160.
**Mongolian Hunting Society,** Tel: 360 248, Ulaanbaatar 36.
**WWF Mongolia,** Tel: 311 659. Trade Street 5. Email: wwfmon@magicnet.mn

*Herders take a break from their chores in Bayankhongor.*

# MONGOLIA'S MONSTERS OF THE DEEP

If the fact that northern Mongolia is reminiscent of Montana in the days of Lewis and Clark is not reason enough fish there, perhaps more enticing is the chance to hook and land a freshwater fish the size of a small tarpon.

This giant of a fish, the *taimen* (with the wonderful scientific name: *Hucho hucho taimen*), is a carnivorous monster that eats other fish (including its own kind), as well as rodents unlucky enough to get caught in the stream. It is by far the largest member of the salmonids—the family that includes trout, salmon, char, and grayling. This family of fish are found in rivers from central Europe in the west, all the way through Eurasia to the Pacific coast of Siberia.

According to Siberian lore, Russian fisherman have netted 90 kilogramme taimen. The days of landing a taimen in Russia, however, are long gone as they have been poached to near extinction. Only in Mongolia do these ferocious beasts survive in relatively large numbers.

Western anglers on fishing safaris to Mongolia also pursue the much smaller lenok (*Brachymstax lenok*), a salmonid rather similar in size and behaviour to the cutthroat trout of the American West. Averaging 18-20 inches in length, with a small mouth like a sucker's, the lenok has beautiful,

*Fly fishing in the north with camels.*

*Bagging the taimen.*

iridescent pink, parr-like markings along its sides. This fish subsists heavily on insect hatches, and readily takes dry flies—especially grasshopper imitations.

While the taimen and the lenok are the prime targets for visiting anglers, Arctic grayling (*Thymallus arcticus*) should not be overlooked, especially if you have a lightweight fly rod available. They are often found in faster water—in places where they are reasonably sheltered from the depredations of prowling taimen—and simply love small dry flies.

The rivers of Mongolia form part of the upper drainage of the great Selenge system, which heads northeast into Siberia and eventually ends up in Lake Baikal. The top fishing is in Khövsgöl Aimag and the other provinces south of the Russian border. The beautiful, broad rivers of the region wind their way through hills and mountains wooded with larch and poplars; the countryside is particularly lovely in late season, when the larches turn yellow before they drop their needles. Interspersed are grassy plains and hills, where Mongols graze their horses and cattle; it is not uncommon to be casting while under the gaze of a lone Mongol horseman.

Many travel agencies, both Mongolian and foreign owned, run trips that cater to the serious fisherman looking for rustic comfort. The more cost effective trips are done by jeep, but travellers willing to spend more can be flown directly to remote fishing lodges in the huge (and noisy) Russian built helicopters. Several travel companies maintain excellent lodges complete with shower block and dining lodge. Guests are housed in wonderfully comfortable *gers*, each with a stove, sitting area, ample shelving, and two beds. With a vested interest in the rivers, some companies have taken it upon themselves to protect the rivers and the fish that live in them. When choosing a travel company, ask what, if any, environmental projects they support in the areas they operate.

Daily routines are maintained at the lodges. After breakfast its time to suit up: breathable Gore-Tex waders over polar fleece long johns are advised, since it can be bitingly cold on the river in the early morning, and the river waters are always chilly.

Once at the river, you can fish by wading or in three-person aluminium boats with jet outboard motors. There are too many rocks in the rivers for propellers. Wading is relatively easy since the rivers flow gently and the bottoms are gravel—a fisherman friendly experience for any age. Have with you two fly rods, an 8 to 10 weight for taimen and a 3 to 5 weight for the lenok and grayling.

By midday the boats put into a likely picnic spot along the river for a shore lunch, then the fishing starts again in earnest until it is time to head into camp for a hot shower, a drink, and dinner.

While both taimen and lenok are usually taken with wet fly patterns like large, ugly Wooly Buggers, it is more fun is to fish for taimen by casting mouse patterns with floating lines. The trick is to quarter these mice downstream, skating them on the surface with a riffle hitch. The take of a taimen is heart-stopping: it literally crashes the fly as it hits, then begins an awesome fight.

The Vermillion brothers (who run Sweetwater Travel) discovered how to keep these monsters from getting away: once the fish has taken, set the hook with the stripping hand, then keep on stripping hard until the rod has a large bend in it. Only then can you be assured that the taimen is really on. If the fish is truly big, move the boat to shallow water, get out and fight it on your terms, not his. Then have someone take a photo of you and your fish, revive it gently, and kiss it goodbye. All fish have to be released, without exception.

So do the taimen really get up to 90 kilos as the Russians attest? Unlikely. The average Mongolian taimen is around 82 centimetres and 4.5 kilogrammes. In the two times that I have fished there, my biggest fish was 135 centimetres long, and weighed about 25 kilogrammes. The record catch for an angler at a Sweetwater camp is 157.5 centimetres (that's 5 feet 2 inches!), taken on a mouse pattern. A few years back, a British angler hooked what was probably a 100 centimetre fish, only to have another taimen from Hell come up and eat it! Incidentally, my big one was targeted by guide Jeff Vermillion, who spotted it lurking under a cut riverbank while he stood on the cowling of the outboard.

Do not expect a taimen on every cast. These are industrial-strength freshwater fish, and like the trophy brown trout of New Zealand, they do not tolerate competitors in their neighbourhood, and have either driven them away or eaten them. You will probably hook at least five lenok to every hit by a taimen, but the lenok are fun as well, especially on dries. For the lenok, make sure that you bring a wide range of mayfly, caddis, and hopper imitations—even when they are rising actively, they can be pretty selective about what they will eat, and you will face a challenge in trying to "match the hatch". Grayling, thank God, are a lot dumber—any small, dark dry will do the trick.

Keep in mind that this fishery is a bit temperamental. Early and late in the season is best: mid-summer rains will 'blow out' (muddy) rivers. Since the murky waters make for awful fishing, the camps will close at this time. The camps are also unpredictable; one may get a lot of hits one week, then go cold while a another camp is doing well. As you might guess in such a frontier operation, the biology and habits of this great sport fish aren't yet well known.

But rest assured. If you manage to take one of these creatures with a topwater mouse cutting a wake across the river's surface, you are in for the fishing experience of a lifetime.

*By Michael D. Coe*
*Professor of Anthropology, Emeritus, Yale University*
*and long-time fishing enthusiast*

# Ulaanbaatar

For the traveller eager to discover the steppe, the nomads, and the wide open spaces, the arrival in Ulaanbaatar may be disconcerting, and even disturbing. This is a city of Stalinist architecture, with sad uniform buildings, wide avenues, and the inevitable central square seen in most Soviet towns.

Beyond first impressions, 'UB', as its known by expatriates, has a quiet charm about it. For those who like walking, a stroll through the town centre can be pleasant, particularly on a late afternoon in summer. Most places of interest for the traveller are accessible by foot, and getting away from the concrete requires just a short bus ride to the wooded Bogd Uul Mountain on the southern edge of town.

The city, located at 1,351 metres above sea level, stretches in an east-west direction across the Tuul River valley. It has a population of around 735,000 and a surface area of 135,800 hectares. Mountains surround it: the Bogd Uul to the south, the Songino to the west, the Bayanzurkh to the east, and the Chinggeltei to the north.

The town centre is surprisingly modern, with very little in the way of pre-Communist-era architecture. In 1930, Ulaanbaatar was still a city of monasteries and gers, all surrounded by high wooden palisades. Tall buildings were forbidden until the 20th century, lest they should disgrace the monastery rooftops. Most of the modern town sprung up after WWII, and the hideous high rise apartments are products of the 1960s.

Tourists arriving from the airport pass conflicting scenes of old and new. Huge belching power stations and concrete factories are the backdrop for the ger suburbs, residential areas composed of gers and small wood homes. These areas, which surround the city, have no sanitation system and residents must collect their water from pump houses.

One third of Mongolians make Ulaanbaatar their permanent home. But nearly all rural folk have friends and relatives in the capital, and many make it their 'second home', a place for business, work and study opportunities. Linked by train to Russia since 1950 and to Beijing since 1955, and having the largest airport, it is also the transit hub of the nation. The city is divided into eight districts: Bayanzürkh, Bayangol, Songino-Khairkhan, Chinggeltei, Sükhbaatar, Khan-Uul, Nalaikh, and Baganuur.

Around Sükhbaatar Square, the political and cultural centre of the city, is the Government House, ministries, embassies, political party headquarters, the university, teaching institutions, museums, theatres, cinemas, the national news agency and the Central Post Office.

Factories are located to the south-west of the centre, on the road to the airport. An area west of the Square, centred on Gandan Monastery, is known for its Buddhist heritage; two other temple complexes and a nunnery are located nearby. Peace Avenue, once a quiet boulevard used by the odd bus or horse cart, is now crammed with off-road vehicles, Korean taxis and flashy European imports. It is the main east-west thoroughfare, and strung along it are shops and restaurants. The third & fourth micro-district is another popular area for shopping.

The districts that make up the capital are named after mountains, in accordance with an old Mongol tradition reintroduced after the fall of communism, which used a terminology more in keeping with proletarian ideals.

## THE HISTORY OF URGA

In October Ulaanbaatar celebrates its birth year, said to have occurred in 1639. At that time it was located more than 400 kilometres to the west at Da Khuree Monastery. The city, however, was portable; and every few years, when the grass was deemed unacceptable for the herds, it moved. Until 1780, the Great Circle (Ikh Khuree) was an immense nomad camp of monasteries and *gers*, which had been located in twenty different sites one after the other.

The term *khuree*, 'circle'—and by extension 'monastery'—alludes to the arrangement of the nomad camp in a circle around the *ger* of the prince, and reflects both the nomadic and monastic origins of the town. As it gradually grew in importance, the buildings became more permanent.

In the 1800s, through foreign influence, the town took the name **Urga**, a deformation of the Mongolian word *Örgöö* which means 'camp' and by extension, 'palace'. By the 1830s, Urga was more or less settled, and divided into two circular complexes.

**Züun Khuree** (Eastern Circle) was the larger of the two complexes and enclosed about a hundred Sino-Tibetan temples, including the Maidar temple and the Golden Palace of the Bogd Gegeen. The Palace was the political centre and the seat of the Mongol government. There were also five monasteries and the large temple to Maidar, which housed a gigantic statue of the Buddha Maitreya. From this area radiated the living districts of the monks. Each *aimag* (district) had its own temple halls, artisans, astrologers and doctors. Nothing remains today of Züun Khuree except for the three *ger*-temples of Dashchoilin which were preserved to house, in 1940, the state circus.

The other complex was **Gandan** (Gandantegchilin), the western part of Urga, which was begun in 1809 on a hill located to the north-west of town. Preserved as a museum by the communists, it came out of the 1930s storm mostly unscathed.

The centre of the Gandan district included most important constructions: the monastery of Gandantegchilin, the temples of the fifth and seventh Bogd Gegeen, and the temple of Mejid Janraiseg (Avalokiteshvara), with a huge statue of the bodhisattva. Gandan formed a veritable independent town within Urga. It was here that one received the highest and best religious education, and that the highest scholastic degrees were given.

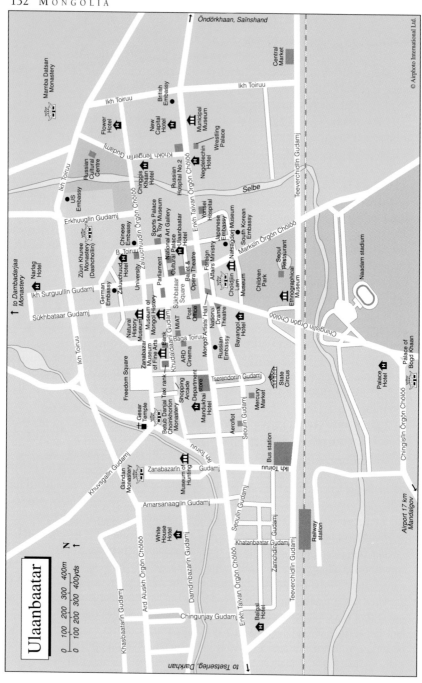

Ulaanbaatar

0  100  200  300  400m
0  100  200  300  400yds

N

© Airphoto International Ltd.

Öndörkhaan, Saïnshand

Central Market

Mamba Datsan Monastery

Ikh Toiruu

Ikh Toiruu

British Embassy

Flower Hotel

New Capital Hotel

Municipal Museum

Khökh Tengeriin Gudamj

Wrestling Palace

Ikh Toiruu

Russian Cultural Centre

Chinggis Khaan Hotel

Russian Hospital No 2

Negdelechin Hotel

Selbe

Teeverchidlin Gudamj

US Embassy

Erkhuuglin Gudamj

Zaluuchuudiin Örgön Chölöö

Chinese Embassy

Sports Palace & Toy Museum

National Art Gallery

Ulaanbaatar Hotel

Yönsei Hospital

Japanese Embassy

South Korean Embassy

Natsagdorj Museum

Marksiin Örgön Chölöö

Züün Khuree Monastery (Dashchoilin)

to Dambadarjaa Monastery

Narlag Hotel

Ikh Surguullin Gudamj

B. Toiruu

Zaluuchuud Hotel

University

Parliament

Cultural Palace

Ballet & Opera Theatre

Foreign Affairs Ministry

Choidjin Lam Museum

South Museum

Children Park

Seoul Restaurant

Ethnographical Museum

Chingisiin Örgön Chölöö

Enkh Taivan Örgön Chölöö

Naadam stadium

German Embassy

Sükhbataar Gudamj

Natural History Museum

Museum of Fine Arts

Zanabazar Museum

Khudaldaan Gudamj

Bank

Museum of Mongol History

Sükhbataar Square

Post Office

MIAT

Baga Toiruu

National Drama Theatre

Mongol Artists' Hall

Russian Embassy

Bayangol Hotel

Chingisiin Örgön Chölöö

Palace Hotel

Palace of Bogd Khaan

Freedom Square

ARD Cinema

Tserendorin Gudamj

State Circus

Airport 17 km Mandalgov

Gesar Temple

Betub Danjai Choinkhorlin Monastery

Taxi rank

Shopping Arcade

Department store

Mandukhai Hotel

Mercury Market

Aeroflot

Seoulin Gudamj

Bus station

Ikh Toiruu

Khuvsgalin Gudamj

Gandan Monastery

Zanabazarin Gudamj

Museum of Hunting

Mkh Toiruu

Amarsanaaglin Gudamj

Seoulin Gudamj

Railway station

Khasbaatarin Gudamj

Ard Aiuskh Örgön Chölöö

White House Hotel

Damdinbazarin Gudamj

Khatanbaatar Gudamj

Zamchdiin Gudamj

Teeverchidlin Gudamj

Chingunjay Gudamj

Enkh Taivan Örgön Chölöö

Seoulin Gudamj

Baigal Hotel

to Tsetserleg, Darkhan

The lay population lived in districts located outside the perimeter of Züun Khuree and Gandan, to the south of the two circles. A new map what of the Mongolian capital looked like at the turn of the 20th century, sold in tourist shops, offers a clear view of the monasteries and districts that surrounded them.

Most of the population still lived in *gers* at the beginning of the 20th century. The town was then in the hands of high-ranking lamas, usury traders, and above all, the Manchus. The representatives of the Manchu administration (*amban*), located next to the residence of the Bogd, held the de facto power. Chinese, Russian, American, Japanese, German, English firms had also set up shop and turned Urga into a centre of international trade.

The 1930s changed everything. In the space of a single decade, nearly all the temples of Urga were destroyed or burnt, their treasures stolen, buried, sold abroad, and their building materials reused for other constructions. Some halls were kept only to serve as warehouses, schools, or offices.

Very little remains today of the temples of old Urga. The best places to catch a glimpse of the original architecture and atmosphere are the Choidjiin Lam museum temple, just south of Sükhbaatar Square; and the palace of the eighth Bogd Gegeen, in the southern part of town. The grounds in both temples are enclosed, grassy and usually quiet. Other monasteries, including Gandan, Gesar and Dambadarjaa, offer both new and old buildings. Dashchoilin Monastery, located amid high-rise apartments, contains a few *ger*-temples that belonged to the old monastic complex of Züun Khuree, before becoming the venue of the state circus and the circus school in 1940.

## SOVIET ERA MONUMENTS AND ART

The **Monument to Sükhbaatar**, built in 1946 for the 25th anniversary of the Revolution, represents the young revolutionary hero on the back of a rearing horse, pointing to the rising sun and summoning his people to fight. It was Sükhbaatar who rode to Russia with a secret note stashed in his riding whip, seeking the assistance of Lenin to help rid Mongolia of the Chinese. On the monument are carved the words attributed to him after driving the Chinese from Mongolia, "If we, an entire people, unite in common effort and common will, there is nothing in the world that we cannot achieve, learn, and succeed in." Any number of photographers will gladly snap your photo in front of the statue, for about Tg800.

Located to the south of Ulaanbaatar, the **Zaisan Memorial**—erected on the 50th anniversary of the Communist Revolution—serves to honour the Soviet and Mongolian soldiers who died in the fight against Nazi Germany. At the top of the cement column, the emblem of the hammer and sickle can be seen side by side with the Soyëmbo, the national emblem of Mongolia. Next to the monumental statue of the soldier, a mosaic composition on a large circular panel in reinforced concrete illustrates the theme of friendship between the Mongol and Soviet peoples. In the centre of it, a large granite bowl holds an eternal flame. The fact that this flame no longer operates is perhaps symbolic what became of the friendly Mongolian-Soviet relations. From the top of the memorial, a good view can be had over the capital.

The 'Revolutionary Mongol' tank brigade monument is located to the south of Chinggis Khaan Avenue, not far from the palace of the Bogd Gegeen. It was built for the 25th anniversary of the Mongol tank brigade, which, with money from the people of Mongolia, was presented to the USSR in 1942 as part of the war effort against Nazi Germany. In the late 1990s there was talk of replacing the monument with a giant bronze horse, to better reflect the true spirit of Mongolia. Financial problems, however, have left the project on hold.

Mongolia's appreciation for the bloodstained dictators who ran the country during communism has not waned, as evidenced by the continued presence of the **Marshal Choibalsan and V.I. Lenin statues**. Choibalsan, the director of the 1930s purges, is in front of the main entrance to the State University of Ulaanbaatar. You can find Lenin on his pedestal in front of the Ulaanbaatar Hotel. Additionally, a giant bust of Lenin, and a mosaic dedicated to communism, can be found inside the 'Lenin Museum', behind Freedom Square. The large **Stalin statue**, which used to stand in front of the National Library, was taken down during the Democratic Revolution of 1990. It was left to rot in a barren field for several years until it was rescued by a private businessman in 2001; he purchased the four metre statue in an auction and re-located it to his beer bar for use as a decoration. The bar, called Ismuss, is located in Bayanzurkh district.

On the airport road, at Buyant Ukhaa, an **inscription** in Mongolian on the side of the mountain commemorates the 25th anniversary of the Mongol Revolution.

# Monasteries and museums

## GANDANTEGTECHILIN MONASTERY

To get some of the atmosphere of historic Urga, one must stroll through the Gandan area where the layout of the old town has been preserved. The *gers*, hidden behind fences, are set up around the monastery in a ring.

The university at Gandan monastery was at one time much larger than its current size. It specialised in several fields of teaching, including: astrology and divination, philosophy and theology, mathematics, medicine, demonology and the suppression of demons. Various methods of divination were used in Mongolia, including dice, and the interpretation of the cracks produced on the shoulder blade of a sheep when thrown in the fire. Certain datsan were specialised in yoga and in white magic. The *otoch*, or warrior-healers, represented more than 10 per cent of the total number of lamas before the Revolution. They practised traditional medicine and used some 3,000 drugs. This medicine has survived to some extent at Gandan in osteopathy, cauterisation, and massage.

Before communism, it was customary for the Mongol pastoralists to send one of their sons, at five or six years old, to study with a lama chosen through an astrological consultation. At the age of 10, the disciple (*bandi*) would enter a monastic school and swear an oath of allegiance to Lamaism. At 15 or 20, he would go into one of the datsan of the university and study there for fourteen years, at the end of which he would have to pass an exam.

The destruction of the major part of the monastery of Gandan and the dispersal of its belongings began in 1937. A major portion left in ruins were the 28 stupas on the north end. Religious activities resumed at Gandan in 1946, but in a completely different context. It served solely as a showcase to foreign visitors as proof of 'religious freedom' in Mongolia. At that time, Gandan was the only monastery in the country open to the public. The monks (less than one hundred of them) had the status of civil servant, and the highest authority in the monastery, the Khamba Lama, was named directly by the Central Committee of the Party.

Apart from its datsan, Gandan also had art schools and printing presses. An art school has since re-opened and in 2000 its director, the Venerable G. Purevbat, put on a huge exhibition in the Cultural Palace, featuring mandalas, *thankas*, models and masks. Plans are underway to send the exhibit abroad. For details, visit: http://www.tibet.ca/english/index.html. And search 'Purevbat'.

Gandan continues to heal itself and new temples have been built on the grounds in recent years. Remeber that this is a fully active monastery and should be respected as such. Do not photograph people or ceremonies without permission. The grounds are free to walk upon, but a US$1 fee is required for entry into the main hall, which is open from 9 am to 4 pm. Services are usually held in the mornings. The following are temples within the complex.

*The Vajradhâra (Ochirdara) Temple*
Built in 1840–1841 in brick and stone, with a tiled roof, this temple houses the main religious object in Gandan: the statue of Vajradhâra, a primordial Buddha (Adi-Buddha) in the Tantric schools, made in 1683 by Zanabazar, the first Bogd Gegeen. The statue holds in its hands a vajra and a bell, expressions of the inseparable unity of the masculine and feminine principles. It is here that the main religious services and the purification ceremonies (*Balin ariun tsever*) are held.

*The Temple of Züü (Temple of the Jewel)*
Once known as the 'Temple of the Remains of the seventh Bogd Gegeen', it was built in 1869 to house the relics of this spiritual leader, who died at the age of

*The Mejid Janraiseg (Avalokiteshvara) Temple*

nineteen. Among the treasures here are a 19th century statue of the Buddha and two of his disciples, as well as a wooden statue of the goddess Lkhamo (Shri Devi, the only female among the eight Dharmapala protectors).

## The Didan-Lavran Temple

The fifth Bogd Gegeen built this two-storey temple with a glazed-tile roof as a library. The 13th Dalai Lama lived here in 1904 when, fleeing the English, he sought refuge in Urga with one hundred of his followers. A fourth temple, built in 1926, now serves as a library and contains over 50,000 unique books and manuscripts, including the Tibetan Buddhist canon, translated into Mongolian in the 17th century. This vast compilation is composed of two collections, the Ganjur in 108 volumes, which contains the fundamental Buddhist teachings (*sutras, tantras,* and texts on monastic discipline), and the Danjur in 225 volumes, composed of commentaries on the Ganjur, including works by Tsongkhapa, the Dalai Lamas and other Tibetan authors, as well as by more than 70 Mongol lamas. The library has a rich collection of manuscripts in Mongolian, Oirat, Sanskrit, and Pali, and contains hundreds of Tibetan and Mongol sutras inlaid with gold, silver, and precious stones. It is not regularly open to the public and you will need to seek special permission for a visit. To the east of these temples stands a stupa built in 1958 by the monastery monks, and a statue of Tsongkhapa (1357-1419), the Tibetan king and reformer who founded the Gelugpa school (Yellow Hats).

The halls of Didan-Lavran also include painted or embroidered *thankas* in gold on black and red backgrounds, the embalmed mummy of the eighth Bogd Gegeen, the tombs of the third, fifth, and seventh Bogd Gegeens, and a bronze statue of Zanabazar. You can also ask to see the statue of Tsongkhapa in silver made by Oirat craftsmen in the 16th century.

*Temple interior at Ganden Monastery, the largest in Mongolia.*

On a more contemporary note, the halls also include a statue of the Buddha Shakyamuni made in 1956 by the monks from Dambadarjaa Monastery (for the 2500th anniversary of the birth of the Buddha), and a statue of the Buddha presented in 1957 by the Indian Prime Minister Nehru.

### The Mejid Janraiseg (Avalokiteshvara) Temple

This temple was built in 1911–1912 to celebrate the end of Manchu domination and, it is said, to heal the Bogd Gegeen of blindness. It is in a mixed Chinese and Tibetan style, and its unusual height allows it to accommodate an immense statue. The 25.6 metre tall Avalokiteshvara-Janraiseg, is a standing deity and arguably the most well-known piece of art in the country. The original was disassembled and taken in pieces to the USSR in the 1930s. A new statue, built in the mid-1990s with donations from Japan and Nepal, stands in its place. The deity, consecrated in 1996, is hollow and contains a storehouse of precious items including sutras, medicinal herbs, bundles of Buddhist mantras and even a furnished *ger*. Entry fee is US$1 for foreigners. In front of Mejid Janraiseg is one of the few stupas not to have disappeared during the purges.

## THE BOGD KHAAN MUSEUM

Located to the south of Ulaanbaatar near the Tuul River (south of the Tank Monument), this complex is composed of a two-storey winter house in European style, seven halls and a triumphal arc erected in 1912 to celebrate the end of Manchu reign and the birth of an independent theocratic monarchy headed by the eighth Bogd Gegeen, Agvanluvsan. The temple complex is known as **Sharavpeljiilin Süm**, that is 'Monastery spreading Wisdom'. The first building is the **Hall of Makharaji** (*Lokapāla*), with the statues (in coloured paper and clay) of the guardians of the Four Quarters. The colour of each one corresponds to those of the four continents around Mount Sumeru, the axis mundi of Buddhist cosmology: yellow for the north, blue for the south, red for the west, and white for the east.

The second hall, Ravsa houses musical instruments used by the monks during the religious ceremonies. Religious pictures, *thanka*, appliqués, gold, silver, and jewellery are also found here.

Next come two small halls placed in the east and west. The 'Hall of Painters' (*Uran zurgiin süm*) and 'Hall of Appliqués' (*Ezegi naamlin süm*) contain paintings and appliqués on silk, cotton, and brocade (a great speciality of Urga artists), made by Mongol artists at the end of the 19th and early 20th centuries.

In the next temple, religious ceremonies carried out by sixteen of the best lamas of Urga were held to ensure that the Bogd Gegeen would enjoy long life and happiness. Here one can see the 'tiger sticks', made from snow leopard tails, fur, and a long white cord. These sticks were used to beat back the throngs of faithful as the hierarch came through, trying to return to his palace. The long white cord on display was used by the Bogd Gegeen to bless the faithful from his balcony, so that he did not have to leave his palace. In the days of old, believers often stood in long lines for a chance to grasp the cord and feel the 'energy' delivered by blind Living Buddha.

The eighth Bogd Gegeen used the **Nogoon Lavran** (Green Labrang) as his private oratory. The works displayed here—made by the top Mongolian, Tibetan, and Chinese master-sculptors of the 18th and 19th centuries—represent the gods of the Buddhist pantheon. The thousand Ayush (Amitayur, the Buddha of Infinite Life) were made by special order in Poland. There are also representations of Tsongkhapa, the sixteen Arhat, and a self-portrait of Zanabazar done in 1680.

The **Jüdkhan süm**, located to the south of the Green Labrang, houses the portrait of Ngawang Losang Gyatsho, the 5th Dalai Lama (1617–1682).

**The Winter Palace of the Bogd Khaan** is a European-style two-storey construction, commissioned in 1905 by Tsar Nicolas II for the Mongol hierarch-king. It houses a number of treasures, in particular works by Zanabazar, and sumptuous clothing such as sable and fox fur inlaid with precious stones that belonged to the Bogd Gegeen and his wife Dongogdulam. Also on display are the many presents given by kings, emperors, and foreign political figures (from Russia, Manchuria and Tibet, to name a few) to the eight Bogd Gegeens between 1636 and 1924. On both levels, visitors will see the personal collection of stuffed animals of the eighth Bogd, a collection that included penguins, seals and a giraffe among others. Note that the giraffe's neck has been shortened to accommodate the room. The Bogd's belongings became state property after his death in 1924 and the entire complex was converted into a museum in 1961.

Located on Chinggis Khaan Avenue near the tank monument. Open from 10 am to 5 pm (sometimes to 6 pm in summer), but closed on Wednesday and Thursday in the winter. Tel: 342 195. Take bus no. 7 or 19 from the Bayangol Hotel or Ard Kino. Admission is Tg2,000 and an extra fee is charged for taking photographs.

## THE CHOIDJIIN LAM MONASTERY-MUSEUM

This complex of temples, located south of Sükhbaatar Square, was built between 1904 and 1908 for the *Choidjiin Lam* (a monastic title) Lubsankhaidav, the state Oracle and younger brother of the eighth Bogd Gegeen. Considered one the most beautiful monasteries in Mongolia, it was closed as a place of worship in 1938 and converted into a museum in 1942.

Its last major restoration work was done in 1960-61, and although now a bit shabby in appearance, it is well worth a visit. The entrance is on the south side, facing the Children's Park. It includes five halls and five arched gateways. Many art and religious objects are on show here, including paintings, sculptures, embroideries, and masks from the 17th to the 20th centuries. The following list describes the five temples inside the complex.

**The Hall of Makharaji**, at the entrance, is dedicated to the guardians of the Four Quarters (*Lokapāla*), whose statues are made of papier-mâché.

The **Main Temple (Temple of Spreading Compassion)** to the right of the Buddha and two of his disciples is a portrait of the Choidjiin Lam Lubsankhaidav, who died in 1918. To the left is the embalmed mummy of Baldan-Choimbol, the preceptor of the seventh and eighth Bogd Gegeens. The Bogd Gegeen's throne stands at the centre of the temple.

In front of the altar, religious objects and musical instruments are placed on tables called 'seats of Javdan'. Above these seats hang *thanka* representing Yamantaka, Devi, Vajrapani, Mahakala, Sita Tara (the White Tara), Avalokiteshvara, Amitayus, and Vishnu. Among the objects on show are the masks of the divinities that were used in the celebrations of the Tsam mysteries, each are decorated with precious stones. Some of these date back to the 18th century, but most were done by Puntsag-Ossor, the well-known 19th century sculptor. The masks made by Urga masters were known for their great expressiveness.

The Tsam ceremonies were held for the first time in Mongolia in 1737 at Erdene Züü Monastery. Black and white photographs displayed in the temple show the last

Tsam ceremony held in Urga prior to the communist intrusion.

On the east side of this hall are the 108 volumes of the Ganjur, brought from Tibet by the fourth Bogd Gegeen. On the west side, are the 225 volumes of the Tibetan manuscript of the Danjur.

A series of small paintings show in a very realistic way the terrifying torment that awaits sinners in Hell. According to the seriousness of their acts, they may be tortured in burning hells or freezing hells. These paintings, known to all the nomadic herders, would have helped their submission to the powerful Lamaist clergy.

The **Gonkon** hall (the room behind the main temple) was devoted to the esoteric activities of the state Oracle. It was here that he would go into his trance, contact the spirits and pronounce his oracle. The Bogd Gegeen consulted the Oracle on all important government matters. The walls of the temple are decorated with appliqué embroideries of the Urga school representing, among other tutelary divinities— Vishnu, Vajradhara, and Yamantaka.

The **Hall of Züü**, located to the west of the main temple, is dedicated to the three Buddhas of the Past (Kashyapa), Present (Shakyamuni), and Future (Maitreya), flanked by two disciples. To either side of the door, are the Sixteen Arhat represented as hermits seated in solitary meditation in their grottoes.

The **Hall of the Yiddam** (once forbidden for most people to enter it) is located to the north of the main temple. It is dedicated to the yiddam, tutelary divinities who can be invoked for protection. They are generally represented in their angry aspect and in sexual union (*yab-yum* in Tibetan, meaning 'father-mother') with their feminine double (*Shakti*). It is here that the secret Tantric rituals were held. The liturgy relating to the yiddam required the presence of mandalas, or meditation diagrams.

*Temple entrance at Choidjiin Lam Monastery.*

This temple contains the amulets of the Choidjiin Lam, statues of divinities made in India and in Tibet, and, in the centre, a bronze sculpture of one of the 84 Indian mahâsiddha, ascetic wise men who played a vital role in the transmission of Tantric Buddhism, and who created the rituals dedicated to the yiddam. The 'Great Accomplished Ones' lived between the seventh and the 11<sup>th</sup> centuries and were reputed to possess great powers. Through asceticism and yogic techniques, they went beyond the duality of subject and object, reaching a state of consciousness of universal vacuity. To the right are bronze statues of Tantric divinities (including *Vajradhara*) united with their feminine doubles (*Shakti*). One of these is the famous statue of Sitasamvara, sculpted by Zanabazar. To the left is a wooden statue of the Dharmapâla Begtse, one of a group of eight Protectors of the Law and the tutelary deity of Mongolia. On the tables lay various ritual objects made around the turn of the 20<sup>th</sup> century.

The **Amgalan Temple** (Öndör-Gegeen Temple) is located to the east of the main temple, this hall contains bas-reliefs representing the Sixteen Arhat. It also houses a self-portrait of Zanabazar (in the north part), and various other works, including statues of Ayush, Mintuk, Ratnasambhava and Maitreya. The most important deity here is Zanabazar's Siamatara—the Green Tara, an extremely popular deity in Mongolia since the 12<sup>th</sup> century. Images of the Green Tara can be seen on practically every Mongol altar in temples and *gers*. Known as the 'Mother of all Buddhas and bodhisattvas', the 'Mother who helps cross the Ocean of Existence', Tara symbolises purity and is always seated on a lotus. One day, says the legend, tears fell from the eyes of Avalokiteshvara into a valley, forming a lake. A lotus appeared on the lake with Tara seated amidst its open petals. The faithful could speak to her directly without having to go through the monks. Öndör Gegeen Zanabazar himself was considered the reincarnation of the Tibetan scholar Taranatha, who greatly contributed to the development of the cult of Tara. This hall also contains a bronze stupa from the 10<sup>th</sup> century, made in India and brought to Mongolia by Zanabazar in the 17<sup>th</sup> century.

The complex is located on Jamian Street, south of Peace Avenue, near the Bayangol Hotel. Open from 10 am to 5 pm (sometimes until 6 pm in summer), every day except Thursday. Tel: 324 788. A fee of Tg2,000 is charged at the south gate; it will cost an extra Tg5,000 to take photographs.

### The Choidjiin Lam Monastery-Museum

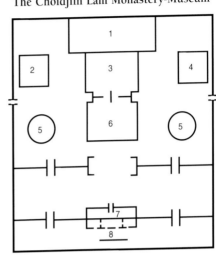

| | |
|---|---|
| 1. The Temple of Yiddam | 5. Souvenir Shop |
| 2. Hall of Zuu | 6. Main Temple |
| 3. Gonkhon Hall | 7. Hall of Makharaji |
| 4. Amgalan Temple | 8. Wall of Dragons |

## OTHER TEMPLES AND MONASTERIES

The **Dambadarjaa Monastery** (Damba Darjalin Khiid), located in the northern suburbs of Ulaanbaatar, is called Temple propagator of the Faith'. It was built in 1765 by the Manchu Emperor Qianlong to house the remains of the second Bogd Gegeen who died in 1723. These relics were moved from Bogdiin Khuree to Dambadarjaa at the same time as the transfer, in 1778, of the remains of Zanabazar to the monastery of Ambarbayasgalant. A funerary stupa, in the north-west of the wall surrounding the monastery, was built in 1774 in honour of the second Bogd Gegeen.

The **Narokhajid** (**Vajrayogini**) **Monastery** first appeared in 1991 as a *ger*. Permanent structures were built for it in 1993 and it was inaugurated in June 1995 by monks from Gandan Khiid and Bakula Rinpoche, a Ladakhi Tantric master and former Indian ambassador to Mongolia. It replaces an older temple of the same name, built at the beginning of the 20th century north of the Tuul River, and dedicated to Padmasambhava, the great Indian master from Kashmir who introduced Tantric Buddhism to Tibet in the eighth century.

The teachings of Padmasambhava form the doctrinal basis of the Nyingma school, the so-called 'Red Hats', and the Narokhajid temple belongs to this branch, which officially reappeared in Mongolia after 1990. This is the first monastery to be run by nuns since the beginning of the revival of Mongol Lamaism. It also houses the first Buddhist school of higher education for women. Religious services are held every day from 9 am till midday. Bus stop: hospital no. 3 (fourth *khoroolol*)

The **Dechin Choinkhorlin Khiid**, dedicated to Padmasambhava and belonging to the Nyingma Red Hat branch of Tantrism, was built in 1991. A guild of astrologers who give consultations live here. It is located in the Bayangol district, south of the Örgöö cinema.

**Betub Danjai Choinkhorlon** is a newly-built Ladakhi-style monastery inaugurated in 1999 in the presence of Indian Vice President Krishan Kant and former Mongolian president Orchirbat. This monastery, a gift from the Indian Ambassador to Mongolia, is considered a symbol of cooperation between India and Mongolia. It houses a conservative religious school that teaches the old Uighur Mongolian script. Located between the Bömbögör market and the Gesar Temple (near the Hanamasa restaurant).

The **Gesar Temple**, across the street from Betub Danjai Choinkhorlon, is built in the Chinese style, and closely associated with Gandan Monastery. Legend tells that the Elephant Head Hill behind the temple was slowly moving south, and the temple was built to halt its progress. Elephant Head Hill has long been topped by an *ovoo*, a sacred mound of stones, and is a good place to survey downtown. Plans have been made to place a 12-metre high Buddhist statue here.

## THE MUSEUM OF NATURAL HISTORY

Located near the town centre, on Sambuu Street, this museum was founded in 1924. The section on natural sciences is divided into several sub-sections: geography, geology, botany, fauna, and palaeontology. Researchers have listed more than 2,270 plant varieties in Mongolia, including 600 medicinal plants and 160 comestible plants. Of the 86 species defined as endemic, two-thirds of them grow in *gobi* areas. Medicinal products are extracted from about thirty different varieties of plant.

The palaeontology section contains more than 800 objects from the Lower Cambrian (500 million years ago) to the Quaternary (10,000 to 15,000 years ago). Among the treasures on display are a wide variety of fossils including: vertebrates, plants, leaf prints, dinosaurs, and mammals. Most fascinating is the rich collection of dinosaur bones and skeletons, which date from 220 to 270 million years ago. The specimens vary in size from a few centimetres to over 30 metres tall, and several are found only in Mongolia. One of the most spectacular examples in the museum is a gigantic complete skeleton of a Tarbosaurus, an Asian cousin of the American Tyrannosaurus, which was discovered in 1948.

The **Golden Camel Museum** (on the second floor) is a recent addition to the building, and provides everything you ever wanted to known about these two-humped desert dwelling beasts.

The Natural History Museum is open daily in summer from 10 am to 4.30 pm (closes at 3 pm on Monday). In winter is it closed on Monday and Tuesday. Admission is Tg3,000 and an extra fee is charged for photography. Tel: 321 716.

## THE ZANABAZAR MUSEUM OF FINE ARTS

Dedicated to Zanabazar, this building contains some of the greatest works of this famed 17th century sculptor. On view are a White Tara (Sita Tara) represented as a young girl, a Green Tara (Siama Tara), and gilt bronze statues of Amogasiddhi, Amitabha, Vairocana, and Akshobhya. One of the finest pieces is a cast iron and gilt bronze statue of the bodhisattva Manjusri holding his two attributes, a sword and a book. Also worth looking for is the famous stupa (Bodhi Subugan) in gilt bronze, with touches of polychromy, characteristic of a new form of Lamaist stupa that appeared at the beginning of the 17th century. The panels decorating its base represent the mounts of the Jina of Esoteric Buddhism: the elephant, horse, peacock, and Garuda.

Zanabazar used the lost wax technique for casting his sculptures, as well as a heavy alloy similar to that used by Nepalese bronze casters. The hall includes paintings done by Zanabazar, including a self-portrait, portraits of his mother and of his preceptor Choijijantsan, as well as a painting of the Green Tara. The museum is located at Builders' Square (Barilgadchidin Talbai) on Trade Street. Open daily from 9 am to 6 pm. Tel: 326 060.

# NATIONAL MUSEUM OF MONGOL HISTORY

This was once called the Revolutionary Museum and is still known as such by locals. The museum does an excellent job of weaving through several millennia of history in Mongolia—beginning with the Stone Age, running through the Turkic and Mongol empires, the rise of Buddhism and the communist experiment. It ends with a colourful display of contemporary society. The first floor is dedicated to pre-Mongol history; showing off examples of ancient Turkic stones and tools used by early man. The third floor offers excellent displays of the Mongol Empire, including old texts, weapons and a wax statue of Chinggis Khaan. Exhibits are marked in English. The second floor features an ethnographical section, with costumes and accessories of the various ethnic groups in the country. Special exhibitions are sometimes shown; in 2000 the museum hosted a documentation of the 1990 Democratic Revolution.

Outside the museum, the large modern sculpture is a memorial for the victims of the 1930s political repression. The bronze figure is shown struggling against the black tyranny afflicting the nation.

The museum is located north-west of Sükhbaatar Square. Open daily (except Wednesdays) from 10 am to 4 pm, and Thursdays from 10 am to 2.30 pm. Tel: 325 656. Admission fee is Tg2,000, and an additional fee is required for photography.

# MUSEUM TO THE VICTIMS OF POLITICAL REPRESSION

Opened in 1996, this museum is dedicated to the tens of thousands of Mongols who died during the purges of 1932–1950. This building was once the residence of Prime Minister Genden (see p. 66), until he was exiled to Sochi on the Black Sea, and then shot in Moscow at Stalin's order. His fate, like thousands of others, was locked away in secret archives until 1990.

The museum, operated by Genden's daughter, chronicles the history and reasons for the purge, and is particularly critical of the role played by Marshal Choibalsan. The second floor display cases, sometimes presented in graphic horror, show how prisoners were arrested, interrogated, shot, and buried in mass graves. The first floor contains a memorial wall dedicated to the victims; names are still being added as research is on-going. An estimated 27,000 died in the purges. In an adjoining room is a mock-up of Genden's former office. Some exhibits offer English explanations, but a guide is useful.

The museum is located on Karl Marx Street, between the Wedding Palace and the Foreign Ministry. Hours are 10 am to 4.30 pm Mon–Fri, and 10 am to 2.30 pm on Sat–Sun. Admission charge is Tg1,000.

# OTHER MUSEUMS AND GALLERIES

The **Municipal Museum** presents the history of the Mongol capital from its foundation in 1639 to modern times, showing various documents and paintings, as well as a panorama of the town carved on an elephant's tusk. It is located inside a period building that the revolutionary hero Sükhbaatar was said to have used as an office. On Peace Avenue in front of the Wrestling Palace. Open Mon–Fri, 9 am to 6 pm, and Saturday 9 am to 3 pm.

The **Natsagdorj Museum** is dedicated to the Mongolian poet/author considered the pioneer of modern Mongol literature. Secretary to Marshal Choibalsan, Natsagdorj was arrested in the purges of 1936 along with many other intellectuals. Freed a few months later, he died soon afterwards at the age of 31; the cause of death remains a mystery. Located near the Choidjiin Lam Museum.

Mongolians have a great history of hunting. During the days of the Empire, great hunts organised for the khaans involved thousands of men, and were designed to develop war tactics. The **Hunting Museum** offers exhibits of stuffed game and history of the sport. It is located in a two-storey yellow building on Zanabazar Street, a few hundred meters south of Gandan Monastery.

More than 500 Mongol and international games and toys are displayed in the **Toy Museum**, located in a four-storey building west of the Sports Palace on the Little Ring Road.

The **Theatre Museum** and National Gallery traces the history of Mongolian theatre since 1921. The displays include old photos costumes and puppets. It is located on the third floor of the Cultural Palace. Enter from the north side of the building. A few steps east of this door, another section of the building houses the National Art Gallery—a collection of mostly Soviet era paintings done in the Western style. The subjects often portray the countryside with colourful and sweeping landscape scenes and horsemen tending to their flocks.

The **Mongolian Artists Exhibition Hall** features a variety of exhibits put on by local artists, making this one of the more unique displays of art in Ulaanbaatar. The café here makes this a good place to have lunch or a beer. Located on the second floor of the marble building on the corner of Peace and Chinggis Khaan avenues (near the Central Post Office).

# Sites around Sükhbaatar Square

There are a few small monuments located around the square. Close to the Foreign Ministry is a large **stone block** with lyrics to the national song *Haluun Elgen Nutag*, loosely translated as 'My Lovely Country', carved into it. In the small park just east of the Post Office is the **0-kilometre marker**; which marks the spot that all distances in Mongolia are measured from. A little further east is the 'Peace Bell', which hangs in a small, Buddhist-style overhang.

High above the Post office, one can see the **Ulaanbaatar city clock**, which chimes

*Sükhbaatar Square, ringed by Soviet era buildings, after a rain storm. The salmon-coloured building on the right is the Opera House. The Cultural Palace is on the left.*

on the hour. Across the street is the **Monument to S. Zorig**, the leader of Mongolia's peaceful democracy movement of 1990. Zorig, assassinated on October 2, 1998 at the age of 36, is portrayed with his briefcase under one arm and a cigarette between his fingers: seemingly off to work with his fellow Ulaanbaatarites. He is best remembered for the calm direction he took during the 1990 protests, when, on several occasions, he dissuaded the masses from attacking the defence forces deployed by the government. Zorig served as a Member of Parliament and was the acting Infrastructure Minister prior to his murder. His death deeply shocked the nation as many saw it as an attack on Mongolia's young democracy. Sükhbaatar Square was filled with candle-bearing mourners for three days after Zorig's death, and, on the day of his funeral, a serious scrum formed as people desperately tried to enter the Government House where his body laid in state.

Despite a massive police search, the killers were never found and the true motive for the attack has given way to much speculation. Flowers gather around the monument every year on April 20, Zorig's birthday.

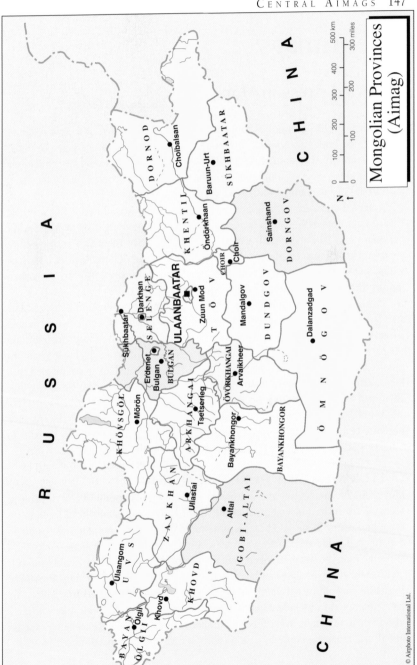

Mongolian Provinces (Aimag)

© Airphoto International Ltd.

# The Aimags

## Protected Areas in Mongolia

In the early 1990s, a group of Mongolian scientists suggested at a conference of international biologists that all of Mongolia be designated as one giant National Park. Eventually they settled on a goal of preserving 30 per cent of the land as protected areas. It is an ambitious plan but as of 2001, about 13 per cent (20.6 million ha) of the country was already under protection.

Protected areas are nothing new in Mongolia. Bogd Khaan mountain, south of Ulaanbaatar, was designated a protected area in 1788, making it the world's oldest national park. The mountain had been venerated since the 12th century. Before communism, the protected areas were patrolled by teams of *karaul*, guards, most of whom were monks. In more recent times, the WWF has teamed up with Mongolian monks to enforce protection laws in local areas.

'Protected Areas' in Mongolia charge admission for people and vehicles. The standard daily fee is Tg1,000 per person and Tg3,000 per car. Mongolians are charged a fraction of this price, but the fees are still reasonable and go towards maintaining the park. Some parks, located in remote parts of the country, may get just a handful of visitors per year, so your fee is welcomed. The protected areas are divided into four categories: Strictly Protected Areas, National Parks, Nature Reserves, and Historical / Natural Monuments.

To find out about the current legislation in these zones, and to buy the entrance permits, contact, NSPAE, 5 Trade Street. Tel: 326 617. Fees can also be paid to rangers who make patrol sweeps in the parks.

### CULTURAL SITES: A WORD OF CAUTION

Mongolia's archaeological and cultural sites are poorly signposted and difficult to access. Very little information is available on historic sites and local legends are often impossible to verify. These factors should encourage visitors to travel with an experienced guide and driver when searching for sites in remote areas.

Some monuments mentioned here may have been moved to museums and it is recommended to ask local authorities about the status of cultural sites. Provincial museums and protected area offices are good sources of information. Lastly, we have attempted to include a maximum number of sites, but not all may warrant a visit in their own right. Travellers with limited time can often find excellent examples at cultural remains simply by visiting the national and provincial museums.

CENTRAL AIMAGS

# Töv

Töv Aimag (Central Province) surrounds the Mongolian capital Ulaanbaatar, which itself maintains the status of an autonomous municipality. The aimag, with a surface area of 77,400 sq. km, links the Siberian taiga and the Gobi Desert. The rugged Khentii Mountains are strung across the north, while the easternmost tip of the Khangai chain is located in the west. Its capital is Zuunmod, sometimes simply referred to as 'Töv Aimag'.

First called 'Aimag of the Bogd Khaan Mountains', it was given its current name in 1931. The Tuul River runs through the middle of the province, and the Kherlen River divides it from Khentii Aimag in the east. North of Ulaanbaatar, the highest peak of the aimag is Mount Asralt Khairkhan (2,800 m).

The eastern part of the province is well watered, and supports groves of larch, birch, cedar, pine, aspen, dogwood, and elder. Fauna is also rich: sable, wild boar, elk, wolf, fox, lynx, bear, roe deer, eagles, cranes, and pheasants all make their home here. There are several worthwhile sites for the traveller in Töv, notably the spectacular Terelj National Park. Khustai Nuruu, the rehabilitation site for the *takhi* horse, is a good day trip. For locals, the pilgrimage site of Eej Khad, a sacred rock, is extremely popular.

## ZUUNMOD AND SURROUNDINGS

The small town of Zuunmod, which means 'hundred trees', is 43 kilometres south of Ulaanbaatar and easily visited on a day trip. Zuunmod has two museums, a recently-built monastery, and retains a laid back atmosphere that is a welcome relief to Ulaanbaatar. Public mini-vans travel between Ulaanbaatar and Zuunmod by the hour, from the bus stop it is another seven kilometres to Manzhir Monastery and the Bogd Uul Protected Area.

In Zuunmod, the **Provincial Museum** on the south-east side of the park has a display on local fauna and flora. At the time of research, the nearby **Ethnographical Museum** was undergoing repairs. **Dashinchoinkhorlon Khiid** (monastery) is on the eastern part of town, and holds services in the morning.

### MANZHIR, THE MONASTERY OF MANJUSRI

The main reason to visit Zuunmod is to access **Manzhir Khiid**, an 18th century monastic complex that is now a museum, tel: 341 176. The monastery was left in ruins after the communist purges of the 1930s, but several years of restoration work has brought some of the buildings back to life. Because the monastery is located in the Bogd Khaan Protected Area, visitors must purchase a park entry fee.

# THE AIMAG AND POPULATION CENTRES

In the 17th century, during the period of Manchu domination, Khalkh Mongolia was divided into four large aimag, or provinces, each named after the main prince who nominally governed it. From east to west were the aimags of the Tsetsen Khaan, Tüsheet Khaan, Sain Noyon Khaan, and Zasagt Khaan. The westernmost region was called Khovd Area, and the far north was designated for the Bogd Gegeen's livestock. The Dariganga pastures in the south-east were grazing grounds for horses owned by the Manchus.

In 1923, the princely titles were replaced with names of mountains. The first became Bogd-Khaan Aimag, the second Mount Khan Khentii Aimag, the third Tsetserleg Mandal Aimag, and the fourth was labelled Mount Taishir Aimag. In 1929, a fifth aimag was added: Mount Chandman Aimag, which included the Khovd region. Each of these aimag was subdivided into *khoshuun* or 'banners', old princely privileges.

Another shake up occurred in 1931 when the five large aimags were divided into thirteen smaller provinces. This number jumped to 18 in 1941, and remained as such until the 1990s when three provinces were added.

Today, there are 21 *aimags*: the 18 provinces of 1941 as well as the autonomous municipalities of Darkhan Uul, Orkhon, and Gobi-Sumber. Each aimag has between 18 and 24 *sums*, of different sizes and population. There are 357 sums in all.

The term 'brigade' once designated an administrative, economic, and geographic unit formed of a group of pastoralists specialised in one particular task. This was characteristic of the organisation of pastoralism into socialist cooperatives. The cooperatives covered the same area as the prefectures (sum). Within each sum, the pastoralists were divided into four or five brigades grouped around a permanent non-nomadic centre. These brigades were themselves formed of a cluster of two or three families which formed a *sur* and which were specialised in the breeding of animals of strictly determined species, sex, and age, intended for a specific use. This is no longer the case today, and the 'five snouts' may once again be bred side by side. The brigades have become 'bag', but the term brigade is still used by many Mongols to designate small 'villages'.

The formation of population centres has largely been Soviet influenced, but is not a new thing. For centuries, groups of *gers* have come together at the crossroads of caravan routes, at oases, at markets, and above all at monasteries. On the location of summer and winter camps, monasteries and fortresses; part of the population would settle into fluid, unstable semi-sedentary 'villages', without any organised character to them. The appearance of aimag centres developed around these semi-sedentary arteries.

Some formed on **monastic sites**. This was the case of Tsetserleg (Arkhangai), Ondörkhaan (Khentii), Bulgan (Bulgan), Mörön (Khövsgöl), and Arvaikheer (Ovörkhangai). Lastly, the old monastic centre of the Kherlen River valley grew into Choibalsan, the capital of Dornod Aimag. In its day, this was an important commercial axis between China and Siberia.

Other urban areas formed on the site of **old military fortresses** built by the Manchus on Mongol territory. Commercial and crafts districts rapidly grew around the Manchu garrisons, as was the case at Khovd City (Khovd) and the old Ouliassoutai, now called Uliastai (Zavkhan).

A variety of other reasons caused urbanisation. In some cases, urban areas appeared around factories, or around stops along the railway line, such as Sükhbaatar and Darkhan (Selenge). Zuunkhara was founded around a petrol field discovered in 1940–41. (*after D. Maidar*)

This once important monastery was built on a rocky spur projecting southwards, overlooking a pretty valley with streams, surrounded by small pine forests. Several foundations of constructions around the rebuilt temples, set on an east-west axis, testify to the size and importance of the original monastery, which had between 14 and 17 halls, and existed for over 200 years (1733–1937). Traces of an artificial lake about 10 metres wide are in front of what used to be the main temple.

The construction of the monastery began in 1733, and more halls were added until 1867. In 1750, the 'Temple for the spreading of the Faith' was placed under the jurisdiction of the Bogd Gegeen.

Manzhir Khiid was renowned throughout Mongolia for its religious services and its celebrations of Tsam, held every year in the autumn. It is said that more believers came here than to the great monastery at Urga. The **masks** used at Manzhir for the ceremony are kept in the Bogd Khaan Museum in Ulaanbaatar.

According to some historians, Manzhir was built on one of the four camps (*ordo*) of Chinggis Khaan, where six of the imperial consorts lived. It was also the site in 1696 of a decisive battle between the Manchu Emperor Kangxi and Prince Galdan, head of the Western Mongols. The Manchus defeated the Mongols thanks to field artillery designed by the Jesuits. Following this, terms were made by the Diet of Doloon Nuur to hand over Mongol territory to the Manchus, who occupied the country for two centuries.

During the 1921 Revolution, Manzhir Khiid served as a refuge for the Bogd Gegeen, who stayed there in secrecy after fleeing his palace at Urga where the Chinese army held him prisoner.

**Rocks engraved with Buddhist images** are located near the temple. One represents Tsongkhapa (1357–1419), founder of the Gelugpa school of Tibetan Buddhism, and a second one shows the Bodhisattva Manzhir (Manjusri), considered the patron of the Manchus. The name 'Manchu' is said to have come from that of 'Manzhir.' A third rock is engraved with a design of an elephant, hare, monkey, and bird, known as the 'allegory of cooperation'.

A small **museum of flora and fauna**, built in 1972, is located on the grounds. Here visitors will find a model of the original temple, as well as small, skilfully done images made from natural elements (wood, sand, feathers, stones and fur) from the surrounding mountains. Also on display are a few **documents** dating from the end of the Manchu period to the Revolution, and a few stuffed animals. Not far away is a reconstruction of a **hunter's hut** made from bark, with traps on display.

Open-air **archaeological remains** at the site include a large cauldron, two metres wide and one metre tall, with inscriptions in old Mongolian. While one of the inscriptions dates the cauldron to the summer of 1730, another explains that it was used to boil water for the tea offered to pilgrims. A large bell, one metre in height, dates to the reign of the Manchu emperor Qianlong (1736–1795). A line of stone statues, from the sixth to the eighth century, once stood near some ancient tombs. One represents a ram, symbol of the power of the *kaghan*.

The **Öndör Dov**, located eight kilometres west of Zuunmod and 22 kilometres south Manzhir, is a popular accommodation option in the area. Facilities include a restaurant, *ger* accommodation and horse trekking. The small *ger* camp at Manzhir itself is a pleasant, albeit basic, option. The town of Zuunmod has two functional hotels close to the Square.

## THE SANCTUARY OF EEJ KHAD

**Eej Khad**, the 'Mother Rock', is about 100 kilometres south of Ulaanbaatar, near Mount Avdarkhangai in Sergelen sum. The route passes through Zuunmod. This rock, to which the Mongols attribute special powers, has long been the object of a popular cult. Its popularity has enjoyed a revival since 1990 and Mongolians now flock here on summer weekends.

According to legend, the spirit of the rock is that of a virtuous shepherdess who used to come here to graze her flock of lambs. She became a spirit after her death, and turned to stone along with her animals. Avoid walking on the nearby white stones as they are the 'Mother's flock'.

A new *ger*-shaped building encloses the rock-statue, which itself is almost completely covered with blue silk scarves (*khadag*). The pilgrims line up to greet the 'Mother', and will ask her to grant three wishes, whispering them into her ear. Money and offerings are slipped into the scarves or placed on an offering table. Only the most faithful will have their wishes granted, so pilgrims try to visit three times per year.

Surrounding the *ger* structure is a wall of tea brick, which pilgrims will walk around three times while flicking spoonfuls of milk at the *ger*. The pilgrims will then visit the other stones in their area. The 'Dog Rock' is particularly popular and, if rubbed against, is said to cure health problems. A few kilometres away is 'Rich Rock', upon which one must rub their wallet for financial rewards.

Special vans travel to Eej Khad in the summer from the long distance bus station in Ulaanbaatar. A Tg4,000 ticket is good for one round trip and about two hours at the rock itself. The three-hour ride, however, is bumpy and these vans are very crowded, so hiring your own car is another option. Pack a lunch and water as there are no facilities at the site.

# Bogd Khaan Mountain Protected Area

The oldest protected area in the country is located just south of Ulaanbaatar. The Bogd Uul has been protected since 1788 and revered since the 1200s. Centuries old laws forbid hunting, development and the felling of trees. Before the 1900s, a breach of these laws spelled death for the transgressor. The reserve has an area of 41,600 ha, of which 18,100 ha are forest. The lower elevations of the reserve are steppe land, while forests of conifer—a southern extension of the mountainous *taiga* of Khentii—are abundant in the higher parts. Manzhir Khiid, an 18th century monastery, is located on the southern end of the reserve, and well worth a visit.

## BOGD KHAAN MOUNTAIN

Bulging mountains surround Ulaanbaatar on all sides; four are venerated with the utmost respect. The most important is the Bogd Uul (uul means mountain), south of the capital, whose master-spirit, Dalkha-Tunchin-Garbo, has the appearance of the great mythical Garuda bird. In the 12th and 13th centuries, the Bogd Uul was called Khaan Uul (the Mountain of the Khaan) because the leader of the Kereit tribe, Van Khaan, lived there. It was later named 'Bogd Khaan khairkhan', *khairkhan* meaning 'dear' or 'loved one', a term often used to designate sacred mountains, or to avoid having to say their real name.

*Children rounding up sheep in Töv Aimag. Mongolia is home to over 28 million head of livestock.*

The highest point along the broad ridge is **Tsetseeguun** (2,268 m). If viewed from the town centre, it is to the south-east, almost hidden by the meandering ridge. A small temple once stood here and every year the Bogd Gegeen of Urga would carry out religious ceremonies, followed by a feast and a great *naadam* (sports festival). Inside the temple were housed a horse's bit, a saddle, a whip, and armour, said to have belonged to Avdai Khan, the founder of Erdene Züü Monastery.

This region offers good possibilities for hiking, and there are more or less well-marked trails. The southern approach to Tsetseeguun, from Manzhir Khiid, is about a three-hour walk. Plan for two hours from the Observatory or six hours from the Zaisan Memorial. Bring water, food, and a tent if you plan to sleep out. At the top are two large *ovoo*, a few rocks covered with inscriptions, and some ruins. **Rock carvings** dating to the Bronze Age have been found in the Ikh Tenger Valley.

After Tsetseeguun, the highest peaks on the mountain are Tusheeguun (2,200 metres), Dzuun Shireet (2,150 metres), and Baruun Shireet (2,004 metres). At the summit of Baruun Shireet, not far from a large rock, is a small grotto called the 'cave of Öndör Gegeen' (Zanabazar).

The Bogd Uul Mountains have some 300 plant varieties. Its forests are mixed with elm, cedar, Siberian sorb, aspen, poplar, birch, fir, and pine. Fauna include wild boar, deer, fox, steppe fox, wolf, hare, squirrel, eagles, kites and woodpeckers. A deer farm is located on the west side of the mountain. They can be seen in large numbers in the Nuukh't valley.

The **Nuukh't, Zaisan, and Törkhurakh valleys** were developed in the 1950s as rest areas for members of the Politburo and Party cadres. Some of the Dachas and rest homes; Nuukh't, for example, have been converted into hotels for foreigners. The valley of Zuunmod, including Manzhir Khiid, is on the south-facing side of Bogd Uul, whereas those of Zaisan and Iarmag are on the north sides. Each year in July, a vast camp of tents, horses, and camels forms at **Iarmag** as Mongols from the whole country gather to take part in the great national Naadam of Ulaanbaatar.

## OTHER SACRED MOUNTAINS AROUND ULAANBAATAR

The three other holy mountains surrounding Ulaanbaatar are easily accessible, and worth climbing for their excellent views. To the west, **Songino** (Onion) Mountain contains a master-spirit that is portrayed as an old man with a blue face and two large fangs in his mouth. North-west of town is **Chinggeltei** (1,949 m), whose master-spirit resembles a wild boar. To the east is **Bayanzurkh**, whose master-spirit resembles a wolf. The master-spirits of these four mountains played an important role during the great Tsam ceremonies held in the monasteries of old Urga.

# Gorkhi-Terelj National Park

One of Mongolia's best national parks lies under an hour's drive away from the capital. Terelj was founded as a park in 1994 and is located on the edge of the strictly protected zone of Khan Khentii. Its 286,400 hectares of territory contain plenty to do for the visitor, including rafting, horse riding, hiking, camping and excellent mountain biking trails. The village of Terelj, on the Terelj River, has some supplies, but most equipment needed by the traveller should be brought from Ulaanbaatar. Beyond the river, the wilderness takes over and most of the terrain is accessible only by foot or on horseback.

'Terelj' is the name of a plant (Latin *ledum*), very abundant in the area, which flowers at the end of spring just before the leaves appear on the trees. Edelweiss is also very common here. This flower, symbol of eternity, is used to light the first fire in the *ger* of a newly-wed couple.

The forests are full of birch, cedar, pine, willow, larch, and aspen, as well as foxes, wolves, and squirrels. Some herders live in the park and visitors will encounter their horses and yaks.

This particularly beautiful region has been chosen as backdrop for a number of Mongol films, in part for its impressive, strangely-shaped rock masses. Some of the rocks resemble the long spiky bodies of the prehistoric animals. The most popular is **Turtle Rock** (Melkhii Khad), which is just off the main road into the park. Nearby are concrete models of dinosaurs, giving the place a slightly Jurassic aura.

## THE TRAGIC STORY OF A MANCHU PRINCESS

At the end of the 17th century, the Manchu emperors tried to increase their influence in Mongolia by forming family ties between themselves and the ruling Mongol nobility.

In 1722, Dondogdorj, the heir to the Tüsheet Khaan (an important Mongol title), married the young daughter of the Manchu Emperor. The marriage contract stipulated that the son born to the couple would become the heir to Zanabazar. The Mongol princes, understanding that the influence of the Manchus would be reinforced if the emperor's grandson became the spiritual leader of the country, emphatically opposed this.

In 1724, when the princess gave birth to a son, they secretly replaced it with another baby, the son of a Mongol concubine of Dondogdorj, and had the real heir killed. When Zanabazar died in 1725, the false heir was designated as his successor.

The princess was unaware for a long time of the death of her son and of the substitution that had occurred. When she learned the truth, she became deeply depressed and died in 1739–40, after a long illness.
(adapted from an article by L. Darsuren in *Mongolia*, January 1990)

Access to Terelj is via the Ulaanbaatar to Nalaikh road. The road splits near Nalaikh; the left fork goes to Terelj. This road travels for 18 kilometres before heading past a checkpoint, where visitors are required to pay a fee. There are several *ger* camps in the vicinity; one of the mainstays is Juulchin, which operates a hotel-restaurant, *gers* and log cabins. The buildings were constructed in 1964 as a holiday place for the *nomenklatura*, as well as accommodation for foreign guests. About two kilometres beyond this are some stone cist graves from the Xiongnu period.

## GUNJIIN SUM: THE PRINCESS' TEMPLE

This tomb of a Manchu princess, which dates to 1740, is a curious find for people trekking inside the National Park. It is located at **Baruunbayar**, about 30 kilometres north of the village of Terelj, in the Zaan Terelj Valley. Next to the tomb is a stele— once set on the back of a stone tortoise—with an inscription by the Manchu Emperor Qianlong addressed to Tüsheet Khaan Dovdon-Dorj.

A sanctuary, surrounded by a wall of white stones, was built near the tomb according to Manchu customs. At one time, the interior included a temple hall and the funerary vault, housing a sandal-wood coffin containing the remains of the princess. Inside the vault, were statuettes of divinities, jewel boxes, precious stones, vases and bowls in Chinese porcelain, which belonged to the deceased. The wall was taken down in 1941 and its bricks used to build a primary school. The treasures disappeared under strange circumstances and have never been traced.

## KHAN KHENTII STRICTLY PROTECTED AREA

The 1.2 million hectares of wooded area north of Terelj Park is little explored despite its relative proximity to the capital. The area is home to some 50 species of mammals, including moose, bear, elk and wolf, as well as more than 250 species of bird. Historians have identified around 800 burial sites here, one of which might be that of Chinggis Khaan or another khaan of the great empire. At 2,800 metres, **Mount Asralt Khairkhan** is the highest point in the protected area, as well as the whole of eastern Mongolia. It was first climbed in 1951, and can be covered with snow even in summer. Some travellers reach the area from the west, where the roads are better. On the east side of the protected area is **Khagiin Khar Nuur**, a pretty lake that can be reached from Möngön Mor't sum. It may also be worth visiting **Möngön Mor't** to find the **stone cist graves** in the area. Not far from the sum centre is the *balbal* funerary site of **Zuunburkh**.

# Other sites in Töv Aimag

## NALAIKH AND BAGANUUR

Located about 30 kilometres south-east of Ulaanbaatar, this industrial town grew up around the coal mines that feed the power stations of Ulaanbaatar. The town is actually considered a suburb of Ulaanbaatar, and administratively separate from Töv Aimag. Once a bustling community, Nalaikh is now sedate. The state-funded mine shut down in the early 1990s and the capital now receives its supply of coal from the mine at Baganuur.

Coal mining here dates back to 1912, when ox carts formed long cart-trains that moved slowly to and from the city. This was the country's biggest industry in the early 1900s, but it was the Chinese who were largely profiting from this trade.

In 1938 a railway line linked Ulaanbaatar and Nalaikh. Mining activities increased to keep up with demand and by 1940, a reported 200,000 tonnes of coal had been extracted from the earth. The increased loads required more manpower and Kazakhs, who lived in the western part of the country, migrated to Nalaikh. A 6,000 strong Kazakh community still lives here; their small mosque is located in the *ger* district east of the town centre.

After the mine closed down it was stripped for parts and is now in very bad shape. Locals in the area still work the tunnels by hand, a precarious job that takes

*The green hills of Gachuurt from the Tuul River.*

a few lives each year. The town square has a large bronze statue of a miner emerging from a cave. Vans from the long distance bus station in Ulaanbaatar leave every hour or so to Nalaikh. But it may be easier to hire a taxi for Tg300 per kilometre.

The major coal mine now serving Ulaanbaatar—at **Baganuur**—is a two hour drive west of the capital. Baganuur has a couple of surprisingly nice hotels, which cater to the foreign technical advisors who periodically inspect the mine. The town is just off the eastbound highway to Khentii Aimag.

## GACHUURT

There are a few **rock paintings** near this small village, located a mere 20 kilometres from Ulaanbaatar. Gachuurt has become a new suburb for the Ulaanbaatar elite. Two-storey private homes have been built just outside the town, along the Tuul River. *Ger* camps open up here in the summer, offering horseback riding and fishing.

## MONUMENT TO TONYUQUQ

One of the better examples of the Turkic remains in Mongolia can be found about 17 kilometres past Nalaikh, on the road towards Janchivian. The site, in a fenced-off area with a few decapitated statues, includes a block of stone dedicated to **Tonyuquq** and inscribed with a long text in the runic characters of the Orkhon

Turks. Tonyuquq, a Turkish nobleman, was born in China between AD 645 and 650; he became a general and then counsellor to the Turkish kaghans Qutluq Elterish (681–691), Qapagan (691–716), and lastly Bilge (716-734) of whom he was also the father-in-law. The monument, discovered in 1897, dates back to the second Turkish Khanate, and was probably erected around 725.

The 62-line text of the inscription on the stele traces the life of Tonyuquq and the historical events he took part in. The influence of this great military strategist over the three Turkish sovereigns seems to have been considerable. When Bilge Kaghan, inclined towards Buddhism, decided to build a fortified Chinese-style town in the Orkhon valley, the 'wise' Tonyuquq opposed him with great determination, counselling him as Chinggis Khaan would when addressing his sons a few centuries later, "You must remain nomads". To the nomads, sedentary life represented a threat, and mobility constituted the only veritable tactic. Buddhism was inappropriate to these warrior nomads. The site, also known as the inscription of Bayantsogt, is thought to predate those of Khöshöö-Tsaidam (see the Arkhangai section), and to be the model for all the later monuments. There is no public transportation to this site, take a taxi from Ulaanbaatar or Nalaikh.

If you are heading south from here, you could stop at a **Khureet Dov**, north of the Bayan sum centre. Here are faded and scattered remains of a **Xiongnu-era town**.

CENTRAL AIMAGS

*The takhi (Przewalski's horse) have returned to Mongolia,*
*thanks to a successful reintroduction programme.*

## BORNUUR

North-west of Ulaanbaatar, in Bornuur sum, a group of large *kurgan* identified as the tombs of Xiongnu princes were discovered in 1912. The site is in the **Noyon Uul** mountains at 1,500 metres above sea level. A felt carpet found in one of the tombs was decorated with scenes of a fight between a yak and a tiger-bodied chimera, as well as a griffin attacking a deer. This object is now at the Central Museum in Ulaanbaatar.

Another tomb revealed 85 women's braids of hair, kept in cases, which led to the suggestion that the deceased was accompanied by his entire harem, represented by their hair. Horse's skulls, saddles, bridles, parts of carts, and household objects were also buried in the tomb. The village of Bornuur is off the main road to Darkhan.

A short drive west of Bornuur is **Jargalant sum**. The village itself isn't much, but to the northwest is a **stone statue** and **funerary site**, both worth looking for.

## WEST OF ULAANBAATAR

Located 100 kilometres south-west of Ulaanbaatar (80 km west along the main road, then 20 km of track south of the main road) is the **Khustain Nuruu National Park**. This 90,000 hectare reserve was created in 1992 as part of the programme to reintroduce the *takhi*, the Asian wild horse better known in the West as Przevalski's horse, which disappeared from Mongolia in the 1960s.

For centuries, the *takhi* were one of the most revered animals on the steppes; but hunting and competition with livestock forced their numbers into decline—so much so that by the 1960s there were completely extinct in the wild. The *takhi*, however, were still very much alive in zoos and private farms in Australia and Europe. When Mongolia opened up to the world in 1990, the opportunity to reintroduce these animals to their native territory came to pass. Khustain Nuruu is one of the two protected areas that these animals are currently confined to. The other is in distant Gobi-Altai Aimag.

Visitors to Khustain Nuruu may want to travel another 20 kilometres west (down the Tuul River), to the **Öngöt archaeological complex**. The site, which dates from the Ruan-Ruan Khanate, has about a dozen stone figures, stone lions, and many stone *balbal*. Of the 35 figures found, about 25 have human faces. (More than 200 *khün chuluu*, stone men, have been identified in Mongolia). The link between this site and the Ruan-Ruan khanate, however, is only conjectural.

The next stop west is the rather dull **Lun sum**. Just north of here, off the main road, is a town called Bayankhangai. With a little luck, you may find here the remains of the ancient town site of **Khermiin Denj**, on the banks of the Tuul River.

The last stop before leaving Töv Aimag is Erdenesant sum. Here, at place called **Omogiin Khötöl**, are **stele with deer carvings**. Nearly twenty rectangular funerary stones with carvings of deer, swans, bustards, and human figures can be found. From Erdenesant the road continues west to Kharhorin.

## MOUNT NAGALKHAAN NATURE RESERVE

Ninety kilometres south-east of Ulaanbaatar, in the sum of Bayandelger, and about five kilometres from the source of the Janchivlan, is the **Mount Nagalkhaan Nature Reserve**. This 130 square kilometre protected area includes over 500 hectares of Siberian larch forests. Several funerary sites from the Turkish and Kirghiz periods have been located across the reserve.

## DELGERKHAAN SUM

The rolling hills of the steppe can be monotonous in this region, but there are some ancient sites here worth investigating. The **monument to the Khaan Kuli-Chur** (Köl-Ich-Chor), is located in the Ikh Khöshööt valley. This Turkish Period site, discovered in 1912, was part of a funerary complex similar to the Tonyuquq site near Nalaikh. The 29-line inscription, on a two-metre tall granite slab, has been badly damaged by time. It is a eulogy, dated to 722, of military campaigns and feats by one of the most eminent dignitaries of the Eastern Turkish khanate.

Also in Delgerkhaan sum are the three rock inscriptions at **Taitiin Khar-Khad**, by Prince **Tsogt Taij**, who lived during the Manchu era. The inscriptions are known as the 'black rock that resonates'. You will need a knowledgeable guide to locate these sites.

North-west of Delgerkhaan, as you head back to Ulaanbaatar, is **Büren sum**. It may be worth a stop here to inquire about some **bronze Age stone cist graves** at a place called **Ongon Khairkhan**. If you are heading east from here, the next stop is **Bayan-Önjuul sum**, where **rock paintings** have been found on **Mount Zorgol-Khairkhan** and the area of **Altanbulag**.

*Deer stele are scattered across Mongolia, particularly in the west. This one is near Ikh Chuluu, on the Tamir River, Arkhangai Aimag.*

# Arkhangai

Arkhangai (Northern Khangai) is one of the most spectacular aimags, full of forests, rugged terrain, lakes and snowy peaks. Many Mongols often dream of going on holiday here. The province's 98,400 people—mostly of the Khalkh ethnic minority—are largely engaged in livestock breeding: water is abundant and pastureland excellent in Arkhangai. It is here, say some Mongols, that herders make the best fermented mare's milk in the country.

Arkhangai has an average elevation of 2,414 metres above sea level. Its name literally means 'northern Khangai', and refers to its forests, which grow on the hilltops of the northern slopes, catching the humidity arriving from Siberia. The flora here is rich, with some 1,700 plant varieties, 20 per cent of which contain valued medicinal properties. Xiongnu tombs are quite numerous in Arkhangai. More than 20 were excavated in 1956 and 1957, all in the bed of the Khunui River.

## TSETSERLEG

Tsetserleg (1,691 metres) is located on the southern slopes of the Bulgan and Mant Mountains, four kilometres from the **Tamir River**, in a superb setting. The town, one of the greenest in Mongolia (Tsetserleg means 'garden'), is one of the most attractive provincial centres in the country. It is 453 kilometres west of Ulaanbaatar by the most direct road, and 493 kilometres via the road through Kharkhorin. The latter route is actually quicker as it is metalled for a large part of the way.

The administrative centre of Arkhangai since 1923, Tsetserleg developed on the site of one of the most important religious centres of western Mongolia. **Zayain Khuree Monastery**, founded in the 17th century, housed over 1,000 monks before its closure in the 1930s. This complex included several groups of Tibetan and Manchu style halls. The Labrang, in the centre, escaped destruction by being turned into a warehouse for food and *arkhi* (alcohol) after the 1921 Revolution. The complex was also the centre of trade. At the turn of the 19th century, Russian and Chinese merchants settled in Tsetserleg and founded businesses there.

From 1960 on, the monastic buildings were used as a museum, and some of the religious objects were saved. Some 78 monastic complexes with more than 200 temples were once found in Arkhangai.

The **Ethnographical Museum** of Tsetserleg was created out of the buildings formerly part of the Zayain Khuree Monastery. Even if it is closed, try to visit the inner courtyard to see the stele dating to the Turkish period set on a stone tortoise. The top of the stele has a pair of carved wolves instead of the usual imperial dragon. This is the so-called '**Sogdian stele of Bugut**', dating to the second half of the sixth century. It bears the oldest inscription testifying to the appearance of Buddhism in

Mongolia, which was previously thought to have occurred some seven centuries later. The museum contains religious objects taken from the nearby temples.

Not far from here is **Buyan Delgeruulegch Khiid**, which was part of the monastic complex of Zayain Khuree. Religious services are held here most mornings.

Behind the museum is a high cliff with three peaks, the 'Three Bulgan', with large Buddhas carved on the rock face. **Mount Bulgan** (1,980 metres) was declared a protected site (18 sq. km) for its fauna and flora.

A statue of the **Buddha Maitreya** is located about two kilometres south of the petrol station, on the banks of the Tamir River.

There are three hotels in Tsetserleg—the Bulgan, Sasa and Sundur. All three are rather basic but the Sundur tends to be cleaner than the others. The bank, post office and other facilities are located near the central square. The airport is one kilometre south of town.

## AROUND TSETSERLEG

The **Taikhar Chuluu** stands 22 kilometres north-west of town, on the banks of the Khoit-Tamir, just off the main road. This curious 16 metre tall boulder is covered with about 150 inscriptions and engravings in various languages. The oldest (in red) are thought to date back to the Stone Age. Among them are several forms of *tamga*, or clan marks, in black and red. Other *tamga*, are still in use today to mark cattle. The remaining inscriptions include texts in the Orkhon runic script of the Turkish period, in Chinese, Uighur, Tibetan, and Manchu. The Mongolian inscriptions date from the 13th to the 19th centuries. Unfortunately, much of this has been covered in 20th century 'graffiti'. Next to the rock is the Taikhar *ger* camp, which offers *ger* accommodation, meals and trips on horseback.

There are several areas of **hot springs** near Tsetserleg, including **Tsenkheriin Khaluun Us**, 20 kilometres south of Tsetserleg, and **Shivert**, located 35 kilometres north-east of Tsetserleg. Visitors to the Shivert valley can also look for the numerous **deer stele**. The **sulphur springs of Tsenkher-Jiguur**, which emerge from the ground at 86.5°C, were outfitted for tourists in 1996. The facility includes outdoor and indoor baths, showers, and accommodation in *gers*.

The rock carvings of **Mount Khongorj** are located about 30 kilometres north-east of Tsetserleg. Follow the metalled road that leads to Rashaant sum in Khövsgöl Aimag. There are over 100 Bronze Age engravings on the slopes of Khongorj, representing, among other things: horses drawing two-wheeled carts, deer, birds, men with bows, and cattle brands (*tamga*). Numerous rock carvings can be found at **Khöröögiin Üzüür**, the top of a small hill 18 kilometres north-east of the Ikh-Tamir sum centre. The deer theme is the dominant one here, although livestock, hunters, and herders are also represented. These date from the Bronze and Iron Ages.

CENTRAL AIMAGS

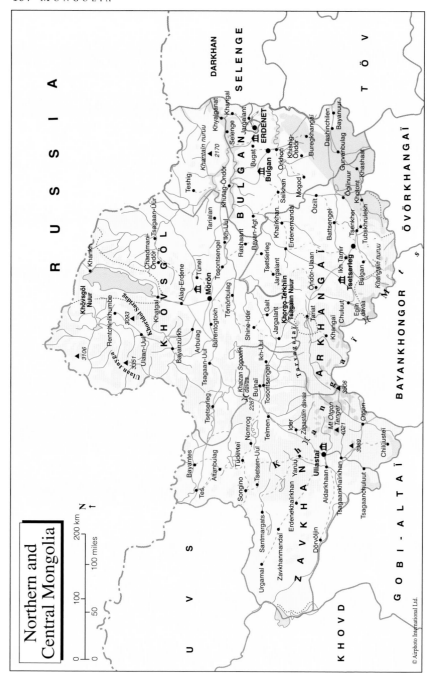

Northern and
Central Mongolia

© Airphoto International Ltd.

## OLZIIT SUM

**Seven ancient monasteries** and other historical sites lie in Olziit sum, an area on the eastern fringe of Arkhangai, north of Ögii Nuur. Olziit carries a unique history. About 70 per cent of its inhabitants are from the Ööld minority, an ethnic group from Khovd Aimag. They are the descendants of a battalion of western Mongol soldiers retreating from a campaign in the east. Their leader was Galdan Boshigt (1651–1697), who launched an attack on Zanabazar and the Khalkh Mongols, but was defeated when Zanabazar enlisted the aid of the Manchus, and won a decisive battle in 1696. The Ööld remained in Arkhangai and preserved their tongue—some older people in the village still speak the dialect. The temples here are unique in that they have flat roofs, rather than the normal, Chinese influenced, hanging eaves. In December 1999, President Bagabandi paid a visit to the village and encouraged the locals to preserve their monasteries for the sake of tourism.

*Ox carts and gers in Arkhangai Aimag.*

## BATTSENGEL SUM

This sum, near the Khoid Tamir River (71 kilometres north-east of Tsetserleg), offers several historical sites including **Xiongnu fortifications**, found at Tsorgiin Shuudai. **Duguin Khiid** is a purely Tibetan-style monastery located at Battsengel. There are several old *thankas* on display here. Nearby is a more recent temple built in the Chinese style.

# Natural sites

## ÖGII NUUR

This 25 square kilometre lake is located at the edge of Bulgan Aimag, not far from the main Ulaanbaatar to Tsetserleg road, and attracts a large number of migratory birds. West of the lake, in the Orkhon valley, are the ruins of the 17th century monastery of Shilin Khiid. About 25 kilometres south of the lake is the Turkish stone site of **Kööshöö Tsaidam**.

## KHORGO CRATER REGION

Arkhangai is a volcanic region with numerous faults and gorges, some of which, in the Orkhon Valley for example, are 10 to 20 metres deep. Approximately 180 kilometres north-west of Tsetserleg, in Tariat sum, is a magnificent region of extinct volcanoes. The highest, the **Khorgiin Togoo**, is located on the east shore of **Lake Terkhiin Tsagaan** (2,100 metres). From its summit, which is covered in *ovoo*, one has a splendid view over the whole region and the lake. The latter, a lake about 20 kilometres long, was formed when volcanic lava dammed the Suman River, cutting a large gorge through the basalt. Khorgo was once one a favourite holiday place for the Politburo members of the communist era, and now attracts foreign tourists.

In the middle of **Lake Terkhiin Tsagaan** is a small island called the 'Head of the Lake', which rises about 30 metres above the surface of the water. This is a favourite spot for **bird watching** in summer. In both summer and winter, colonies of wild geese, ducks, and swans live here and along the **Suman River**. This river is full of fish, including Siberian salmon, pike, perch and gudgeon. If you plan to catch some, bring your own fishing equipment from abroad or Ulaanbaatar.

The **Chuluutiin Gol Gorge** is a huge fault 30 kilometres long that forms a canyon along the aptly named 'River of Pearls' (Chuluutiin Gol). At the start of the gorge, a bit before the bridge, are some rock carvings.

**Choidogiin Borgio** is another very pleasant spot for walking or fishing, located between Terkhiin Tsagaan Nuur and Tariat, east of Khorgo, where the Suman and Chuluut rivers meet. There are more rock engravings here, most of which date from the Bronze Age.

**Zuun Salaa Mod** is a sacred forest containing age-old trees with misshapen and deformed trunks. One of the most ancient and most remarkable is an immense *ovoo* tree, decorated with prayer flags and surrounded by offerings. Like other sacred forests in Mongolia, this place has one particular feature—if someone has lost something important, he should spend the night by this tree, and the place where he lost the object will appear to him in a dream.

# Archaeological and cultural sites

The green valleys of Arkhangai Aimag are extremely rich in archaeological remains, dating from the Bronze Age to the 13<sup>th</sup> century, with deer stele, statues of 'stone men' (*khün chuluu*), and Xiongnu tombs. Most of Mongolia's 450 deer stele are located in the basin of the Altai and Khangai. Until 1990, about 100 had been located in Arkhangai. Further exploration between 1990 and 1993 identified another 40, in the region of the Khanui River.

### DEER STELE AND *KHÜN CHULUU* (MAN STONE)

An excellent stele with a horse's head is located in the Khunui Valley of Erdenmandal sum. Another well-preserved stele is in the Artsat Gorge on the north side of the Tsagaan Davaa (White Pass). *Khun Chuluu* can be seen on the right bank of the **Chuluut River**, at the end of the Shavart Valley next to a ritual offering stone, decorated on one side with engravings of cone-shaped motifs. Others can be seen south of Sediin Tolgoi, near the winter camp (*övöljöö*) of **Dadag**.

### KHÖÖSHÖÖ TSAIDAM

About 25 kilometres south of Ögii Nuur and about 60 kilometres from the old imperial town of Kharkhorin, in the Orkhon Valley, are two important monoliths located near one another. The first funerary monument is dedicated to the Turkish prince Kul-Tegin (685–731), and the other to his brother **Bilge-Khaan** (716–734).

The **Monolith of Kul-Tegin** is the oldest dated monument of Turkish literature in Mongolia, linked to the tomb of prince Kul-Tegin. The grey marble stele is decorated on the top with a pair of interlaced dragons and its back surface is covered in Chinese inscriptions. Nearby is a decapitated stone tortoise that would have been its base. Several other decapitated statues can be seen lying around nearby. The stele and the statues were part of a funerary complex that included the tomb itself, a tile-roofed temple hall, as well as marble statues of animal and human figures. The stele stood in front of the temple. At the top of one of its sides, is the seal (*tamga*) of the khaan, while the other side bears the date the monument was dedicated: August 1, 732. To the right of this are traces of runic characters (the old Turkish script, also called Orkhon script).

*Following pages: the pastures of central Mongolia.*

The inscriptions on the stele are a condemnation of the expansionist policy of the Chinese Tang dynasty in Central Asia, listing some of the events that played an important role in the history of the Turks, leading to their unification. However, vandals have caused serious damage to the stele.

The carved statue of Kul-Tegin himself, of which fragments have been found, led a procession of several hundreds of *balbal* (non figurative stones that represented the enemies killed by the deceased or in his name).

One kilometre away is the **monument dedicated to Bilge**, brother of Kul-Tegin, which was carved three years after the Kul-Tengin statue. Bilge's reign marked the final decline of the Turkish khanate. Ten years after he was poisoned, the entire area between the Altai and Lake Baikal was incorporated into the Uighur Empire, which lasted a century.

**Bilge's statue** is in a bad state of preservation and has been broken into four parts. It still carries inscriptions in runic characters and is surrounded by decapitated statues. These two dated monuments to Kul-Tegin and Bilge are important points of reference for the study of other inscriptions in runic characters.

At the confluence of the Urtiin and Ongiin rivers, in Zuun Bayan Ulaan sum, is a hill with the **funerary monument of Elterish-Khaan**. Inscriptions on the monument are dedicated to the parents of Kul-Tegin and Bilge.

In 2001, a joint Mongol-Turkish archaeological expedition made extraordinary finds in this area (along the Arkhangai/ Övörkhangai border). The most significant was the excavation of **Bilge Khaan's grave**, which included a golden crown, gold cups, a belt, gold deer statues, earrings, precious stones, a tea-pot, a trinket box and more than 1,500 silver coins. The golden crown, engraved with a mythological bird, was the most important find. These items are now on display at the Central Museum in Ulaanbaatar. Övörkhangai Aimag is assuming responsibility for some of these Turkic sites, and plans to build a museum dedicated this period.

## RUINS OF THE FORTRESS OF KHAR BALGAS

This Uighur site is located not far from the Khotont sum centre, south of Ögii Nuur, on the banks of the Orkhon, only 25 kilometres north-west of Erdene Züü Monastery. The town of **Khar-Balgas** (Black Ruins), the old Ordo-Balik (Camp Town) was the centre of the Uighur Empire (745-840). Founded in 715, it was destroyed in 840 by the Yenisei Kirghiz. This once enormous city was excavated in 1890, 1933, and 1949. Only ruins of it are left. There are traces of town quarters, the remains of temples and of a Buddhist stupa and parts of the ramparts flanked by watchtowers. The plan of the fortress is almost square. The ramparts, about 12 metres tall, are formed of a thick wall of unbaked brick covered in a layer of earth and grass, and surrounded by a wide ditch.

Judging by the surrounding stone blocks, this great agglomeration was likely to have been twin cities laid side by side, destroyed one after the other and rebuilt nearby. In the centre of the town was a second rampart surrounding the khaan's residence, which had two gates on the southern and northern ends. The commercial and craft centre lay to the south-west of the fortress. Water was brought to the town by irrigation canals, traces of which can still be seen.

Several stone stele with inscriptions in Turkish, Uighur, and Sogdian can still be seen in the town. One of these, in all three languages, was erected in honour of a Uighur khaan. Some of the stele writings refer to the 'great religions', including Buddhism and Manichaeism, or to changes in the way of life of the Uighur, who are generally recognised by historians as having a high level of culture.

*Following pages: Yaks are valued by Mongols for the high quality of their milk, Övörkhangai Aimag.*

# Övörkhangai

Övörkhangai means the 'Southern Khangai', referring to this province's location in comparison to the Khangai Mountains. The aimag, with 113,000 inhabitants and a surface area of 63,000 square kilometres, supports great herds of livestock, including the largest number of horses and cattle in the country, a testament to the lush grasses they feed on.

Thousands of yaks inhabit the Orkhon Valley, and another native beast, the Orkhon sheep, is famed for its fine wool. Övörkhangai is also known throughout Mongolia for the timber used in the construction of *gers*.

The province is rich in history and includes important sites related to the Mongol Empire and the founding of Buddhism. It is also strongly connected to the Turkic tribes of the eighth and ninth centuries. New archaeological projects funded by Turkey revealed important finds in the north of the province in 2001. This period of history is now being promoted in Övörkhangai and plans have been laid for a museum and a monument to **Bilge Khaan.**

## ARVAIKHEER

Arvaikheer (1,913 metres) means 'barley steppe', and is located in the southern part of the Khangai Mountains in a transitional zone. To the north is green pastureland, while to the south is arid *gobi*-style steppe. The town grew from a large religious centre founded in the early 18ᵗʰ century. The important monasteries were located near mineral springs, which are common here. A **hydrotherapy centre** is located 25 kilometres south-west of Arvaikheer, while the spa at Khujirt is to the north-east.

Övörkhangai was once home to 38 monastic centres and hundreds of temples. The largest monastery, which grew into the town of Arvaikheer, was called Arvaikheeriin Khuree. **Gandan Muntsaglan Khiid**, a small temple complex located a few hundred yards north of the town centre opened in 1991. A *thanka* on display here shows a reproduction of the layout of the old monastery.

There are two **museums** in town, one focusing on the works by Zanabazar and his disciples (he lived in Övörkhangai). The **Aimag Museum** boasts fossils, stuffed animals and about a thousand years of man-made artifacts.

Not far from Arvaikheer, in two locations, are the **rock carvings of Shatar Chuluu.** The rocks are covered in thousands of carvings representing wild camels, deer, men riding horses bareback and sometimes holding bows and arrows, hunters with lances and spears, and symbols of the sun. Another place to look for carvings is on the slopes of **Mount Bug-Sogot**, about 15 kilometres from town. This complex of rock art includes mammoths, rhinos, and men training wild horses.

Arvaikheer is more developed than most provincial capitals, and offers a few different options for both **accommodation and food**. The Khangai, Alt Ovoo and Bayan Bulag hotels are all near the town centre. The Alt Ovoo is the flashiest of the bunch, with gleaming white tiles and crisp sheets on the beds, although its a bit pricey at Tg15,000 per person. For food, try the unnamed restaurant north-west of the main square.

If you are flying, the airport is south-west of town. But the drive to Arvaikheer from Ulaanbaatar isn't too bad—nine hours on a mettaled (and pot-holed) road.

## UYANGA SUM

There are two important historical sites worth exploring in Uyanga, a sum northwest of Arvaikheer. The **stele of Ongin** (*Maantiin Khööshöö*) dates to the Turkish period. It is located near the Ongin River, used to be in the centre of a funerary complex, and is included on a list of historical monuments recognised by UNESCO. Believed to have been erected in 731, it has a nineteen-line inscription. The inscription is an epitaph dedicated to a general or high dignitary of the khaans Elterish and Bilge. Its contents are similar to that of the inscription of Khööshöö-Tsaidam (see the Arkhangai section).

The second site of importance in Uyanga is the 'man stone' known as **Uuvshkhai**. In the 18th century, a wooden temple was built around it and permanent services held by the monks. Each year the local administration gave the monks a gift of 25 sheep. It is worth noting that a centuries-old cult, long predating Lamaism, developed around these stone statues to whom offerings are made and who are 'fed' by the locals. Observe the traces of grease around the mouths of the statues.

Uyanga is also well-known for the **Eight Lakes of the Navel (Khuissin Naiman Nuur)**. Fed by the Urkhit River, and surrounded by volcanic craters, these lakes are located at an elevation of 2,500 metres above sea level. The protected area covers some 11,500 ha, and was created to preserve the delicate lake ecosystem.

## KHARKHORIN: THE MODERN TOWN

Located 373 kilometres from Ulaanbaatar and 138 kilometres north of Arvaikheer, this important village is the administrative centre of Kharkhorin sum and owns one of the two most important mechanised farms of the country, built in the mid 1950s. Agriculture has been practised here for centuries, and wheat, rye, oats, and barley are grown. A diversion canal from the Orkhon brings irrigation water to Kharkhorin, which also has an important mill.

Kharkhorin also happens to be on the of the top tourist destinations in the country, and every summer tour groups are taken here to admire the Erdene Züü Monastery and the remains of the imperial site of Karakorum. Despite this, Kharkhorin's tourism industry is rudimentary. Most travellers stay and eat at the *ger* camps outside town. And if you are expecting to find anything interesting in the village you will be

*A stupa at Erdene Züü, Mongolia's first monastery, built in the 16th century.*

disappointed. The modern town is a Soviet creation of concrete blocks, just slightly more developed than other sum centres.

There are a few **hotels** in town where you could get a bed for under Tg6,000 per night. The two best are the Bayan Burd and the Mongon Mod. The former has a sauna. Outside town there are several *ger* camp options. For around US$30 per night you get a comfortable *ger*, meals and pretty scenery. One of the better places in the area, if just for the location, is the Orhon Hotel, south-west of town.

# Karakorum: the imperial city

The imperial site of Karakorum is located on the right bank of the Orkhon River and on the north-eastern slopes of the Khangai Mountains. Karakorum existed for 140 years but was the capital of the empire for only 32 of those. It served first of all as a base camp for the leader of the Kereit tribe, before being used by Chinggis Khaan in 1222 as a supply point for the Mongol armies. Cereals were grown there to feed the army, and agricultural implements and weapons were cast there.

In 1235, Ögödei, son and successor of Chinggis, surrounded it by a rampart measuring approximately 1.7 kilometres by 1 kilometre; it was during his reign that

Karakorum became a true urban, diplomatic, and commercial centre. Despite this, it managed to retain a strongly nomadic appearance. The palace was built only for official receptions, and the court did not live in town and instead set up their camps in the surrounding area. The town was largely inhabited by foreigners including officers and secretaries of the court in the service of the empire, merchants, diplomats, and artists. The artists in particular were there against their will, having been captured in conquered areas during the military campaigns. Their talents put to the service of their new masters. After the conquests, the Mongols needed foreigners to fill administrative posts and therefore created a heterogeneous body of Muslims, Nestorians, and Buddhists to work for them.

The choice of the location of Karakorum as the imperial site in the 13th century perpetuated an ancient habit of systematically placing the centre of the successive 'empires of the steppes' in the Orkhon Valley, and more precisely within a perimeter of some 50 kilometres around the sites of Erdene Züü and Karakorum. The Mongols simply continued the old tradition followed earlier by the Xiongnu (third to second centuries BC), the Ruan-Ruan (fourth to sixth centuries AD), the Turks (Tujue, sixth to eighth centuries), and the Uighur (eighth to ninth centuries). The remains of the Uighur capital, Khar Balgas, or Ordo Balik, are only 25 kilometres north-west of Erdene Züü Monastery (see Arkhangai Aimag).

Neither the Turks (who came originally from the Altai) nor the Mongols (who came from the Khentii) departed from this tradition. The Orkhon Valley was located in the most favourable microclimatic zone of central Mongolia, but above all, its choice as the centre of power allowed identification with the earlier powerful confederations and brought with it an undisputed legitimacy.

Almost nothing remains of the imperial site of Karakorum. The bricks and stones of the ruins were reused to build Erdene Züü Monastery. The most important remains of the imperial capital are the **two granite tortoises**. These probably once served as pedestals for inscribed stele. There used to be four of them. Of the two that remain, one is located near the tomb of the wife of Avdai-Khan (see Erdene-Züü) and serves as an *ovoo* for the local population. The other tortoise is poorly preserved. It can be found on the summit of a nearby hill, from which there is a panoramic view over Erdene Züü and modern Kharkhorin.

**The Palace of Ögödei** (Palace of the 10,000 Prosperities) was built in the south-west part of town, on the shores of an artificial lake. Only its foundations remain. Excavations carried out in 1949 uncovered ceramic and metallic objects, some of which are on display at Erdene Züü. The others are now in museums. These objects include large iron cauldrons used by the Mongol army, pieces of glazed tiles, stone statues and stone inscriptions. The excavations also revealed Buddhist frescoes, evidence of the presence of a temple on the palace site. This palace was of some importance, as testified by the large tumulus, which still remains. The main courtyard of the palace had a surface area of 1,200 square metres. The emperor lived there only twice a year, at the beginning of spring and in summer.

It is likely that monks brought one of the stone lions in Kharkhorin from one of the ancient funerary sites of the Orkhon valley, such as Khöshöö-Tsaidam (see Arkhangai). Between the lion sculptures are bases of columns. These seem to have served as supports for two stone cups. The only other evidence of old Karakorum are the barely visable remains of the diversion canals built under Ögödei.

## ERDENE ZÜÜ MONASTERY

Located north-west of the imperial site at Karakorum, this monastery was built on the site of the ruins of the ancient Mongol capital. It was the first great Buddhist monastery of northern Mongolia, and for centuries one of its most important. In its time, it rivalled Urga as the main centre of Buddhism. It was not a simple monastery but a veritable fortress, surrounded on four sides by powerful walls and towers. Each wall had a gate, similar to the building designs of the old Qidan and Mongol towns.

Having met the Dalai Lama in 1577 at Khökh Khot (the present-day capital of Inner Mongolia, Hohhot) the Khalkh khaan Avdai built, in 1586, three temples to house *thanka* offered by the Dalai Lama. These temples were to be the basis of Erdene Züü.

A few years earlier, **Altan Khan**, the descendant of Chinggis Khaan in the 25th generation, had invited a hierarch from the Tibetan Gelugpa school, and had granted him the title of 'Dalai Lama'. Buddhism was still a relatively new phenomenon then in Mongolia. In 1260, Kubilai made it the official religion, but it had remained confined to the Mongol aristocracy. The meeting between Altan Khan and the Gelugpa high monk was followed by the arrival of aggressive Tibetan monks who succeeded in the destruction of all shamanist 'idols' (*Ongon*) and the conversion of a large part of the Mongol population.

### ERDENE ZÜÜ AND THE VAGARIES OF HISTORY

The construction of Erdene Züü began in the 16th century and continued until the middle of the 19th century. The temples often suffered fire or attack over the years. In 1731, they were violently attacked by the Western Mongols, and between 1760 and 1814, they were restored several times. At the beginning of the 20th century, there were more than 600 temple halls and places of worship there, making it the most powerful of the Khalkh monasteries. But the purges of the 1930s finished off most of the temples and today only three remain.

What was left of the great monastic complex was turned into a museum in 1965. The remains from the old capitals of the khaans and from the palace-monastery were displayed here. Erdene Züü re-opened as a place of worship in 1990, although it also serves as a museum. This double status as museum and working monastery is a source of conflict between the administrative authorities of the museum (who consider the presence of the monks as a danger to the treasures housed there), and the monks, for whom the *Lavran* (see p. 183) is above all place of worship.

The temples have been built in a mixed style. Between the 16th and 20th centuries in Mongolia, besides the Mongol style proper, which originated in the shape of the *ger*, two other styles coexisted. One was the Chinese style, which is dominant at Erdene Züü; the 'three züü' (see p. 182) are characteristic examples. The second style was Tibetan. The *Lavran* (Labrang in Tibetan) in the north-eastern section is in a pure Tibetan style. There is also a composite Sino-Tibetan-Mongol style. Not a single nail was used in the building of these temples.

## THE 108 STUPA ENCLOSURE

A wall of 108 stupas (*suburgan* in Mongolian), 400 metres by 400 metres, surrounds the monastery. It was built between 1734 and 1804 and each stupa was erected in commemoration of a particular event, related in the inscriptions on each one. The stupa is formed of three parts: the base, the reliquary, and the spire of thirteen rings crowned by a cosmic emblem. Some harbour the remains of great lamas, mummified in salt and mercury and wrapped in strips of cloth covered in ashes, clay, and gold or silver.

The **Golden Stupa**, or **Bodhi Suburgan** is located near the centre of the monastery. It was built in 1799, stands at 10.5 metres in height, and honours the fourth Bogd Gegeen. This stupa belongs to a type known as 'of the sacred Tree of Enlightenment'. Inside it are representations of 100,000 different Buddhas and 55,070 bodhi-suburgan. It is surrounded by eight smaller stupas.

In the western sector, the most sacred section (the male side of the *ger*), holds several notable buildings. The first is the **Hall of the Dalai Lama**. Built in 1675 in red brick and in gold, it is composed of two small prayer chapels and was used as the museum archives office. Behind the hall are strange-looking barriers made of cross-shaped tree trunks. Designed to frighten evil spirits, they form a limit that must not be passed by pilgrims on horseback.

Also in this sector are two **brick tombs**: the tombs of Avdai khaan, the founder of Erdene Züü, who died in 1587, and that of his son Gombodorj. The tomb of the wife of the Tüsheet Khaan Gombodorj is located outside the monastery walls, in the female sector, not far from the famous tortoise of Karakorum. Gombodorj's son is best known in Mongolia by his title **Öndör Gegeen Zanabazar**. He was the first Bogd Gegeen, the first of the eight pontiffs of the Lamaist church among the Khalkh. He founded a number of monasteries, and created the Soyembö alphabet; one of the letters of this alphabet became the symbol of the Mongols' independence. Zanabazar was also a great bronze caster, goldsmith and political leader.

# MISSIONS FROM EUROPE

Much of the current knowledge about the ancient and city of Karakorum comes from the reports given to Europe by the two Franciscan missionaries who travelled there in the 13th century.

John of Plano Carpini (c. 1182–1253) and William of Rubruck (13th century) left the world with interesting descriptions of the Mongol court, which the former visited in 1246, and the latter in 1254. The Pope and the King of France sent them to the Mongol homeland on missions that were diplomatic, political and religious.

In 1241, Ögödei had launched a vast military expedition against Eastern Europe, a campaign that sent shock waves to Rome and the rest of the continent. At that time the Church was going through a profound crisis, torn apart by schisms and heresy. Jerusalem had fallen in 1244 to the Muslims, and Emperor Frederic II had been accused of heresy and sacrilege at the Council of Lyons, held in 1245 and initiated by Pope Innocent IV.

But word had it that there existed at the court of the Great Khaan, and in the countries under Mongol rule, Nestorian Christians who had converted Mongol princes. There was a persistent rumour, heard across Europe, about a certain 'Prester John', a lone Christian monarch among the potentates of Central Asia. This became the common denominator behind a series of missions sent across Asia at the time of the Mongols. To Pope Innocent IV, the Mongols, still hesitating in their choice of an official religion, were potential allies in the struggle against the Muslims, if only they could be converted.

Even before the opening of the Council, the Pope sent Friar John Carpini to the Great Khaan on a mission to convert him. Not only did Friar John fail in this but he came back from Karakorum with alarming news, the Khaan Guyuk was preparing to attack the West and demanded the Pope's submission.

A little later, King Louis IX of France in his turn sent Friar William of Rubruck off, bearing letters addressed to the Great Khaan. In December 1253, the monk managed, with some difficulty, to reach the camp of Emperor Möngkh—who had succeeded Guyuk—and to stay in Karakorum until August of the following year. He was impressed by the cosmopolitanism that reigned at the court of the Great Khaan. There were ambassadors from the caliph of Baghdad, Persian and Chinese scholars, Russian princes, Indian princes, Muslim merchants, and a small community of French made prisoner in Hungary. Among the French were, a Norman bishop from near Rouen, a woman from Metz in Lorraine, and a Parisian goldsmith, Guillaume Boucher, the creator of an extraordinary silver fountain that stood in front of the Great Khaan's palace. Shaped like a tree, it poured out mare's milk and other bracing drinks through the mouths of golden dragons. A model of this fountain can be seen in the Central Museum in Ulaanbaatar.

Friar William was impressed by the cosmopolite appearance of Karakorum, but even more so by its ecumenism at a period when religious intolerance was the rule in Europe. "There are twelve idolatrous temples of various nations, two mosques where the law of Mahomet is proclaimed, and a church of Nestorian Christians at the end of town", he relates. The Nestorian Christians belonged to the eastern branch of the Syriac church. Nestorianism had made its way among the Turkish peoples—as testified by the indirect Syriac origin of the Mongol script via the Uighur script. Further, the leading Mongol clans were related to Nestorians through a network of family alliances. The Empire still had to decide on a state religion, and the Great Khaans enjoyed organising theological disputes between the followers of the various faiths. Friar William, however, failed in his mission. He left Karakorum on August 16, 1254, with instructions from the Great Khaan to demand on his behalf the submission of the King of France and of the leaders of Christianity.

As soon as he arrived on the throne, in 1260, Kubilai, grandson of Chinggis Khaan and founder of the Mongol Yuan dynasty in China, transferred the capital to Beijing (Khanbalik, Marco Polo's Cambaluc). After the fall of the Yuan Empire, in 1360, Karakorum was razed to the ground and burnt by the Ming armies. Attempts were later made to revive it, but it never regained its former glory. Its ruins were eventually used to build Erdene Züü Monastery.

Today, the sites related to the history of the Mongol Empire are still the object of much research and controversy. We now know that Karakorum was not the only important town of the empire (see Khentii Aimag, p. 221), but the site still retains great importance for the Mongol nation.

There have been recent discussions about moving the capital back to Kharkhorin from Ulaanbaatar—an idea particularly encouraged by the 15,000 residents of Kharkhorin. In contrast, an opinion poll showed just seven per cent of Ulaanbaatar residents approved of the idea.

Nevertheless, a team of researchers and politicians have conducted feasibility studies for such a plan, and concluded that the a move should begin in the year 2020 and end in 2030. These years coincide with the 800-year anniversary of the founding and completion of the original capital. A final decision on the matter is still pending, and will surely incite a flurry of nationwide debate.

## THE THREE ZÜÜ

These three temples, which date to the founding of the monastery, are located in the north-west, that is, in the most sacred sector to the Mongols. *Züü* means 'respect' in Tibetan. In front of these temples, a large Chinese-style incense burner is used for burning juniper.

Gol Züü, or the 'main züü', was built in 1586. It houses a statue of Shakyamuni with, Otoch Manal (Bhaishajyaguru), the god of medicine, on his left, and Amithaba, symbol of the purity of the spirit and of spiritual enlightenment, on his right. The presence of the god of medicine is not surprising: Erdene Züü, renowned for its doctors and its astrologers, was considered the greatest scientific centre of the country. In front of Shakyamuni, stand the *arhat* Ananda, the Buddha's favourite disciple, and Kashyapa, one of the Buddhas of the past who was once the guru of the historical Buddha. Four Golden Tara, works by Zanabazar, used to be included among the treasures of this temple. The cult of Tara was particularly popular among the Mongol nomads; feminine aspects (Shakti) of Avalokiteshvara, the Bodhisattva of Compassion, there are twenty-one of them in the Mongol Tantric tradition of which the White Tara and the Green Tara are the most important. They are believed to have become incarnate as the two wives of the great Tibetan king Songtsen Gampo (617-650), who is considered to have introduced Buddhism into Tibet.

The goddess Lkhamo (Shri Devi) guards the entrance to the temple. One of the eight Dharampala, Mahâkala, the 'Great Black', joins Shri Devi at this post. Both serve as guardians of the Buddhist Law and protectors of monasteries. Mahâkala became very popular in Mongolia after the Dalai Lama ordered the destruction of all Shamanic *ongon* in the country.

The **Eastern Züü** has a coffered ceiling decorated with images of Taras and *mandalas*. In the centre are three large statues representing Shakyamuni, with the Bogd Gegeen on his left and Janraiseg (Avalokiteshvara or Chenrezi in Tibetan) on his right. A model of the züü made of sandalwood is also on display.

The **Western Züü** has a ceiling decorated with representations of Taras and *mandalas*. The main statues in the temple represent Sanjaa, the first propagator of the faith, and Maitreya, the Buddha of the future, on either side of the present Buddha, Shakyamuni.

The roofs of these three züü are held up by a complex system of bracketing. Each züü contains paintings made on a base of clay mixed with straw and stucco. Various ceremonies were held in front of the three züü, including the Tsam, a religious play executed by masked dancers. The Tsam, which has Tibetan origins, was held for the first time in Mongolia at Erdene Züü Monastery almost 200 years ago.

The **Avdai Khaan** invited the Dalai Lama to Erdene Züü for the consecration ceremony of the monastery, but the Dalai Lama only sent a representative. It is said that on the day of the consecration, a rain of yellow flowers fell on Erdene Züü and that the monks kept the petals in one of the temples.

### THE BUILDINGS IN THE EASTERN SECTOR

The **Lavran (Labrang) Temple** was built in a purely Tibetan style in 1760 to serve as residence for the Bogd Gegeen when he stayed at Erdene Züü. The top storey is dedicated to Mahâkala. Since the Lavran has once again become a place of worship, the upper storeys are closed to visitors. The middle storey is dedicated to Gombo-Guru and Otoch Manal (Bhaishajyaguru), the god of medicine, and the ground floor is used for public religious services. These services usually last from 11 am to 3 pm.

The **Courtyard of Happiness and Prosperity** to the west of the Golden Stupa, about 30 metres from the lion sculptures and the column bases, is a round area paved with large, flat stones that served as the foundation of a gigantic *ger* erected in 1658. Legend has it that it served as a ceremonial *ger* for Avdai Khaan. This enormous *ger* could hold up to 200 people and could be used for the great annual assemblies when all the Mongol nobles gathered together. The monks later set up a wooden platform to use during religious ceremonies. In front of this great pedestal one can see a depression covered in grass. This marks the location of an old artificial 'sacred lake', which was filled with water from the Orkhon.

All the Mongol princes made it a point of honour to have their own hall built within the complex of Erdene Züü. Construction continued into the 19th century, and some of the halls were built outside the limits of the enclosure. The monks' living quarters were located around the temples, according to the principle of the *Khuree*. There seems never to have been more than 500 monks living within the monastery.

### THE PHALLIC STONE (*BOOVIIN CHULUU*)

Not far from the site of Erdene Züü, below the second tortoise, is a stone set up in the 16th or 17th century to serve as a lesson to the young monks who did not respect the rule of chastity in force among the Gelugpa. According to one of the many versions of the story surrounding this stone, a monk who had broken his vows was castrated and his sexual organ put on public display as an example to others. The stone, intended as a warning to the monks, is a symbolic reminder of this event. The mountain towards which the phallic stone is orientated is meant to suggest the form of a woman lying on her back, symbolically reflecting the safe distance which should be maintained between the two sexes. It now seems to be a place of pilgrimage for women who want a child.

CENTRAL AIMAGS

# Other sites in north Övörkhangai

## THE STELE OF BAYAN ULAAN

Located in the sum of the same name, this stele is decorated with motifs of stylised deer and set in an enclosure of stone slabs. Local lore states that Chinggis Khaan spent the night here with his army.

## SHANKH KHIID

Located in Kharkhorin sum, 20 kilometres south of Erdene Züü in a plain watered by the Sarnai River (near the Shankh Mountains). This monastery, formerly known as **Baruun Khuree** (Western Monastery), was once one of the most important in Övörkhangai Aimag. Founded in 1647, Shankh Khiid was nomadic before being fixed in its present site in 1787. More than 23 temple halls were built here, the last in 1885. In 1921, Baruun Khuree still had some 1,500 monks.

Before 1990, all that remained of this great monastery were a few buildings with broken roofs that had served as warehouses during communism. Its history is linked to Zanabazar, and the official hagiography attributes its founding to him when he was only 13. The temple complex is being gradually restored and monks have returned to celebrate services here and to teach in the recently rebuilt school.

The monastery used to be flanked by a small wooden building that housed a white scarf, said to have belonged to Tsaagadai (Jagatai), the son of Chinggis Khaan, as well as a trumpet known as the 'warrior trumpet of Chinggis Khaan'. A certain number of monks devoted their entire lives to looking after the relics.

Of the original buildings, only three small halls and the main temple (Tsogchin) remain, built in the mid-1700s. The fifth Bogd Gegeen gave its present name, **Puntsagdarjalin Khiid**.

## TÖVKHÖN KHIID

The excellent location of Tövkhön Khiid was selected by Öndor Gegeen Zanabazar on his 19th birthday. It was built in 1653 and he named it 'Land of Happy Solitude'. The hermitage of Tövkhön is 68 kilometres from Erdene Züü, in the wooded Shiveet-Ulaan Mountains of Bat-Ölzii sum.

Not far from the summit of the mountain, on a first platform, are several temple halls, one of which is made from wood. To the west of these, having passed some large rocks, one can see a footprint attributed to the first Bogd Gegeen, and a **small cave** (*uran darkhni agui*) where Zanabazar meditated. Climbing further up, one arrives at a second platform from which a spring runs out. Another cave is located here—the *Ekhiin Khevlii* (Mother's belly), which is just big enough to stand in, although you have to crawl to enter it. This is a veritable *regressus ad uterum* to which the pilgrims appeal in the hope of having their faults washed away in the next rebirth. From there one can climb higher and reach the summit of the mountain where there is an *ovoo* and rock called the 'place of *naadam*'.

Öndör Gegeen Zanabazar was the first leader of the Mongol Lamaist church and led an intense intellectual, religious, and artistic life. His biography includes work as a bronze caster, goldsmith, translator, compiler, founder of monasteries, and creator of a new alphabet for the phonetic transcription of Mongolian, Tibetan and Sanskrit. Much of this work was done at Tövkhön Khiid

Travellers should note that women are not allowed to climb to the summit of the mountain and the monks make sure that this rule is followed. In 2001, a Tg68.5 million **restoration project** on the monastery was completed, bringing the temples back to their original glory.

## KHUJIRT
Khujirt sum is located 54 kilometres south-west of Kharkhorin in the Khangai Mountains, at an altitude of 1,600 metres. The sum centre was built and designed as a spa town during the Soviet era, but fell into disrepair in the 1990s. Recent renovations, however, have improved the facilities, and the hot tubs and mud baths make for a good day trip.

The forty hot springs in the area have long been known for their therapeutic virtues. Long before the Mongol period, many tribes from Central Asia made use of this remedy as testified by the ancient tombs discovered nearby. There are notably some at the foot of Mount Shunkhlai, a mountain with a statue of a deer at its summit. The statue recalls the legend of a hunter named Shunkhlai who once, long ago, came across a badly wounded deer coming down from the mountain. He saw the animal lie down on the riverbank before returning towards the forest. The next day, he saw the deer return to the same spot. Intrigued, the hunter explored the area and found a hot spring. The deer, which should have died from its wounds, had been restored to health thanks to the therapeutic powers of the spring. The mountain was then called **Shunkhlai**, and since then the spring has been used in the treatment of a variety of ills.

## THE ORKHON VALLEY
A spectacular region of volcanic craters and rushing streams, the area also offers long lava flows south of the Orkhon River. The highlight of the valley is the 24 metre high **Orkhon waterfall**, located 80 kilometres west of Khujirt. The falls, sometimes known as Ulaan Tsutgalaan, are situated on one of the bumpiest tracks in a country of many bumpy roads. If you can manage the journey, this is an enjoyable side trip in good weather. The route is through volcanic landscape, and hot springs dot the surrounding hillsides. The waterfall is most impressive in late summer after the heavy rains. In early summer it may be completely dry.

The black volcanic rocks that carpet the landscape exploded from the earth 20 to 30 million years ago, when the nearby Togoo crater was still active. The eruption is likely to have also created the waterfall, as the faultline shifted and cracked the valley floor. About eight kilometres before the falls is Üürtiin Torkhoi, a good place to stop and explore the river canyon. A smaller waterfall (**Bag Khukhree**) is also in the vicinity.

Close to Bag Khukhree is a **funerary site** in the Valley of the Camel's Stone (*Temeenii Chuluunii Am*), a site that dates between the seventh and third century BC. It is located near the Tsagaan Gol River and includes several **tombs** and **deer stele** lying on the ground. The site's name comes from one of the standing stones on which is an engraving of a group of small figures in red, preceded by a man leading a camel.

*The Orkhon Waterfall, a well-known traveller's destination in central Mongolia.*

*Shepherds moving their flocks in central Mongolia.*

About 10 kilometres south-east of the Orkhon waterfall, the **Mogoit hot springs** bubble up from the ground at temperatures between 45°C and 72°C. The site is in a pretty wooded valley, under mountains that top 3,000 metres. Visitors will find free basic baths inside small wooden cabins at the hot spring site. Ask the locals for the exact spots to choose according to the ailment to be treated. Unless your driver is confident of the right track, you will need to ask local advice to find the springs.

To the south of these springs, is a high rocky massif called the **White Rock of the Khangai**, at the top of which grow three Siberian pines, the tallest of the forest. Other nearby curiosities include two huge **caves** at **Aguit** and **Shar Khad**, both located in Bogd sum.

## BATKHAN UUL NATURE RESERVE

The Batkhaan Uul Nature Reserve, about 218 square kilometres in size, is located 250 kilometres south-west of Ulaanbaatar, in Burd Sum (about 10 km south-west of Erdensant Sum, Tov Aimag). These mountains are the eastern-most extremity of the Khangai chain and reach a height of 2,178 metres, with sand dunes stretching away from their base to the south-west. The impressive rocky massifs include **Togoot Ulaan Khad**, a huge red cliff. The reserve contains **Kirghiz tombs**, some impressive rock engravings and a variety of fauna including grey antelope, lynx, wildcat, fox, wolf, and deer.

## Other historical and natural sites

### GALDIIN KHAD

This is a beautiful region with strangely-shaped rocks, grassland and hills, located about 20 kilometres from Nariintel. Galdiin Khad makes for a convenient side trip for travellers heading on the main east-west highway between Bayankhongor and Övörkhangai aimags.

### THE ROCK CARVINGS OF TEVCH UUL

These are in the extreme south of the aimag near Khovd sum. The most interesting drawings represent chariots drawn by four horses. This type of vehicle, which dates back to between the third and first centuries BC, is the ancestor of the wheeled cart that was widely used in Mongolia between the seventh and 13th centuries. On the cart is a banner with an *argali* drawn on it. Beside it walks a warrior pulling a bow. Inscriptions dating to the Turkish period, *tamga*, and drawings of human figures, can also be seen.

NORTHERN AIMAGS

# Selenge

Located in the basin of the Orkhon and Selenge rivers, and giving onto Siberia to the north, Selenge is one of the smallest aimags at just 41,200 square kilometres. Its population of 103,000 inhabitants endure a harsh continental climate, with top temperatures in summer reaching over 40°C, and falling as far as –42°C in winter. Selenge has large areas of conifer and deciduous forests, but it also accounts for 70 per cent of the wheat harvest in Mongolia. The agricultural lands are located in the basins of the Orkhon and Selenge rivers. Selenge also has a comparatively well-developed industrial sector, helped largely by the Trans-Mongolia railroad, which runs through it. Visitors travel to the eastern part of this aimag to dip into the Yeröö hot springs. In the west is the famed **Amarbayasgalant Khiid**. A good metalled road passes through the province on its way to Russia.

## SÜKHBAATAR AND SURROUNDINGS

The capital of the province is located at the junction of the Orkhon and Selenge rivers, 626 metres above sea level and some 311 kilometres from Ulaanbaatar. This is an important frontier town, located near the Russian border town of Naoushki, through which the Trans-Siberian railroad runs. Sükhbaatar is not a large town, having just 20,000 inhabitants, but stores large reserves of petrol, thanks to smuggling across the frontier. About ten kilometres south of the town, less than a kilometre west of the main road, is a **sacred tree**, honoured by believers in shamanism. The tree, draped in silk scarves, receives visitors wishing to appease local spirits.

The town has several hotels, the best of the lot is probably the Selenge, located close to the train station. The Station Hotel and the Orkhon Hotel are the other options. The train journey between Ulaanbaatar and Sükhbaatar takes 9.5 hours. From Ulaanbaatar, trains depart at 10.30 am and 9.05 pm. Trains depart from Sükhbaatar at 6.10 am and 9.30 pm. All trains stop at Darkhan.

**Altanbulag**, a the small frontier town 24 kilometres east of Sükhbaatar, is just across the border from the Russian town of **Khiakhta**. At the time of writing, Westerners were not allowed to cross the frontier here, and must cross by train at Sükhbaatar. A new 'Free Trade Zone' was completed near the border post, boosting the town's image and business opportunities. In 1921, Altanbulag was, for a short time, the provisional capital of Mongolia. In June of that same year, the troops of the Red Army, with help from the small Mongol army of Sükhbaatar, defeated the Mad Baron's army at Altanbulag, then called Amgalanbaatar. A **monument** to the liberation of Khiakhta and Altanbulag stands at Tölgö Bulag.

*Following pages: Amarbayasgalant Monastery, the main attraction in Selenge Aimag.*

NORTHERN AIMAGS

## DARKHAN

The second largest town in Mongolia, Darkhan is actually the centre of a tiny independent aimag called Darkhan Uul, which includes the sums of **Shariin Gol, Orkhon,** and **Khongor.** Now home to more than 90,000 people, forty years ago it was little more than a tiny train station on the Trans-Mongolian line.

In 1961, the 14th Congress of the MPRP decided to create a new industrial centre, the second largest of the Mongolian People's Republic; it chose Darkhan for the minerals in the area and for its proximity to the important oil fields at Shariin Gol. The town, nicknamed the 'blacksmith of Socialist Solidarity'—Darkhan means 'blacksmith'—was built with aid from 'brother countries', and workers from Czechoslovakia, Poland, Hungary, and Bulgaria.

Darkhan doesn't quite sprawl, but the city is spread out over four districts: the 'old town', near the station, the new town, just south of the latter, the northern industrial district, and the southern industrial district. Most of the buildings are Soviet-style except a few log cabins near the train station. The pride and joy of the city is a 16-storey apartment building, the tallest in Mongolia. Darkhan produces the best leather goods in Mongolia, intended mainly for export. It also has several professional and technical schools that attract students from across the country.

The new town has most of the facilities for the traveller, including restaurants, the post office, the bank, the Cultural Palace (which includes a cinema), the central hospital, the provincial museum near the bus station, and a radio station. Darkhan has no airport. There are several hotels in this part of town. The two best are the Darkhan Hotel and the Nomin Hotel.

The coal seams of **Shariin Gol**, with their open-air excavations, are 63 kilometres from Darkhan. Their reserves are estimated at 500 million tonnes at least. A railway line linked to the Trans-Mongolian takes the coal to Darkhan, Erdenet and Ulaanbaatar. Trains run between Ulaanbaatar and Darkhan five times a day; the journey takes 7.5 hours. A bus journey, on a good metalled road, takes six hours to travel between Darkhan and Ulaanbaatar.

**Kharaagiin Khiid** is a recently built temple located to the south of the 'old town'. There used to be four monasteries around Darkhan, and the province of Selenge boasted 55 monastic complexes, but they all suffered the fate of other Mongol temples during the purges, except for part of the monastery of Amarbayasgalant, 70 kilometres north-east of here, on the Darkhan-Erdenet road.

South-west of Darkhan is **Zuunkharaa**, mainly a goods redistribution centre with one distillery. The mountain scenery and the small wooden homes make this an attractive area. The hunting areas to the east of here are popular with Ulaanbaatar's 'weekend warriors'.

*In Mongolia, children are jockeys. Most learn to ride at the age of three.*

# Natural sites

### THE SPAS OF THE YERÖÖ BAYAN

Just south of the town of Yeröö and about 100 kilometres from Sükhbaatar, along the Yeröö River, are hot springs that have been turned into a spa area with wooden houses built directly over the springs. Near the spring area, is a small temple and nearby, slightly higher up in the mountain, is a large tree-*ovoo*, surrounded by forests. The area is a favourite with foreign hunters, who come here mainly for the *argali*, elk, and wild boar. **Deer stele** can be seen at Khuder-Khar, in Yeröö sum. This mountainous area is cut by the Yeröö River and covered in forests of pine and birch.

### THE SELENGE RIVER

This large river has a number of affluents, including the Orkhon, the Tuul, the Ider, the Delger-Mörön, and the Chuluut. Its waters eventually flow out to the Arctic Ocean. In 1998, a group of Japanese kayakers paddled from Lake Khövsgöl, down the Eg River to the Selenge, and onto Russia.

# Archaeological and cultural sites

Bronze Age **rock carvings** have been found close to the Tushig sum centre. Other carvings have been located in the **Kuiten Mountains**, south of old Darkhan, and in **Orkhon** sum. Most of the **man stones** in Selenge are in the Selenge River basin. North of the Gart Mountains and on the southern slopes of the **Tsagaan Tolgoi** stands a figure holding a ritual cup in his right hand. To the south of the statue, are several *balbal* stones aligned towards the south-east.

## AMARBAYASGALANT MONASTERY

The 'Monastery of Tranquil Felicity', once one of the three largest Buddhist centres in Mongolia, is located near the Selenge River, in the Iven Valley, at the foot of Mount Büren-Khaan. Built between 1727 and 1736, it is one of the very few monasteries to have partly escaped the destruction of 1937, after which only the buildings of the central section remained. The entire contents: the *thankas*, statues, and manuscripts, were looted by the communists, or hidden until more fortunate times. Restoration work began in 1988 and some of the new deities were commissioned in Delhi, India.

The monastery was originally built to house the remains of Zanabazar, the first Bogd Gegeen, or Öndör Gegeen, the 'August Light'. At the time of Manchu expansion in Mongolia, Zanabazar allied himself with Emperor Kangxi (1662–1722). The aim of the Manchus in founding this monastery was to seal with great pomp this alliance between the Mongol Lamaist church and Manchu power. Monasteries were still mostly nomadic ones then, and this edifice, built to last and financed by the imperial Manchu treasury, constitutes in the terms of Corneille Jest, 'an imperial seal affixed to the submissive Mongol soil'.

Unlike the monastery of Erdene Zūū, which is composed of an ensemble of temple halls of different styles, Amarbayasgalant shows great stylistic unity. The overall style is Chinese, despite some Mongol and Tibetan influence. The plan is symmetrical, and the main buildings succeed one another along a north-south axis, while the secondary buildings are laid out on parallel side axis.

The entrance to the monastery is located in the south and preceded by a screen meant to prevent evil spirits from entering. It leads to the small **Hall of the Seal** where the tablets bearing the imperial edict on the founding of the monastery were kept. The main doorway was often closed and not the usual entrance, the passages to the right and left of it were kept open.

On the eastern and western sides of this courtyard were two identical halls, the **Bell and Drum Towers**, and to the north stood the **Hall of the Heavenly Kings**, the guardians of the four directions. Past that, one came to a second courtyard with the

Tsogchin Dugan, the main hall, set on a terrace, and flanked on either side by hexagonal pavilions, called the 'Halls of History'. On the walls of the pavilions are inscriptions relating the history of the monastery.

In the early 1900s, the 8,000 monks of Amarbayasgalant were divided into six aimag, or communities, each one with its own main hall within the monastery complex. The Tsogchin was the congregation hall where all the monks assembled. Behind the Tsogchin, and on the central axis, is the Hall to Shakyamuni. To the east of it is the chapel for the remains of Öndör Gegeen Zanabazar (1635–1724), and to the west, the chapel that housed the remains of the fourth Bogd Gegeen. Between these two and the Tsogchin is the Hall of the Mandala to the west, and the Hall to Ayush (Amitayus), the Bodhisattva of Long Life, to the east.

The last hall on the central axis is the Labrang, which served as residence to the visiting Bogd Gegeen. To either side of it are halls to Narokhajid and Maidar (Maitreya).

To the east and west of the third and fourth courtyards, and surrounding them on all sides, are the 'Ten White Halls'. The monks' gers were laid out from east to west, in rows separated by narrow streets.

Amarbayasgalant Khiid was inaugurated for the second time in September 1992. Gurudeva, a Mongol monk living in Nepal, led the ceremonies. He has been instrumental in the restoration of this unique complex.

The monastery itself is deceptively remote. It is best reached from Darkhan, can be reached from Erdenet, and is sometimes used as a stopover en route to Khövsgöl. Jeep tracks zig-zagging through the grass have stumped many a driver, but there are gers on the way from which you can ask directions. Comfortable accommodation can be had at the Amarbayasgalant ger camp, located seven kilometres south of the monastery. Basic rooms are available adjacent the monastery, in a small guesthouse run by the monks.

NORTHERN AIMAGS

# Bulgan

Located in the basin of the Selenge River and its long affluent, the Orkhon, this aimag of 48,800 square kilometres and over 60,000 inhabitants, has some of the highest rainfall in Mongolia. The majority of its inhabitants are Khalkh, with some Buryat.

The low mountains of Bulgan belong to the eastern part of the Khangai chain. The north of the province is green, with thick forests and magnificent pastureland, particularly at Tarvagatai in Teshig sum. More than one million livestock feed on these grasses. Arid steppe lands dominate the southern part of the province.

Agriculture is facilitated by the presence of fertile soils, wide valleys and low mountains with gentle slopes. There are several former state farms that grow wheat, potatoes, and fodder. The most fertile soils are those in the basins of the Orkhon and Selenge rivers.

Bulgan also has important deposits of copper and molybdenum. The largest mine in the country, and one of the largest in the world, is the copper mine at Erdenet.

This province is considered one of the cradles of the movement that led to the 1921 Revolution. It was here that Baron von Ungern Sternberg, the 'Mad Baron', was captured by the special regiment known as 'the West Road', led jointly by Choibalsan and the Siberian partisan Chetinkin.

Bulgan is rich in archaeological remains, and only recently the History Institute of the Mongol Academy of Sciences announced the discovery of a bronze helmet dating between the eighth and sixth centuries BC, near the Egiin Gol River. In the mid-1990s, there was talk of damming the Egiin Gol, which would have flooded archaeology sites. The hydro-electric project, however, has been suspended.

## BULGAN CITY

The town of Bulgan is located in the Orkhon Valley at an elevation of 1,208 metres. It is 330 kilometres from Ulaanbaatar by the south road, and 467 kilometres via Darkhan and Erdenet. The *ger* districts are in the southern end of town and the industrial zone lies in the north-east.

The centre of town is blessed with a monument dedicated to cosmonauts. J. Gurragcha, Mongolia's first and only cosmonaut, hails from Bulgan. On a nearby hill is the **mausoleum of Khatanbaatar Magsarjav**, which is shaped like a *ger*, and mainly of interest for the view over the town.

Magsarjav, an ex-plenipotentiary, was commander of the troops of the Sain Noyon Khaan and Zassagt Khaan aimags from May to July 1921. He is considered a national hero by the Mongols for the important role he played during the period of domination by the White Guards in Western Mongolia. Having worked under Baron von Ungern

*Left: Two horsemen make their way over a pass in northern Mongolia.*

Sternberg, he turned against the White Guards and, in the night of July 21, 1921, he liquidated their garrison before freeing the town of Uliastai, capital of the present day Zavkhan Aimag.

The centre of town has the usual facilities: hotels, bank, museum and post office. A third hotel, open only in summer, is located about ten kilometres west of town, in the alpine site of Jargalant. The airport is about two kilometres from town.

About three kilometres south-west of Bulgan is **Dashchoirkhorlon Khiid**, set up in 1992. Further south are the ruins of **Vangiin Khuree** monastery, built in the middle of the 17th century and destroyed in 1937. There are a few scattered remains, including the broken pieces of a large white stupa.

## ERDENET CITY

This large town of 70,000 inhabitants is located 371 kilometres from Ulaanbaatar and 68 kilometres from Bulgan, on the south slopes of Mount Erdene. Although within the territory of Bulgan Aimag, Erdenet is actually the centre of a small independent province called **Orkhon**, which also includes Bayan Öndör and Jargalant sums. Erdenet is the fourth largest town in Mongolia and one of its more sophisticated.

A bit east of town, it is hard to miss the gigantic open cast copper mine, which is the cornerstone of the town's existence. The mine, one of the ten largest copper mines in the world, is 51 per cent owned by the Mongolian government and 49 per cent owned by private investors in Russia. Mount Erdene (meaning: treasure, jewel) also contains important deposits of turquoise, lazurite, malachite and other minerals.

Three kilometres from Mount Erdene, a group of monks built a monastery called **Noyon Khutugtiin Khuree**, to protect the sacred mountain. At the time of its construction, the craftsmen and artisans used precious stones from the mountain to make their sculptures and statues. In 1727, not far from the mountain, another great monastery was built, that of Amarbayasgalant (Selenge Aimag, see p. 194) in honour of Öndör Gegeen Zanabazar, who used the copper from this mountain to cast some of the most beautiful statues of Mongol Buddhist art. Later, the Manchus mined turquoise, lazurite, malachite and other minerals here. In the 1940s, Russian geologists pointed out the mining potential of the region to the authorities and prospecting began in earnest in the 1960s.

Erdenet is spread out along Sükhbaatar Street, which has a surprising number of shops and restaurants. There are several hotels to chose from, notably the Selenge Hotel and the Chandman Hotel, both of which serve food and beer. A few businesses have sprung up around the mine. Erdenet is the centre of the **carpet weaving** industry in Mongolia, almost all the carpets are produced for export.

Erdenet can be reached by both rail and road. Daily trains take 14 hours to make the journey and usually travel at night. The station is 10 kilometres east of downtown.

Some travellers going to Khövsgöl will first take the train to Erdenet, then a jeep to Mörön via Bulgan—thereby cutting out a portion of a bumpy ride.

Another idea is to take a mountain bike on the train and do a cycle tour in Bulgan, or ride all the way back to Ulaanbaatar on the paved road. You must pay a small fee for carrying a bicycle on the train.

If you find yourself heading north from Erdenet, you could stop in **Selenge sum** to inspect the **Enkh-Tolgoi man statue**. This is a large figure, three metres tall, in front of which is a stone bowl. The mouth of the statue, covered in grease, reflects the ritual practices of 'feeding' the statues carried out by the locals.

THE MINING COMPLEX

The Erdenet ore-dressing combine is located 4.5 kilometres from Erdenet. During communism, this corporation played a major role in the economic development of the country—at one time accounting for 70 per cent of its currency earnings and also using up 70 per cent of Mongolia's energy. The molybdenum produced by the mine was shipped to Russia to pay off Mongolia's debts (this metal is used for making special steels). The mine fell on hard times in the 1990s, and racked up gigantic debts. The Asian economic crisis of 1998 further exacerbated the situation when the price of copper plummeted. By the end of that year the company was US$60 million in debt. The crisis has since improved slightly, but Mongolia is hoping to one day sell the mine to a financially stable buyer. The mine can be exploited for another 50 to 60 years, and runs twenty-four hours a day, 365 days a year.

There are no organised tours, but visitors are sometimes allowed into the mine if prior arrangements are made. More convenient is the **Mining Museum**, which belongs to the mining company, on the second floor of the Erdenet Cultural Palace.

## BUGAT SUM

The Monument of Bugat, in **Bugat sum** (north of Bulgan City) is a large Turkish era stele discovered in 1956. Set on a stone tortoise, its top is decorated with a carnivorous animal under which is a straight nosed anthropomorphic face. On the sides of the stele is a 29-line inscription in Sogdian relating events that occurred in the Turkish Empire around the 580s. This inscription was made in honour of Mughan Kaghan (553–572), or Mou-Han, by his successor Taspar who converted to Buddhism. In the same sum is the **statue of Züün Türüü**, located west of the Bugat sum centre.

# North-West Bulgan Aimag

The ruins of the city of **Baibalik** are located on the banks of the Selenge River, in **Khutag-Öndör sum.** The town is said to have been visited by Sogdian and foreign merchants, and to have had a community of monks living there who translated texts into Uighur. Also in this sum is the **Stele of Nariin-Tülber**.

North of this sum is the **Eg Tarvagtai** pastureland, a beautiful area of forest and mountain scenery—ideal for walking and camping. Further north is Teshig sum, where you can find the **Stele of Teshig**.

# West Bulgan Aimag

Two protected sites are located about 80 kilometres north-west of Bulgan City, in Khutag-Öndör sum. The first is around the **Uran Crater**, which is 500 to 600 metres wide and 50 metres deep. The crater is located near the main road to Khövsgöl and the ascent is not difficult. Nearby, another protected area takes in the **Tulga Craters**, whose shape is reminiscent of the three stones placed around the hearth in a *ger*. **Mounts Togoo** (1,620 m) and **Jalavch** (1,560 m) are located 12 kilometres south of Mount Uran. Upon looking at the shape of these craters it is easy to understand their names: *togoo* means cauldron and *jalavch* means small cooking-pot. On one of the slopes of Tulga are a dozen *kereksür*, stone cist graves, and a large block of granite.

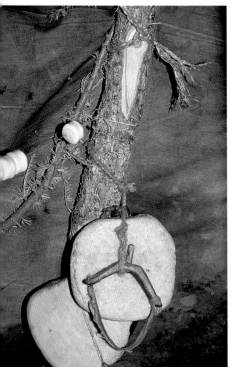

Further west, in **Bayan-Agt sum**, are two more craters—the northern and southern **Khuis Mandal. Lake Sharga** was formed after the northern crater exploded, and dammed the Shar-Burt River with lava.

The monumental **complex of Shiveet-Ulaan** is located on the banks of the Khanui River. It includes a monument with runic inscriptions in Orkhon Turkish, a stone sculpture of a carnivorous animal decorated with a deer, and five stone figures; each leaning on a stick and holding ritual cups. The **deer stele of Khuurai-Khag** is located in the south-east of the sum.

## SAIKHAN SUM

The **monument dedicated to Khaan Moyunchuur**, 3.8 metres tall, is located in **Saikhan sum**, at a site called **Khuremt**. It is thought to date to the eighth century, and bears an inscription in Uighur. The

*Cheese drying inside the ger.*

inscription describes the destruction of the Turkish khanate by a Uighur army, the military campaigns of the latter, and the way in which they built their cities and palaces. It is dedicated to Moyunchuur (746-759), successor to the first Uighur khaan Peilo under whose reign the Uighur reached the height of their power. Moyunchuur launched a series of victorious campaigns against the Kirghiz in the north, and the Qidan to the east. In the middle of the eighth century, the Uighur occupied a territory stretching from the Altai Mountains in the west to the Khingan Mountains in the east, the Gobi in the south, and the Sayan Mountains in the north.

Visitors to the area can also investigate the **man statues of Nariin-Khuremt**. Four or five of these probably date to the Turkish period. One differs from the others in style and is reminiscent of the statues on Easter Island. It is partially buried in the ground with only its head visible.

# South Bulgan Aimag

### MOGOD SUM
This is first of all a spectacular natural area, and the highest peak in the sum, called Mogod, has an elevation of 2,130 metres. Access to this region is, however, difficult

*Two elders stop for a smoke at the local market.*

and the best approach is from the sum centre. Visitors to Mogod will want to investigate the many cultural remains scattered across the landscape, including **rock carvings** near the Orkhon River and **The Stele of Tsakhiurt** east of the Mogod sum centre.

The **funerary monument of Ikh Asgat**, north-east of the Tülee Mountains, is an excellent piece of pre-Mongol art. It has a ten-line inscription in the runic script of the Orkhon Turks. This is the epitaph of a Turkish nobleman, dating probably from 724, and formed part of a larger funerary complex. There are also engraved figures holding ritual cups in their right hand, cone-shaped motifs with an ibex, and a wild ram—symbol of the power of the khaan. Around and in front of it are ritual enclosure stones, *kereksür* tombs, as well as *balbal* stones. The Mongols have venerated this monument since ancient times. The archaeologist Ser-Ojav calls it the "sacred funerary complex of the golden *tamga* (seal)".

Pressing on to the west, there are more historic sights in Khishig-Öndör *sum*. These include a **Turkish inscription at Ar Khana** and a stele north of the town centre, with a representation of the moon and five deer.

## DASHINCHILIN SUM

In **Dashinchilin sum**, one can find the so-called **rock inscriptions of Arslant and of Khangidai**. But the real reason to visit the area is to inspect the remains of several towns and fortifications of the Qidan period, including **Chin Tolgoin Balgass**, an important Qidan town that was founded in 944. These scattered ruins are located to the north-east of a 17th-century ruined monastery built on the site of the Qidan city.

**Khadassangiin Balgass** is located west of Chin Tolgoin Balgass. This was a fortified town with a square plan and four gates. Traces of the irrigation canals remain.

**Derssen-Kherem** and **Taliin Ulaan Balgass**, close to each other, include a few traces of canalisation, which testify to the existence of agriculture. Another site is **Emgentiin-Kherem**, on the north bank of the Khar-Bukh River, where a significant amount of Qidan ceramics were discovered.

The **Ruins of Tsogt Taij** Palace are located on the banks of the Tuul River, about 45 kilometres from the Dashinchilin sum centre. The building of this castle has been attributed by the Mongols to the Khalkh prince **Tsogt Taij** (1580-1637), famous for his fierce resistance to Manchu expansion. He was a cultivated and astute nobleman, a poet and a Buddhist, who decided to join forces with Ligdan Khaan, the last Chinggis-khaanid, in hopes of restoring the old power and unity of the Mongols. They were defeated and the **'White Palace'** of Tsogt-Taij was burnt to the ground.

The walls of the castle and the other buildings were made of slabs of uncarved stone. Tall half-destroyed doors lead into the courtyard; and inside is a half-collapsed Buddhist stupa. An enormous **grinding stone** is located near the ruins.

Despite the attribution to Tsogt Taij, this is actually thought to be one of the most important towns of the Mongol feudal period. The castle was built on the ruins of a much older town, of considerable size, dating to the Qidan or even the Uighur: the town of **Khadassan**. The earthen ramparts are well preserved. Beyond the limits of the town, one can see traces of **irrigation works** and old square fields—city life had developed here more than 1,000 years ago. The town fell to the Jurchen, who razed the homes, palaces and temples to the ground.

Just to the west of the ruins is a large stone with an inscription dated to 1624, attributed to Tsogt Taij. This is the largest rock inscription found in Mongolia.

If you are travelling north from Dashinchilen, you could visit the **Bichigt Gol Valley** (Script River Valley), fifty kilometres from Büregkhangai sum centre. The valley has no less than 43 inscriptions on sheer sandstone slabs, in black and red. Most of them date to the Mongol Yuan dynasty (1271–1368).

## GURVANBULAG SUM

**Khögnö Tarniin Övgön Khiid** is a late 16th-century monastery built near the Tarni River, in the far south of **Gurvanbulag sum**. It is located within the protected area of **Mount Khögnö Khaan**, at the edge of a vast expanse of sand. Of the original monastery, only two pavilions remain and both have undergone restoration work. In the mountains, a few ruins have recently been restored and two small temples have been back in use since the beginning of the 1990s.

**Mount Khögnö Khaan**, a sacred mountain, was venerated by the Orkhon Turks, or 'Blue Turks'. The site of the new monastery of **Övgön Khiid** was the scene of a memorable battle between the Khalkh and the Western Mongols, led by Galdan Boshigt. On the south-east of Mount Khögnö Khaan is a **man-stone**—the **Monument of Shilüüs Valley**.

There are several good *ger* **camps** in the area, making this a destination for travellers seeking a day or two of rest. Some of the families living here in summer will rent horses for reasonable rates.

## RURAL CHORES

*The nomad life is a hard one as chores are constant and never-ending. Top left, a family makes felt using traditional methods. Top right, a goat skin is stretched on a wood rack. Bottom, a herder with a lasso pole has caught an untamed horse.*

# Khövsgöl

Nudging into the belly of Siberia, Khövsgöl is a 100,000 square kilometre chunk of land known for its wild mountains and alpine lakes. The province takes its name from Lake Khövsgöl, the deepest in Mongolia. This is a Turkic word meaning 'lake of the blue waters', which was popularised in the 19th century by Russian travellers as 'Kossogol'.

About 120,000 people live in this province, most of whom are Khalkh, but a few are descendants of Turkic speaking tribes, closely related to the people of Tuva. The minority groups include Khotgoit, Darkhat, Uriankhai, Buryat, Ööld, Dörvöt, and Bayat. The people of Khövsgöl have long been known as rebellious; monks here launched a Civil War in 1932. In recent years, Khövsgöl has proven itself a liberal island in the sea of conservative rural provinces. It supported the democratic candidates during the elections of the 1990s, and in 2000, Khövsgöl elected to Parliament an independent candidate named Gundalai.

Lake Khövsgöl has become a major destination for tourists, and a number of *ger* camps have been set up on the lakeshore to accommodate visitors. An army of anthropologists have descended on the aimag to study shamanism, which is particularly strong in the far north.

In the far south, the aimag is delimited by the **Tarbagatai Mountains** and in the north by the Eastern Saian, whose highest point is **Mount Möngkh Saridag** (3,491 metres), on the frontier with Russian Buryatia. The west bank of Lake Khövsgöl is bordered by a mountainous zone which reaches 3,191 metres at **Mount Tsömörlög**. There are more than ten volcanic craters in these mountain areas. Trekkers may also want to visit Mongolia's highest **waterfall** (70 metres), which cascades down the Arsain River, in the **Khoridal Saridag Strictly Protected Area**.

Apart from Lake Khövsgöl, this aimag includes about 300 lakes of which 200 are located in the Tsagaannuur region. It is drained by the Selenge, Delgermörön, Ider, and Tes rivers and has a number of mineral springs, especially in the area of the Tsagaan, Boom, and Shishged lakes. Hundreds of rivers have their source in the eternal snows of the mountains in this region.

Khövsgöl is the most wooded province of the country, with forests of birch, pines, cedars, and larch. The highest trees in Mongolia grow here, with some reaching over 40 metres in height. This province also has an abundant fauna typical of mountainous *taiga*: deer, wild boar, squirrel, beaver, otter, ermine, marten, sable, and wolf. The tribes living in the forests were traditionally engaged in hunting although they also depended on herding to some extent. The local topography (mountains and taiga) facilitates the breeding of large cattle (yak and *khainak*, a cross between a yak and a cow). Small herds of deer and reindeer, bred for their antlers, exist around Renchinlkhumbe. Sable farms have also been opened in the province.

A few industries have been set up, mostly in wood processing or in the manufacture of structural elements of gers and of Mongol saddles. There are a few food processing plants, factories, flour mills, and a fish cannery. The first cannery was opened in 1942 to process fish hauled out of Tsagaan Nuur, but fishing in this lake was banned when it was realised this industry was not sustainable. Generally, however, the lakes and rivers of Khövsgöl have abundant fish: grayling, white salmon, and *omoul*, an endemic salmonid from Lake Baikal introduced here in 1956. The *omoul*, listed among the protected species, may only be fished privately and not for commercial purposes.

Khövsgöl Aimag is rich in mineral resources: coal, graphite, and phosphorite deposits have all been found there. One of the world's largest phosphorite mines, with reserves estimated at over 500 million tonnes, is located here. There are also relatively important deposits of green jade, chalcedony, and rock crystal.

## MÖRÖN AND SURROUNDS

The town of Mörön (1,283 m) isn't much to look at, but the surrounding area, with high mountains and sweeping grasslands, is decidedly majestic. It is located 671 kilometres from Ulaanbaatar on the north slopes of Mount Erchim, beside the Delger-Mörön River. Mörön, which means 'wide river', was founded as a trade centre next to the Möröngiin-Khuree Monastery, which was built around 1890. This was, in its day, one of the largest religious centres in northern Mongolia. The aimag once had sixty such monastic complexes. A new monastery, **Danzandarjaa Khiid**, opened in 1990 on the site of the old Möröngiin-Khuree, to the west of town, not far from the road to the airport. This is an attractive monastery of Mongol-style architecture, built in the shape of a *ger*.

Mörön is a safe town for visitors, but tensions briefly flared up in December 1997 after an American businessman shot his Mongolian employee during an argument at their timber mill. The American was jailed, charged with 'over-zealous self-defence', but was able to leave the country soon after, by paying compensation to the family of the deceased. After the shooting incident, a car driven by another foreigner was stoned, although there were no injuries.

Mörön has a main square surrounded by administration buildings, shops, a theatre, the bank and the post office. Close by is a statue of **Davaadorj**, a local hero who fought the Japanese at Khalkh Gol in 1939. The provincial **museum** offers a good introduction to the aimag and includes a section of the Tsataan (Dukha) ethnic minority, who specialise in herding reindeer.

The museum also houses a fine statue of a many-armed Avalokiteshvara

(Janraiseg), in a style unusual for Mongolia. There is an arrangement of the flora and fauna of Khövsgöl, and an impressive mammoth's tooth.

Mörön has a few **hotels**. Two worth noting are Hotel Delger Mörön, and the Gov Tourist Hotel. The latter is more upscale. The airport is located five kilometres northwest of the town centre.

To the south-west of Mörön, in the western part of the Erchim Mountains, used to be one of the most important towns of 13th-century Mongolia, the 'white city of **Erchim**'. Only the ruins of it stand today. West of Mörön, one can find a number of tombs and *kereksür*, as well as 14 deer stele, in the **Delger-Saikhan Valley**.

In **Bürentogtokh sum** (west of Mörön), look for the **five deer stele** that form part of a funerary complex. One is decorated with a *tamga* (clan inscription).

# South of Mörön

## JARGALANT
This is a small town of wooden buildings, located on the Ider River, in the southernmost part of the aimag. A large hut-shaped *ovoo*, made of long branches, marks the entrance to town.

The old monastery of Jargalant, **Ariin-Khuree**, was closed in the 1930s, but one of the buildings of the main temple escaped destruction as locals used it as a warehouse for furs and hides. These goods were then sent to Ulaanbaatar to be made into leather goods and carpets. In 1991, a new building was erected and religious services are now held there.

A small **museum**, dependent on the monastery, used to display the photograph of Öndör Gongor, the tallest man of Khövsgöl and indeed of Mongolia. He measured 2.4 metres and was known as Duunii Baatar, the 'man with the resounding voice', as he could be heard some 30 kilometres away! He was taken on as bodyguard to the last Bogd Gegeen, and died in 1929 when he was less than 50 years old. It is said that he was so tall that no horse could be found for him.

Near Jargalant are some beautiful forests of two hundred year-old larch trees, as well as thermal springs. Twenty kilometres north of Jargalant is the magnificent **Tsagaan Burgas Valley**. The peaks of the surrounding hills offer excellent views over the Tarbagatai Mountains.

## SHIN IDER AND GALT SUMS
The **Uran Dösh** crater (2,471 m) is located in the Erchim chain, south of the Tsagaan Burgas pass, on the road to Shine Ider. A **stele group** of Shin Ider sum has engravings of deer and horses.

**Stele in the Nuukh't Valley** include two deer stele that can be found about 10 kilometres north of Galt sum, north-west of a site that includes about 100 Xiongnu-

period tombs and circular stones. The **Galt museum** is worth a visit for its collection of old playing cards. Locally-made cards such as these are still used today by the nomads from Khövsgöl, Arkhangai and Zavkhan.

## SANGIIN DALAI NUUR

This large salt water lake (166 sq. km) with a large bird population, is located on the south-western part of the aimag near the border with Zavkhan. The elevation here is about 2,000 metres above sea level. South-west of the lake, in the Tes valley, is an attractive spot called **Shavar Turuu**.

# East of Mörön

To the south-west of **Rashaant sum** are two **extinct volcanoes**, Ikh Sandal, and Bag Sandal. Geological studies show that they last erupted at the end of the Tertiary era. With some hunting you might also find the remains of a **Uighur town** of the ninth to tenth centuries. It is located some 10 kilometres west of Khutag sum (in Bulgan), north of the Selenge River.

# Khövsgöl National Park

The jewel of Mongolia's national park system, this one is given great acclaim by travel agents. The park, with a surface area of 838,000 ha, is enclosed to the north by the Saian Mountains and to the west by the Khoridal Saridag chain. It was created in 1992 to protect the lake's ecology, which has long been jeopardised by miners, loggers and traders. A large deposit of phosphorous nearby is one of many natural resources eyed by politicians as a revenue earner.

Despite conservation efforts, the park is still overcoming its growing pains. Over-grazing, illegal logging, and the poaching of musk deer are some of the dangers that threaten the park's ecological balance. Mongolia's national parks allow local people to retain their grazing grounds, so don't be surprised if you stumble upon someone's *ger* encampment while trekking through the thicket. The Tsaatan (nomads who breed reindeer), roam the mountainous *taiga* and the wooded steppe to the north and west of the park.

## LAKE KHÖVSGÖL

Lake Khövsgöl, 136 kilometres long and 36 kilometres wide, at 1,645 metres above sea level, is the second largest lake in Mongolia as well as the deepest. Known as the 'Blue Pearl of Mongolia', because of its crystal clear waters, it flows into the **Eg**

*Left: a Tsaatan ger of northern Khövsgöl*

River (Egiin Gol), which then joins the Selenge, and finally reaches **Lake Baikal**. It belongs to the same water drainage (and geologic) system as Baikal, only 250 km away, and like this 'sister lake', has its own endemic fauna and flora.

Almost 70 per cent of Khövsgöl is over 100 metres deep, reaching 267 metres at its deepest point. This is the largest reservoir of fresh water in the country, and represents two per cent of the world's reserves. Such is the clarity of the water that one can see fish down to a depth of a few dozen metres. Among the rivers that flow into the lake, are the **Khankh** and the **Khoroo**; their mouths are important rest sites for migratory birds. From January to April or May, the lake freezes over and is covered for several months by 1.5 metres of ice. Lorries used to drive across it in winter, a practice banned since the 1980s to prevent pollution.

In the centre of the lake are four islands known as the 'Earth navel' (the largest and most wooded island), the 'Stone navel', the 'Wood navel', and the 'Small navel'. Around the lake are a number of caves. Brown bear, musk deer, ibex, *argali*, marten, beavers, elk, lynx, and wolves inhabit the surrounding mountains.

Unlike most Mongols, the locals living around Lake Khövsgöl eat fish. As soon as they are caught, the graylings are slit from head to tail along the backbone and belly, and hung up on a stick to dry in a well-aired place. While some anglers use a handline, others fish at night with a harpoon. The lake has nine varieties of fish, including the famous lenok and *omoul*.

A small ferry called the 'Sukhbaatar' occasionally crosses Lake Khövsgöl from Khatgal to Khankh. There are no scheduled departures so traders carrying goods from nearby Russia usually charter the boat, and allow passengers to tag along. The crossing takes 13 hours and can be very rough if the wind is blowing. On September 20, 2000, a storm sent huge waves crashing against the boat, tossing Tg6 million in cargo overboard.

## KHATGAL

This small, sleepy town, about 100 kilometres from Mörön at the southern end of Lake Khövsgöl, once housed a large colony of Russian traders and loggers. In recent years, it has become the main gateway for foreign tourists to reach Lake Hovsgol.

*The door of the ger, always faces south.*

Khatgal is actually on a small inlet of the lake. A road heads over Jankhai Pass to the settlement of Jankhai (a 17-kilometre trip) on the west shore, it is from here that the whole lake can be viewed. A bit further up the road is the more secluded settlement of Toilogt.

The well run National Park office provides information and photographs of the park. This is a good place to ask about trekking, horse riding and accommodation. Travellers can choose between several *ger* camps in town. Thyme 3 is a Mongolian-UK joint venture and offers some of the best food in region (www.4thworldadventure.com). Jambal's Guesthouse draws weary travellers for its new sauna. Another option is an older hotel called the 'Blue Pearl', which offers standard rooms at reasonable rates.

*A fortune teller relates a customer's future.*

Both Jankhai and Toilogt offer good *ger* camps, horse riding and fishing spots. Thyme 1 (operated by the same people who do Thyme 3) has horse and boat trips, and comfortable *ger* accommodation. While Thyme is geared towards independent travellers, Camp Toilogt caters toward group tours. It also serves as the base for an annual **100 kilometre foot race** called the 'Sunrise to Sunset'. (There is a 42 km section as well) See: www.ultramongolia.com for more details.

Permits for the national park are purchased at a gate 12 kilometres south of Khatgal. The fee is Tg1,000 per night and Tg3,000 per vehicle. If you stay longer than you originally paid for, inform a ranger at the national park office.

## KHANKH

Khatgal's sister city is Khankh, also located within the national park and close to the Russian border. It lies 50 kilometres from Mondi, the nearest Russian town. Foreigners, however, cannot cross at this border post. Lake Baikal is about 200 kilometres away from Mondi. Khankh and Khatgal are joined by road along the east shore of the lake, as well as by boat. The east shore, however, is not as spectacular as the west, and therefore not frequently visited by tourists.

# Northern Khövsgöl Aimag

## TSAGAAN ÜÜR

East of Lake Khövsgöl is Tsagaan Üür sum, of interest primarily for the mysterious **Dayan Derkhii** cave. The cave is located at a site called **Erdene Bulgan**, on the east bank of the Tsagaan Üür River, 30 kilometres south-east of the sum centre.

The cave is an ancient and well-known pilgrimage site where a deified shaman was venerated. According to legend, Dayan Derkhii was a shaman who was turned into a spirit of the surrounding stones and hills. His cult is not limited to Khövsgöl, but can be found throughout Mongolia among the Khalkh, Uriankhai, and Buryats. Dayan Derkhii was considered the patron of shamanistic initiations, and Mongols used to come here from the south of the country to venerate him. Khövsgöl has remained till this day one of the last bastions of shamanism in Mongolia. The cave, 30 metres long, is one of the most impressive in Mongolia, with more than ten side galleries, dozens of openings, and a mineral spring.

## ULAAN UUL SUM

Travelling north-west from Mörön, the road crosses the Öoliin Davaa pass, and enters Ulaan Uul sum, on the banks of the Gun River. In the district of Ulaan Uul, is a path known as the 'road of Chinggis Khaan's chariots', which is associated with the Mongol Imperial conquests. Rock carvings can be seen at **Tol'jgui Boom**, near the Khugii River, at the border between Renchinlkhumbe and Ulaan Uul sums.

It was once possible to reach Ulaan Uul by charter plane from Mörön, but now there is no alternative other than going by jeep on a difficult and marshy trail. On the way, you can stop in **Bayanzurkh sum**, which has rock carvings at **Bichigt Gulag**.

## DARKHAT COUNTRY

Up until the early 20th century, the term 'Darkhat country' used to be applied to the area around Renchinlkhumbe sum, Ulaan Uul, and Bayanzurkh, in the Shishged river basin. This area extends from **Mount Khoridal** (3,130 m) to **Mounts Ulaan Taiga** (3,351 m), **Bayan Uul** (3,093 m), and **Möngkh Saridag** (3,491 m).

The peoples living in Darkhat territory have traditionally engaged in fishing, gathering, and the breeding of reindeer. The name Darkhat ('blacksmith', but also 'free subject, one who is exempt') was given to the local population by the Bogd Gegeen, who became their overlord in the 17th century. Exempt from taxes and services to the Manchu emperor, they paid taxes only to the Lamaist church.

## RENCHINLKHUMBE

Renchilkhumbe was originally an important monastery known as Zöölön (sometimes, Gandannamjilin). At the beginning of the 20th century, this Darkhat monastery-town included one Russian and five Chinese trading posts that bought fish, cattle, and furs from the Darkhat. It is said that the lamas of Zöölön, who suffered from vitamin deficiency, went to the spas of Boom and upper Lake Tsagaan to be treated. When the monastery was shut down in 1938, there were still 1,500 monks living in there. Those not shot were put to work in the local wood, textile or food cooperatives.

## KHIARUUNII SHIVER
About 30 kilometres north of Renchinlkhumbe sum centre, in the Jar and Khiaruun river basin, is a superb forest of trees (willows, cedars, Siberian pines) reaching 30 to 40 metres in height.

## LAKE TSAGAAN (TSAGAANNUUR)
This lake is located north of the sum centre and about 50 kilometres from Lake Khövsgöl. The village of Tsagaannuur, composed mainly of wooden houses, is located in what may be called the 'Lakes Region' as it is here that some two-thirds of the 300 lakes of Khövsgöl province are to be found. The Dukha, or Tsaatan (literally reindeer man), live in the surrounding mountains.

The region of **Tsagaanuur** and **Renchinlkhumbe** is probably the most remote and inaccessible in Mongolia, and serious consideration and planning needs to be taken before travelling there. Communications, hotels and supplies are poor, and the lack of roads means that a lot of it is only accessible by horse. These drawbacks, however, have not stopped groups of western anthropologists from visiting the area in droves to study shamanism, which is very much alive here.

# Western Khövsgöl Aimag

## DELGER-MÖRÖN AND TES VALLEY SITES
In the **Delger-Mörön and Tes valleys**, west of Mörön, are several groups of rock carvings that date to the Bronze and Iron ages. With a jeep, knowledgeable guide and some luck, you may be able to find them.

The first set of carvings is located in a pretty mountain setting, behind the pass leading to Delger-Mörön in Arbulag sum. They are located on the site of the **Palace of the Great Khaan Möngkh** (13th century), discovered in 1956 by Mongol archaeologists. A commemorative stele with an inscription in old Mongolian to honour the khaan used to stand there. Near the ruins of the palace, on three hills, are rock carvings in the shape of reindeer hooves. Nearby are more engravings that resemble the footprints of a panther.

In addition to these carvings, about 50 kilometres from Mörön is a large valley with a ensemble of ruins and a large rock called **Bichigt Khad**, which, despite its

Mongolian name, bears no inscription! It can be found on the left bank of the Delger-Mörön River,

The **Rock carvings** of *Khüükhdiin Ovoo* are a group of rock engravings on the left bank of the Tes river, about 10 kilometres west of the Tsetserleg sum centre. There are also 'hooves' here, as well as anthropomorphic silhouettes and outlines of deer (or reindeer) with very large antlers. Slightly to the east is another site called the 'Children's Ovoo' (*Khüükhdiin Ovoo*).

Another 1.5 kilometres on, a third group of carvings have similar features to the preceding ones, with additional drawings of crosses and circles, as well as a ploughing scene. These carvings all testify to the ancient use of carts and draught animals. They are thought to be between 2,000 and 5,000 years old.

The Russian scholar, A. Okladnikov, has suggested that the hoof represents the male reproductive organ, the circle the female uterus, and the wheel the sun god of Vedic times. It is now accepted that the carvings belong to the Bronze Age, when the Karasuk culture was developing along the Yenisei River.

*The Mongol saddle is decorated with silver artwork. Legend says the buckles were developed by Chinggis Khaan to keep his warriors standing in the saddle.*

Eastern Mongolia

© Airphoto International Ltd.

N

0    50    100    200 km
0    50    100 miles

CHINA

CHINA

RUSSIA

Menengiin tal

Ereentsav
Dashbalbar
Khalkhgol
Ikh Burkhant
(Ancient site)
Sumber
Choibalsan
Choibalsan
Matad
Erden Tsagaan

DORNOD

Bayandun
Gurvanzagal
Dadal
Bayan-Uul
Sergelen
Bayantumen
Bulgan
Kholonbuir
Tsagaan-Ovoo
Wall of Chinggis Khaan

Darigarga
Sükhbaatar
Baruun-Urt
Asgat
Naran
Ongon
Khalzan
Bayandelger

SÜKHBAATAR

Tümentsogt
1284
Burentsogt
Uulbayan
Tuvshinshiree

Monkhkhaan
Bayandun
Bayan-Ovoo
Batnorov
Norovlin
Bürenkhaan
Binder
Bayan-Adarga
Guvanbayan
Berkh
Öndörkhaan
Galshar

KHENTII

Batshireet
Bayan-Ondör
Ömnödelger
Tsenkhermandal
Mörön
Darkhan
Khajuu-Ulaan
Bor-Öndör

Deitgerkhaan
2270
Mongonmorit
Bayandelger
Delgerkhaan

DORNGOV

1682
Ölziit
2042
Arkhust
Bayan

CHOÏR

Bayanjargalan
Choïr

Asralt
khairkhan uul
2800
Batsümber
Partizan
Terelj

Zuunkharaa
Bornuur
Baganuur

Zelter
Sükhbaatar
Altanbulag
Shaamar
Dulaankhaan
Khuder
Yeröö
Zuunburen
Orkhon
Sharingol
Khongor
Bayangol

DARKHAN
SELENGE

ERDENET
Baruunburen
Orkhontuul
Tseel
Ugtaaltsaidam
Bayantsogt
Jargalant
Zaamar
Bayankhangai
Sümber
Khotol
Orkhon

Bayan-Önjüül
Buren
1820
Delgerkhaan

ULAANBAATAR
Altanbulag
Zuun Mod
Erdenesant
1689
Ondorshireet

TÖV

DUNDGOV

ÖMNÖGOV

Khentei Mts

EASTERN AIMAGS

# Khentii

Khentii Aimag, a few hours drive east of Ulaanbaatar, has the historical distinction of being the homeland of the 13$^{th}$ century conqueror Chinggis Khaan. Dozens of sites scattered across this province are associated with his life, notably in his suspected birthplace, Dadal. The prominent ethnic minority is Khalkh, but several villages in the north are dominated by Buryats, a group that probably originated around Lake Baikal and the then migrated south towards Mongolia.

About 20 per cent of the territory's 82,000 square kilometres is covered in larch, cedar, birch and fir trees. The southern part of the province is mostly grassy steppe that rolls right towards the northern reaches of the Gobi Desert. Khentii is drained by two large rivers, the **Kherlen** and the **Onon**, which have their source in the north and belong to the Pacific Ocean basin.

Aside from Chinggis Khaan, racehorses, bred in **Galchar** sum (in the far southeast), are the pride of this province. These horses are famous throughout the country for their great speed and have won prizes in the national Naadam competitions.

Agriculture accounts for about 60 per cent of the aimag's production but there is also a wealth of untapped mineral resources: gold, tungsten, asbestos, uranium, iron, copper, manganese, and tin. There are coal mines at Shandagant and a fluoride mine at Berkh.

## ÖNDÖRKHAAN AND SURROUNDINGS

Located 331 kilometres from Ulaanbaatar, Öndörkhaan is the capital of Khentii Aimag. It is located on a wide grassy plain at 1,027 metres above sea level, on the banks of the Kherlen River in the south-eastern part of the province.

The **Provincial Museum**, west of the theatre, offers facts and details on the historical sites of Khentii, as well as some artefacts from the days of Chinggis Khaan's Empire. The **Ethnological Museum** is one of the more unique museums in the countryside. It is housed in the former palace of the Tsetsen Khaan, the Mongol prince who governed Tsetsen Khaan Aimag during the reign of the Manchus. The buildings, which date to the 18$^{th}$ century, house a rich collection of relics and artwork that belonged to aristocratic families before the objects were confiscated after the 1921 revolution. Dashdeejetlin Khiid, a tiny monastery with five monks, is located next to the museum.

**Gundgaravlin Khiid** is a new monastery complex that first appeared as a temporary *ger* in 1990, and was given permanent constructions in 1992. It is built on the site of the old monastic complex of Öndörkhaanii Khuree, or 'monastery of

Tsetsen-Khan', dating to the 17th century (1660) and which housed the first school of philosophy in Mongolia. In 1938, the monks were arrested, and either sent to camps, forced to return to lay life, or executed. The temple buildings were destroyed in the 1950s. The old monastery had more than 1,000 monks; about thirty monks serve the new temple.

A curious site is the 1.8 metre tall **anthropomorphic statue** (man stone) just west of Öndörkhaan, near the airport (about two kilometres from town). The centre of town is dominated by a long **park**, which contains statues of wild animals and a **monument dedicated to the Soviet fighters** killed during the Khalkh Gol war.

Most visitors to Öndörkhaan stay in the Kherlen Hotel, which is located in the centre of town close to the Ethnological Museum. The other two options are the Energy Star Hotel, the entrance to which is around the back of the Government House, and the Bayan Bulag Hotel near the food market. There are a few restaurants in town, notably the Tiger Café on the main street. **Internet** is available at the telecom office for a reasonable charge.

About twenty kilometres west Öndörkhaan in Mörön sum, are the ruins of the Qidan city of **Züun Kherem** (eastern fortification). This was the most northern of the Qidan Empire towns and it played the role of a vanguard along the northern borders. Crops were grown behind the town, in the Kherlen basin and along the small Mörön River. The **Baruun Kherem** (Western Fortress) was located two kilometres west of Züun Kherem, and had seven gates. The remains of the base of a watch-tower can be seen. The present thickness of the walls is seven to 12 metres, and their height varies from 1.5 to three metres.

## BINDER SUM

Binder is a small village in northern Khentii, surrounded by yellow meadows and pine forests. Here researchers have found the ruins of **Uglekch Fortress,** located on the south slopes of Binder Uul. An outer granite wall encloses a second wall inside. It probably dates to the Qidan period or to the 13th–14th centuries.

The rock carvings here are particularly unique. In 1974, a joint Mongol and Soviet expedition discovered a large number of carvings in the Arshaan Khad Mountains (Mt. Sacred Spring Rocks). The oldest of these carvings date to between the **Mesolithic** and the **Upper Palaeolithic** periods. These old carvings are on a rock, set apart from the others, which is entirely covered on both sides with about 100 signs: circles, geometric figures, and hoof prints in long rows. Some are similar in shape to the drawings in the Upper Palaeolithic caves of Western Mongolia, such as Khoit-Tsenkher (see Khovd Aimag). No examples of these types of drawings have been found in Western Europe.

About 20 metres from this rock stands another stone with representations of three animal figures, one behind the other (rhinoceros, bull, or wild boar). A third rock bears inscriptions in Tibetan, Chinese, old Mongol, and Arabic. A Lamaist

# THE TOMB OF CHINGGIS KHAAN

When a khaan died, the site of his tomb became taboo. It was believed that disturbing the tomb would destroy the khaan's soul. One hundred men-in-arms guarded the royal cemeteries, each chosen from the forests of Uriankhai and thought to possess fearsome shamanistic powers.

The site of the burial of Chinggis Khaan is still unknown, as are the exact causes of his death. Most sources say he died aged 66 (in 1227) from wounds incurred after a fall from his horse. He was on a campaign in China at the time, and on his deathbed told his son how to destroy the Qin Empire. While his body was being carried to its final resting place, all the people on the route of the funeral procession were killed to ensure the secrecy of their location.

There are several versions of what happened next. According to one, Chinggis was buried in the bed of a river (the water was temporarily diverted before being allowed to return to its original course). Another version states that a herd of 1,000 horses were sent charging over the burial place to cover up all traces of it, while according to a third version, the great conqueror's tomb is to be found in one of the caves on Mount Burkhan Kaldun. The Chinese allege the burial place is on their territory, while the Mongols insist it is on theirs.

At the site, soldiers killed the 2,000 servants present. To further ensure the secret, these soldiers were killed when they returned to Karakorum. It is likely, however, that the royal family knew the location. It was recorded that in 1229 Chinggis' son Ögödei had forty beautiful girls sacrificed there, in order to serve Chinggis in the afterlife. Further, several of Chinggis' descendants are presumed buried nearby.

But within a few generations, the unmarked graves of Chinggis and the other khaans were forgotten, and centuries of neglect covered them with overgrowth. For years afterwards, herdsmen in Khentii continued to protect curious sites and graves connected to the khaans, but their knowledge of these places are mere folklore.

When Mongolia opened its doors to the world in 1990, archaeologists and explorers around the world took an interest in finding the legendary site of the great Chinggis Khaan. The first to try were the Japanese, who mounted a three-year project called 'Gurvan Gol'. Armed with the latest advances in sonar technology, the Japan-Mongol team scoured Khentii Aimag, and by 1993 had counted 3,500 tombs dating from the Hun period to the Mongol middle ages, eight of which were thought to date from the court of Chinggis Khaan. But the search, which was financed by the largest daily newspaper in Tokyo, was terminated after an opinion pole in Ulaanbaatar revealed that the project was unpopular. And Chinggis went undiscovered.

*An actor portraying Chinggis Khaan*

The newest theories come from an unlikely source. A recently formed expedition to find the tomb has been organised by former Chicago commodities trader and lawyer Maury Kravitz, a 'Chinggisiphile' who has been mystified by the khaan's legend for forty years. Kravitz's team, which includes Mongolian scientists and a history professor from Chicago, surveyed the hills of Khentii in 2000 and 2001, staking out likely spots to excavate. In true Indiana Jones fashion, the team (financed with US$1.2 million) are searching with tips taken from the ancient chronicle *The Secret History of the Mongols*. En route, they have laid monuments at spots they associate with Chinggis.

At one point, a possible burial location was spotted, but the team had to evacuate after being attacked by a swarm of giant biting flies. (This was seen as an auspicious sign). But work on 'Fly Mountain', as they call it, was postponed when a more likely site was found near Binder sum centre. The 'Ghengis Khan Geo-Historical Expedition', as it is called, counted 60 odd graves in an area surrounded by a huge stone wall.

The 3.2 kilometre long wall is more than three metres high in places. Locals call the site "Chinggis' Castle", "Red Rock" and "Almsgiver's Castle", and say their ancestors have been protecting the site for generations. The team caused a stir in the media when the site was announced, along with news that the government had given them permission to excavate. Digging is set to begin in the summer of 2002, with hope of unlocking one of the world's last great secrets.

representation of the Buddha, on the vertical surface of the rock, conceals older Scythian drawings. A dozen *ovoo*—altars dedicated to the mountain sprits—surround **Arshaan Khad**, the most important one standing on the summit. This mountain must have been venerated and used as a sacrificial place since ancient times. Still more inscriptions, from the Turkish era, are at **Binderiin Rashaan** in nearby Batshireet sum.

# Sites associated with Chinggis Khaan

Throughout the province of Khentii, the birthplace of Chinggis Khaan, history and legend are inextricably mixed.

## TSENKHERMANDAL SUM

Although sources disagree on this, it is possible that Temujin (Chinggis Khaan) was made khaan in this area in 1206; either near the Tsenkher River or at Khokh Nuur. Most locals agree on the latter. (A study in 2001 also suggests a site near Binder) There is a small silver plaque featuring the image of Chinggis at **Khokh Nuur**, which is only accessible by motorbike, horse or foot. **Khangil Nuur**, about 30 kilometres further west, is another site associated with Chinggis. It is believed he occasionally set his camp here.

Researchers have also found **stone slab tombs** within this sum. Try looking at Melzelei Uul, which has a group of tombs from the Middle Kherlen. Pre-Mongol era **rock inscriptions** have been found in the Burgalt Valley.

The Russians founded the sum capital, called Modot, as a logging and mining town. Prison labour was used to extract the natural resources, and a walk up the valley reveals several abandoned mines and old equipment. There is an old wooden hotel in town, and a *ger* camp is sometimes set up in the summer.

## DADAL SUM

This sum, set in an attractive wooded area 254 kilometres north-west of Öndörkhaan, is the legendary birthplace of Chinggis Khaan. Dadal once housed one of the 33 great Lamaist temples of the country consecrated to Chinggis. The temple was razed to the ground in 1936-37. In June 1990, the monks returned and carried out the rituals dedicated to Mount Bayan-Ovoo—west of the museum—and to a second mountain, thought to be Burkhan Kaldun (see p. 222).

Because of its natural setting and association with Chinggis Khaan, Dadal is a destination for tourists. The crowds, however, are small, and you are likely to have the trails and lakes to yourself. Most tourists base themselves at **Gurvan Nuur** (Three Lakes), a camp of log cabins (Tg3,000) about two kilometres from Dadal. Another option is the nearby Onon *ger* **camp**, which charges US$30 per night. Camping is also a good option if you have your own supplies.

Some public jeeps go directly to Dadal from Ulaanbaatar. Jeeps and vans also leave from the Post Office in Öndörkhaan, but there is no set schedule and the wait can often be long. Hiring a private jeep from Ulaanbaatar or Öndörkhaan gives you more flexibility to explore sites in the area. Planes occasionally fly to Dadal (check the MIAT schedule).

The sites in the area include a **Xiongnu funerary site** north of Dadal, the **Buural cave**, 44 kilometres from Dadal and the **Galtai cave**, about seventy kilometres northwest of Dadal. The latter is close to the Russian border and visitors need special permission from the border police before travelling in the area.

There are a few things to see close to the Dadal sum centre (sometimes called Bayan Ovoo). **Khajuu Bulag** is a small spring in the middle of the forest near the Bayan River, from which Chinggis Khaan is said to have drunk. A bit east of this spring is **Deluun Boldog**, which locals consider the birthplace of Temujin (historians may think otherwise). The hill is topped with a stone monument dedicated in 1990 to honour the 750th anniversary *The Secret History of the Mongols*, a 13th century chronicle of the empire.

One of the lakes at **Gurvan Nuur** is known as **Lake Delüün**, or 'Spleen lake'. Legend has it that when Temujin (Chinggis Khaan) was about to be born, his mother was preparing a soup made from the spleen of a white horse. It is also said that in those days, the lakes did not yet exist, but Temujin's family *ger* was pitched here. At the *ger* camp itself, visitors will find a mammoth **10-metre tall monument** decorated with a portrait of Chinggis. Dedicated on May 31, 1962, it celebrates the 800th anniversary of his birth. This was the high point of the festivities organised by Tömör Ochir, then secretary-general of the Central Committee of the Mongolian People's Revolutionary Party (MPRP). Beside the portrait is an inscription that reads, "I have exhausted myself to unite my people. If my body should suffer, so be it! But let not my people fall into confusion".

On June 16, 1962, the People's Republic of China in turn organised great festivities that preceded the construction at Ejiin Khoroo (Inner Mongolia) a museum intended to house the 'relics' of Chinggis Khaan. The news immediately led to a strong debate between Soviet, Mongol, and Chinese historians, in regards to the birth and death place of Chinggis. In October of the same year, the Third Plenary Session of the Central Committee of the MPRP condemned this commemoration, branded it an act of anti-Marxist nationalism and the manifestation of a personality cult, and declared officially that Chinggis Khaan was a "reactionary figure of History".

*"The bandit wars led by Chinggis Khaan threw the people into unimaginable misery. To deny or minimise the reactionary nature of the military exploits of Chinggis Khaan is equivalent to fundamental deviation from the original Party line, and to incitement to nationalism".* (Ünen, August 1962)

Tömör Ochir was removed from his posts, thrown out of the Party, exiled away from the capital, and mysteriously assassinated in 1985. Nevertheless, no order to destroy the monument to the glory of Chinggis Khaan was ever given.

**Mount Burkhan Kaldun** is thought to be the sacred mountain that Chinggis Khaan venerated. When he was still only Temujin, he hid here, surrounded by his enemies, and succeeded in outsmarting them. *The Secret History of the Mongols* describes how he carried out sacrifices to the mountain, kneeling nine times and undoing his belt (as an act of submission), and presenting libations of mare's milk.

According to the Persian historian Rashid al-Din, the 'Great Forbidden Enclosure', **Ikh Khorig**, where Chinggis Khaan and his son Tolui were laid to rest, is located somewhere on the slopes of this mountain.

The exact location of Burkhan Kaldun, however, is unknown. Some have identified it as the present **Khentii Khan** (2,362 m), which borders onto Töv Aimag. This peak is one of three mountains traditionally venerated by the Mongols. In 1995, president Ochirbat decreed that this cult be restored.

*A horseman watches over a few of Mongolia's 2.1 million cows.*

*In summer, travel in Khentii Aimag can be wet and difficult.*

## DELGERKHAN SUM

According to the Mongol scholar Damdinsüren, **Mount Bayan Ulaan** is the old **Khöödöö Aral**, where the great chronicle, the *Secret History of the Mongols*, was composed. It was here that the three great khaans: Ögödei, Möngke, and Yesön Temur, were crowned. This site is located to the west of the town of **Delgerkhaan**.

About 13 kilometres south of Delgerkhaan is the archaeological site of **Avragiin Balgas**, which was discovered in 1969 by the Mongol archaeologist Kh. Perlee. It is believed that the **Palace of Aurug**, built by Chinggis Khaan, was once here. This discovery shocked historians as it was previously thought that Karakorum was the only important town in the Mongol empire.

According to Mongol scholars, Aurug, founded in 1189, is the oldest Mongol population centre and, like Karakorum, was first used as a supply base for the Mongol army. On the site, traces of a foundry, including part of an iron hub intended for a huge cart, have been uncovered.

In the early 1990s, Japanese scholars involved in the **Gurvan Gol project**, which aimed to locate Chinggis Khaan's tomb, identified the foundations of dozens of buildings over a zone of some 40 hectares around Aurug. They believe they may have found a palace (with 13 earthen elevated platforms) and a Chinese-style temple, perhaps built in honour of Chinggis Khaan after his death. The court at Aurug would originally have been nomadic, spreading out along the Kherlen River, and only become permanent later. There is almost nothing to see of these remains (only minor excavations have been made), but the area is still worth visiting to taste water from the **Avarga Toson mineral spring**, which was used by the Mongol khaans.

EASTERN AIMAGS

The water, slightly fizzy, now comes out of a pump operated by a family living in a nearby *ger*. Fill up your water bottles here for Tg100 per litre.

## THE MONUMENT TO CHINGGIS KHAAN

Close to the spring and the site of Aurug, this is one of the few post-1990 monuments in Mongolia. The UNESCO funded granite block is topped by a Chinggiskhaanid standard, on which are engraved the words attributed to the great conqueror, "My body will disappear, but our people will live on eternally". It commemorates the 750th anniversary of the *Secret History of the Mongols*, the most important historical chronicle written by the Mongols themselves at the time of Ögödei, son and successor to Chinggis (c. 1240, or 1324 according to some authors). In August 1990, more than 2,000 people gathered at the monument, among them many scientists and political figures, to watch the grand festivities, which ended in a traditional *naadam*.

In June 2001, a new complex of nine white **Imperial** *gers* was set up, providing some idea of how the khaans once lived. A statue of Chinggis is in the largest tent, and on the walls of the other tents hang the portraits of nine generals and 40 khaans.

### LAKE AND RESORT

The **Khöödöö Aral plain** stretches for over 30 kilometres along the Kherlen River, to the west of Mount Kherlen Bayan Ulaan, at a height of 1,300 metres above sea level. In the middle of the plain, about four kilometres west of the Delgerkhaan sum centre, is the **Avarga-Toson Lake** and adjoining spa resort.

The **mud baths** and mineral-rich lake have been used for centuries as a spa. Each year, in August, dozens of *gers* and tents appear along its shores. The **resort** here offers cabins and meals at local rates, but is geared mostly for Mongolians on holiday. A more upscale option is the **Ondor Givant** *ger* camp ($30 per person), eight kilometres west of the resort. **Camping** spots are plentiful.

## FORTRESS OF CHINGGIS KHAAN

The **remains of fortifications** extend for some 600 kilometres, from Bayan-Adraga sum to the Gan River in Manchuria. Locals in the region call them the 'Fortress of Chinggis Khaan'. Unfortunately, almost nothing remains of these 800 year old walls, most of it was destroyed after the fall of the Mongol Yuan dynasty in 1368. Travellers in northern Khentii and Dornod may pass this wall in different areas; the map in this book on p. 215 shows the direction the wall follows. The area just south of this fortification is called the 'path of Chinggis Khaan's horses'.

# Other archaeological and cultural sites

## STONE SLAB TOMBS AND MAN STONES

Stone tombs are particularly numerous in the province of Khentii and examples can be found in several sums. Travellers will need a guide to track them down, but there are a few places to start, including **Batshireet sum**, at Barkhan and in the Upper Onon (in the northern part of Khentii), **Ölziit sum** at Deed Ölziit (north-west of Öndörkhaan), and on the left bank of the Kherlen and at **Bayan-Ulaan** (west of Öndörkhaan). **Man stones** have been found at several locations across Khentii. In **Batshireet sum**, by the northern branch of the Egiin Gol, at the end of the Jivkhistei Valley, are five statues. Just north of this site is a small, square funerary complex in stone. In front of the figures is a line of *balbal* stones facing south-east. Other figures have been found in central Khentii and in the southern part of the province. The museum in Öndörkhaan can provide more details on the specific location of ancient sites.

## BALDAN BERAIVAN KHIID

The ruins of this monastery, the hidden gem of Khentii Aimag, are located in a remote area in **Ömnödelger sum** near the Jargalant River. The monastery was established in the 17th century by a lama named Tsevendorj, who was given orders to build it from Zanabazar. At first the monastery consisted of *gers*, and was moved eight times before finally settling at its current location during the Manchu period. It became one of the most important temple complexes in the country, and housed 3,000 monks at its height.

The complex included a *datsan* (faculty) specialised in the training of architects, painters and sculptors. The main temple, called Dash Zepelen, was a huge stone building that had 64 doors, 164 pillars and 30 windows. The last *ger*-temples were set up in 1910.

There is more to see here in comparison to the other ruined monasteries in Mongolia. Most of the main building is still in tact and restoration work is underway to bring the facilities to working order. The restoration work is headed by the Cultural Restoration Tourism Project (CRTP), which has a US office and sends volunteers to help at the project site in the summer (until 2005). For more information on this, visit the informative CRTP website: www.home.earthlink.net/~crtp/

# Sükhbaatar

Created in 1941 and located in the eastern part of Mongolia, this province is named after the founder of the Mongol People's Revolutionary Party. This is the fief of the Dariganga people, who originally came from the south-eastern part of the province.

Most of the province, at an altitude between 1,000 and 1,200 metres, is made up of flat, treeless steppe. The Kerülen (Kherlen) River flows along the north border of the province. In the south are vast stretches of sand. The **sands of Moltsog** extend for some 80 kilometres, and surround a few lakes, such as Ganga Nuur. This part of the province is rugged and volcanic. Ancient volcanic eruptions have left lava flows over some 10,000 square kilometres of territory. The highest peak in the province, Shiliin Bogd (1,777 m), is about 10 kilometres from the Chinese border.

Vast numbers of white-tailed gazelle (*Tsagaan zeer*) can be spotted in this province, particularly in the **Ushig steppe** (in the far east of the aimag). The economy is for the most part dependent on livestock breeding, with sheep accounting for 70 per cent of the herds, but there are also coal, iron, and zinc mines, and some light industry such as saw mills.

## BARUUN URT

There is little to say about this unattractive town of 18,000 inhabitants, located 190 kilometres south-west of Choibalsan and 557 kilometres from Ulaanbaatar. Baruun Urt (981 m) features a small town square dominated by the revolutionary hero Sükhbaatar riding a horse. This one is less dynamic than his statue in Ulaanbaatar. A few shops and a couple of hotels are nearby, but there is no town market.

**Erdenmandal Khiid** (monastery) was founded in 1991 as a *ger*-temple. The following year, permanent buildings were constructed. The old monastery of Mandal, destroyed in 1938, was 20 kilometres from this new site. It had seven temples and could accommodate 1,000 monks. Nothing remains of it except two statues from the main hall that have been placed in the new buildings. Before the purge of the 1930s there were many monastic complexes in this aimag, including those of Egüder, Ovoono, and Mandal.

The **museum** is interesting for its local silver jewellery. There is also a Dariganga *ger* on display, which, unlike other Mongol *ger*s, has a framework of poles that are permanently attached to the *toono* (wooden crown) of the *ger*. Also unique is the stove, which is made of dried mud.

The **airport** is one kilometre south of town. Aside from the usual flight to Ulaanbaatar, some flights occasional go from Ulaanbaatar to Dariganga, so check with MIAT. Public jeeps and vans usually wait for passengers in a lot near the monastery. Transport to and from Ulaanbaatar goes daily but a car to Dariganga is less frequent. Because of Dariganga's location on the border with China, travellers going there are required to carry a permit. These are obtained from the police station in Baruun Urt (on the west side of town). Bring your passport.

## NARAN SUM

There are several **stone figures** here, the first place to look is 18 kilometres east of the sum centre. At this site, next to a circular tomb, is a statue with Mongoloid features, a large nose, an earring, and a cup in his right hand. The left hand is placed on his belt. About 700 metres from this, near a circular tomb, is another statue with a large stomach. South of the sum centre, is an inscription on a rock at Zulegt.

Naran sum is the homeland of **O. Dashbalbar**, a popular poet and rebel politician who died in 1999 of liver disease. (Although at the time of his death there was much speculation that he was poisoned). Aside from admiring Hitler and sending birthday greetings to Sadaam Hussein, the long-haired Dashbalbar had become famous in Mongolia for his fiery rhetoric and xenophobic statements. A monument dedicated to him is located in the sum centre.

## ERDENTSAGAAN SUM

This remote sum includes the **Lkhachinvandat** region (1,233 m) and **Araates mountains**, which have been protected for the sake of the elk that live there. The tallest mountain in this area, **Mount Baruun Mognor**, is located on the south-west edge of the reserve. There are several craters in the region, including **Mount Chandmani**.

The sum also offers some historical sites, including an interesting **stone cist grave** at Zun Khovd. You can also look for the statue known as Bor *khushuuni khöshöö*. This 1.2 metre tall statue is located 20 kilometres to the north-east of the sum centre, near a tomb. There is another statue 60 metres to the north-east.

To the west of the Nükh't Mountains, south-east of Erdentsagaan, is a 1.3 metre tall statue. It is located on a small hill, near a square funerary mound surrounded by standing stones. A little further on is another statue with an earring and a beard.

# Dariganga country

During the Manchu era, the grasslands of Dariganga were reserved for the horses owned by the Emperor of China. The centre of this region, sometimes called the 'antechamber of the Gobi', is Dariganga sum. The sum centre (sometimes labelled Ovoot on maps), is 175 kilometres from Baruun Urt. This is a mountainous region with some 180 craters. Many of the mountains have strange shapes reflected in the descriptive names given them: Anvil, Cauldron, Navel, Washing Bucket, and *Ger*

Opening, to name a few. The tallest and most beautiful are the **Shiliin Bogd** (1,777 m), and **Senjit** (1,599 m).

The holy mountain of **Shiliin Bogd** is 70 kilometres south-east of the sum centre. Its crater is two kilometres wide and 300 metres deep, and there are dozens of small *ovoos* covering it. The view from the top—overlooking the grasslands and the Chinese border—is fantastic. Just 14 kilometres to the north-west of Shiliin Bogd is the basalt **cave of Taliin Agui**, which is full of stalagmites and said to be one of the largest in Mongolia (200 metres long, 100,000 cubic metres in size).

The drive to and from Shiliin Bogd is dotted with craters. One of the best known is **Asgat** (1,294 m), a name that refers to the three large stone blocks on it. **Zuun Busluur** (1,302 m) is southwest of Asgat and south-east of the Ongon sand dunes. **Ukhaa Tolgoi** (1,281 m) is 15 kilometres north-east of Asgat. The crater of **Lamtin Dösh** (1,572 m) is south of Shiliin Bogd.

Also notable is the **Zotolkhan Crater** (1,425 m). On the west slopes of this mountain, where the Khargaltai River has its source, are several columns of basalt.

The **Altan Ovoo** crater, which hovers above the Dariganga village, is a sacred mountain venerated in ceremonial rites. In 1990, a stupa was erected on the site of an old golden-roofed temple. From the summit of the crater, Shiliin Bogd, 70 kilometres to the south-west, is clearly visible.

**Ganga Nuur**, a small lake of only four square kilometres, is eleven kilometres from the Dariganga sum centre. The lake has a spring next to it, is near the **sands of Moltsog**, and is part of a reserve that covers some 288 square kilometres. The reserve attracts migratory birds and includes lakes Kholboo, Uizen, and Sumt.

About 21 kilometres east of the sum centre (past Ganga Nuur and on the way to Shiliin Bogd) is a **statue of Toroi Bandi**, built in 1999. Toroi Bandi was a locally famous bandit who stole horses from the Chinese and passed them along to

*An example of the 'man stones' in Dariganga.*

his Mongol countrymen—a Robin Hood of the steppes. The statue shows him crouched on the ground, surveying the Chinese border, which is just a few kilometres away.

## STONE STATUES IN DARIGANGA SUM

The anthropomorphic statues of Sükhbaatar Aimag are different from those of other provinces in the way they are made, the seats upon which the figures are seated, and a number of ethnographical details.

There are several of these 'man stones' in Dariganga, all easily reached with a jeep and a local guide. On the south-eastern slopes of the Altan Ovoo, near the centre of Dariganga sum, are three marble statues near a large kereksür. To the north-east of these, and to the south-east of the kereksür, stands a fourth statue, slightly over one metre in height, with its left hand resting on its knee. In the Khörög Valley (Khörgiin Khööndi), 35 kilometres north of Shiliin Bogd, are two statues. The first is seated wearing boots and a conical hat, his right hand holding a cup and his left placed on his knee. The second one is about 700 metres north of the first. There are said to be more than fifty stone figures in the area.

To see these sites, most travellers base themselves in the Dariganga sum centre. It is possible to drive all the way to Shiliin Bogd and back on a day trip, but you may want to start out in the afternoon, camp at the mountain, and return the next day. All visitors must carry a permit to travel in the area, which is easily obtained in Baruun Urt. Aside from camping, the only place to stay is the Dagshin Hotel, located one kilometre from the village, near the Dagshin Bulag Lake. Ger camps periodically open in the area in summer.

Dariganga is famous in Mongolia for its silversmiths. All work, however, is done at home, so if you want to see or purchase silverwork, its best to ask for help from a local or your guide.

# Dornod

The giant eastern province of Dornod (Eastern) touches Siberian Russia on the north and sticks into China on the east like a thumb. This province of 123,500 square kilometres is known for its great stretches of flatness and golden grasslands. The majority of the inhabitants here are Khalkh, with some Buryats, particularly in Bayan Uul, Bayandun, Dashbalbar, Tsagaan Ovoo and Ereentsav sums. There are also some Barga and Uzemchin in Gurvan Zagal and Khölönbuir sums. About 150,000 people live in this province, half are in the capital Choibalsan.

The steppes of Dornod stretch hundreds of kilometres, including the **Menen steppe**, which is part of the great Dornod steppe. Although this low altitude steppe is dominant, there is rugged terrain in the south-east (the **Khingan** chain), and in the northwest (the Khentii Mountains). In the north, and in the east part of the Dornod along the Chinese border, is a superb area of forests. **Khökh Nuur** (Blue lake), in Choibalsan sum, is the lowest point in Mongolia, 554 metres above sea level. The Dornod steppes are the favourite habitat of the white steppe gazelle, one of the rarest animals in the world. Wolves, red foxes, badgers, and the steppe fox are just some of the 25 species of mammals living there, along with ibex, deer, bears, and beavers.

Agriculture is the economic basis of the province, and the main areas of cultivation are in the basins of the Khalkhiin Gol, Onon, and Kherlen rivers. Wheat is grown over some 30,000 hectares. Dornod is also the second industrial province after Selenge. Coal, non-ferrous metals, gold, silver, fluorite, uranium and oil are all present. Western oil companies have drilled for oil in a couple of locations, notably the Tamtsanbulag area.

## CHOIBALSAN

About 656 kilometres from Ulaanbaatar, this is fourth largest town in Mongolia, with around 47,000 inhabitants. Located at 850 metres above sea level, it is spread out over the site of an important religious centre founded in 1822. Before the 1921 Revolution, the town was called **Sain Beissin Khuree**, named after the prince who founded the monastery and set up his general headquarters here. At the beginning of the 20th century, Sain Beissin Khuree had two monasteries, surrounded by the *ger* districts of the sedentary population, the Chinese and Russian merchant districts, and a palace. Located at the crossroads of important caravan routes linking the centre of Mongolia to Manchuria, and Siberia to China, the town became an important trade centre.

In 1931, it was renamed Bayan-Tümen, and then Choibalsan in 1941, after the infamous figure known as the 'Mongol Stalin', who was born in this province. In

1939 it was connected by rail to Russia, in order to send troops and supplies to the front lines of a battle that was brewing against the Japanese. Later, the railway turned the town into a key trade hub and the most important industrial centre in the east of the country.

Upon first look, Choibalsan is a little disorientating. Most provincial capitals are centred on the Soviet built town square. Choibalsan was the same way until the early 1990s when the government offices and other important buildings were transferred a couple of kilometres to the east. The 'Old Town' still offers museums and a few shops, but most of the facilities needed by the traveller are in the 'New Town'.

The Old Town is dominated by the **Memorial to Mongolian Heroes**, a great arch, under which is a soldier charging to the enemy on his horse. A Soviet army tank is nearby. Across the street is a **statue of Marshal Choibalsan**, hero of the 1921 Revolution. He later played a major role in the purges of the 1930s (see History section). Behind Choibalsan is the **Provincial Museum**. The first floor features paintings, one of which, done by lama Gombosüren, shows the old monastery of Sain Beissin Khuree. The second floor of the building is dedicated to the history of the province, and has a room replicating Choibalsan's office, including a huge radio. The building to the west is the **Natural History Museum**, which includes a good collection of dinosaur bones and animals. About 1.5 kilometres east of these museums, hidden in the ger suburbs, is the **GK Jukov Museum**. This small museum gives a good briefing on the 1939 war against Japan, which took place in at Khalkh Gol in the far eastern section of the aimag. This museum only opens when visitors arrive, so ask for a tour from the caretaker.

The town monastery, **Danrag Danjalan Khiid**, is located in the New Town, north of the main street. The original complex was once one of the greatest monasteries in Mongolia with almost 10,000 monks and seven temples. It was destroyed in 1937, and reappeared modestly in 1990 as a simple ger. In 1991, it was rebuilt as a permanent structure in which more than 30 monks now live.

Choibalsan is not a beautiful city, but the hotel and dining options are better than most aimag capitals. The Kherlen Hotel is the best value with rooms for under Tg8000. The Tovan Hotel is more expensive, but has the best restaurant in town. The Sterk Hotel is a third option. There is an **Internet Café** inside the library, next to the Kherlen Hotel.

The market and bus station are about one kilometre east. About five kilometres further along is the train station. The train departs from Choibalsan on Tuesday and Thursday at 5 pm, and arrives at the border town of Ereentsav around midnight. It returns to the capital the following morning. Foreigners are not allowed to take the train to Russia, but can go as far as the border. No food or drinks are available so come prepared.

EASTERN AIMAGS

## Protected sites

The grasslands of Dornod are the least spoiled and most extensive in the country. More than 1,000 species of plants have been identified there, corresponding to 21 different types of pasture land.

**Ugtam Uul reserve**: (300 sq km) located in the north of the province, about 30 kilometres east of the Bayandun sum centre. This wooded area includes the Ugtam Mountains, the Kharkhan Mountains, and a functioning Buddhist monastery.

**Mongol Daguur protected zone**: (1,030 sq. km) lies in two separate parts. The northern end is a continuation of the Russian reserve of Daurski, and the southern part includes the Ulz River. Six very rare varieties of crane, including the threatened Siberian crane, live here. There is a Protected Area office in the village of Ereentsav.

**Dornod Steppe**: (5,704 sq. km) An exceptional site in the heart of the arid Asian steppes. Divided into sections A (the Menen steppe) and B (the Lagiin Kholoi), it aims to preserve a unique ecosystem, sustaining huge herds of gazelle that can include up to 40,000 animals.

**Degee Nömrög protected site**: (3,112 sq. km) located 420 kilometres east of the town of Choibalsan, at the extreme eastern tip of Mongolia. Moose are endemic in this area of hills and winding streams. Its remoteness has kept this area untouched, and it is perhaps the only place in Mongolia where the destructive affects of overgrazing are non-existent.

To get information on permits and logistics, contact the Strictly Protected Areas office in Choibalsan, in a white building east of the Tovan Hotel.

## Places of Interest

### BUIR NUUR (LAKE BUIR)

Located 285 kilometres from Choibalsan, and at a height of 581 metres, this pretty saltwater lake offers crystal-clear waters and good **fishing** opportunities. Stretching across Khalkh Gol and Sumber sums, this is the largest lake in eastern Mongolia, over 20 kilometres wide and 40 kilometres long. Its north-west shore is in China. Mosquitoes invade this area in summer, so bring plenty of bug repellent and light clothing that will cover your skin. It's worth noting that the Dornod steppes are reputed for being the home of the fiercest mosquitoes in Mongolia—a shame because Buir Nuur has beautiful sandy beaches and a wide variety of fish, including carp, *taimen* and lenok. Along its shores stand several memorials dedicated to the Mongol and Russian soldiers who died in the battle of Khalkhiin Gol. The largest memorial, called Khamar Davaa, is 50 metres tall.

*An elderly man walks through the sandy suburbs of Choibalsan, the capital of Dornod Aimag.*

## THE KHALKHIIN GOL REGION

Located in the south-east, this area was the site in 1939 of a fierce battle between Japan and a joint force of Mongol and Soviet troops. The Japanese, already in control of Manchuria (which they called Manchuguo), planned to invade Mongolia and set up a puppet state there. The Soviets, threatened by Japanese imperialism in the East, were quick to react and bulked up their forces along the front lines. Hundreds of tanks, canons and airplanes, and thousands of troops, faced one another across the Khalkh River. Although border skirmishes had been going on since 1935, the first serious battle occurred in May 1939. The Japanese were pushed back, but then in July launched a massive ground force. Three battles left 18,100 Japanese dead and over 48,000 wounded. As for the Soviets, their losses equalled 8,900 dead and nearly 16,000 wounded. The eighth Mongolian cavalry division played minor roll in the fighting, it lost 237 men.

The Japanese, now seeing the determination of the Soviets in Mongolia (and therefore Siberia), turned towards South-east Asia. Diplomats representing the USSR and Japan met several times after the battle, and finally, in October 1941, all sides signed a document to determine the extent of Mongolian borders. The situation remained tense, however, and huge numbers of Soviet borders guards were strung across the frontier.

The Khalkh River flows through Sumber sum. The main town, Tsagaannuur, is

375 kilometres south-east of Choibalsan. The **museum** here explains in detail the battle of Khalkhiin Gol. A large **Japanese cemetery** attracts many visitors from that country every year.

## IKH BURKHANTIIN TOKHOI

On a hill on the banks of the Khalkh Gol (about 10 km from the sum centre) is an immense Buddhist statue some 40 metres long representing Janraisig. The sculpture is carved into a block of stone, and is reminiscent of the huge statues of the Buddha that can be seen in Afghanistan, Xinjiang, or India; it the only one of its kind in Mongolia. Bat Ochiriin Togtokhtooriin (Tovan)—a rather progressive prince who developed the arts, culture and the local economy—commissioned the statue in 1864. The entire sculpture underwent renovations in the mid-1990s, and was unveiled with much fanfare in 1997.

Note: Travellers to Khalkh Gol and Buir Nuur must carry a border permit, which can be acquired from the police station in Choibalsan.

## THE NORTHERN SUMS

Strung along the northern forests and steppes are the three sums of **Bayan Uul**, **Bayandun** and **Dashbalbar**. The Buryat minority inhabit this area. They are more sedentary than Khalkh Mongols, and many prefer to live in log cabins rather than *gers*. For an introduction into the Buryat lifestyle, visit the local **museum** in Dashbalbar sum.

This region is also home to the now defunct **Erdes Uranium mine**, which was developed secretly by the Soviets in the 1980s, but shut down in 1990 with the collapse of the economy. The mine enjoyed a spark of life when it re-opened in 1997, but closed again a year later. Disgruntled Russian workers staged a protest in 1999, demanding back pay, but were largely unsuccessful.

The town of **Mardai**, south of Dashbalbar and where the miners had their homes, was abandoned. Mongolian looters moved in and stripped the town of anything usable. The private houses look like they were once nice, but the looting left them in tatters. Some Mongolian families have taken to squatting in the houses, but all facilities, including the police station, schools, government buildings, and power station, have been abandoned.

East of Mardai, in the south-west of Gurvanzagal sum, is a small lake called **Sumiin Nuur**. On its shores are remains of constructions believed to date to the 17th or 18th centuries.

# Archaeological and cultural sites

Palaeolithic sites have been found at **Bayandun** and **Tamtsagbulag**. Neolithic sites have been discovered opposite the town of Choibalsan, in Matad sum, at Lam Chuluuniitag, in the north-east of the basin of Lake Kulei, and around Bulgan. In Sergelen sum, at **Erdene Ovoo**, is a **deer stele**.

## TOMBS AND STONE FIGURES

The **tombs of Tsagaan Ovoo**, in the south-east part of Gurvanzagal sum (north of Choibalsan), are surrounded by large stone slabs stuck vertically into the ground, forming a square enclosure. They are thought to date to the end of the Bronze Age. **Götsögiin Bulag** is a site with a large square **tomb**, to the west of which stand several vertical stones, carved with an anthropomorphic face. **Sonkh Tavan Tolgoi** is a site with two stone figures. The first, in grey marble, may be a Qidan noble; the second has been decapitated.

## BARS KHOT

In Tsagaan Ovoo sum, west of Choibalsan, are the remains of three towns grouped under the name of **Bars Khot**. These towns were built by the Qidan and were still inhabited during the Mongol Empire.

Inside **Bars Khot 1** are the ruins of four large temple halls with tiled-covered roofs. In the central hall are the remains of an altar dedicated to the main divinity. Mongol-style decorations have been found on some structural elements, as well as on the bases of the statues. Stupas had been built nearby. Near this complex, one can see two towers, now very ruined.

This appears to have been a religious centre of the Qidan. **Written documents** from the period mention the existence of several monasteries here housing thousands of monks.

One kilometre further east is the second town, **Baruun Dureegiin Kheren**. Various objects and the remains of a town dating to the Xiongnu period have been excavated.

Located 15 kilometres east of Bars Khot 1, the **third fortified town** served as the last camp of khaan Togoon Tömör, the last emperor of the Mongol Yuan dynasty who settled here after being driven from China.

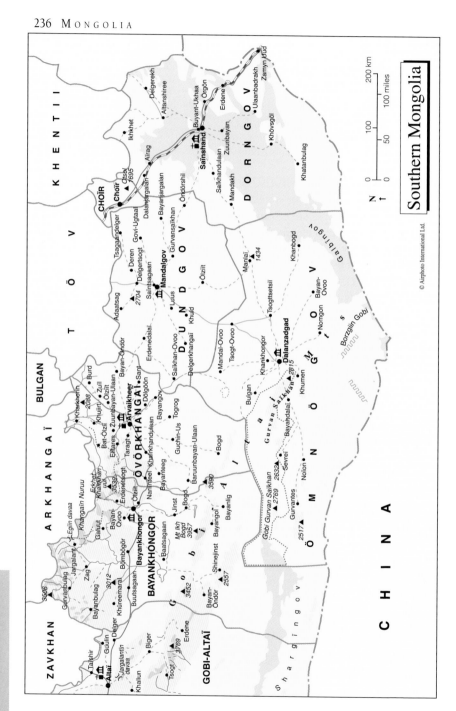

GOBI AIMAGS

# Dundgov

The brown plains and rocky outcrops of Dundgov (Middle Gobi) Aimag stretch over 78,000 square kilometres of territory between Töv Aimag and the South Gobi. The altitude here varies between 990 metres and 1,926 metres. The highest summit, the Delgerkhangai (1,926 m), located in the sum of the same name near Khashaat, is part of a chain stretching from west to east over 45 kilometres. The southern and eastern parts of Dundgov are particularly arid, and much of the province is subject to strong wind and dust storms. The fauna and flora here are typical of the Gobi, with a great variety of medicinal plants. Industry is limited to a few coal mines, food processing and construction factories. Since 1999, Dundgov has been one of the hardest hit aimags in the 'zud' national crisis (see p. 115). In 1999 alone, the province lost nearly 30 per cent of its livestock.

## MANDALGOV
This town of 17,000 inhabitants, located 293 kilometres north of Dalanzadgad and at 1,435 metres above sea level, was founded in 1942. It can be reached by plane in 30 minutes from Ulaanbaatar. It used to take seven or eight days by camel to cover the same distance! The airport is three kilometres south of town.

Mandalgov has a couple of **hotels**. The more popular is the Mandalgov Hotel at the eastern corner of the square. The **museum** prides itself on its 17th-century bronze Buddha made by the great Zanabazar. **Dashgiimpeliin Khiid**, is a new monastery in the northern part of town.

The town has a **monument dedicated to** "Soviet-Mongol friendship", at the top of a hill called Mandaliin Khar Ovoo, north of the central square, from which one can have a good view over Mandalgov.

## Protected areas

Dundgov includes part of what is known as the 'great Dornod steppe', which stretches over the three provinces of Sükhbaatar, Dundgov, and Dornod.

### THE TOGOO SPRING
This cold water spring 34 kilometres south-east of Mandalgov is surrounded by extinct volcanoes, notably the Togoo, Bayan, Borogchin and Suman craters.

## TSAGAAN SUVRAG (WHITE STUPA)

This is the name of a white limestone rock, in Ölziit sum (far south of the province), about 30 metres tall and shaped strangely as a result of wind and water erosion. From afar, it can be mistaken for the ruins of an old city. Locals have long venerated this mountain, and have so much fear and respect for it that they refrain from saying its real name. They call it 'Tsagaan Khairkhan', the 'White Darling'.

Years ago, when an earthquake shook the area around Mounts Ikh Bogd and Bag Bogd in Bayankhongor Aimag, the eastern part of the White Stupa collapsed. So great was this rock fall that the enormous cloud of white dust that rose from the ground completely blocked the horizon for three days. This area is rich in marine fossils as a huge inland sea once covered it.

In 2000, researchers in Ölziit sum found a Has symbol carved on a rock, which they believe dates back 5,000 years to the Bronze Age. The Has, which resembles a swastika, is derived from the position of the Big Dipper in each season. It has long been a part in traditional Asian culture, and is associated closely with Buddhism.

### ULAAN SUVRAG (RED STUPA)

This is a strange blood-coloured ridge is 20 kilometres west of the 'White Stupa' at a place called Sair Us (It's technically in Omnogov Aimag). During strong spring storms, the fierce winds that lift up the thick brown dust are called the 'sand winds of Hormusta Tengri' (*tengri* means 'heaven, sky', and Hormusta Tengri is one of the most powerful Mongol deities). There are many legends associated with these mountains. One states that a long time ago, a male and female dragon, one white and one red, rose up from here. Their long tails remained and became the white and red stupas. In the same area, not far from Rashaant, are a number of rock paintings.

### IKH GAZRIIN CHULUU

There are some interesting granite rock formations here, about 70 kilometres north-east of Mandalgov. A small tourist chalet here is sometimes open in summer

### BAG GAZRIIN CHULUU

More granite rock formations, about 60 kilometres north-west of Mandalgov. The ruins of a small monastery are on the south-east part of this rugged area.

### OASIS OF KHÖKH BURD

This oasis is located in Adaatsag sum, a bit west of Bag Gazriin Chuluu. On a small island in Lake Burd, where swans, partridges, and ducks live, are the ruins of a small 10th-century monastery and a 17th-century palace. South of the lake, the Uudiin Bulag spring is known for its medicinal properties. There is an old resort near here that will open if visitors arrive, ask for the caretaker.

# Archaeological and cultural sites

## GIMPIL DARJAALAN KHIID

This monastery is located in Erdenedalai sum, about 115 kilometres north-west of Mandalgov. Unlike the others in the area, it was not destroyed in the 1930s, but put into use as a warehouse for wool and sheepskins from the local cooperative. It has been done up since 1990 and services are periodically held there.

## YARAKH UUL

This is a Lower Palaeolithic site, between Gurvansaikhan and Öndörshil sums. A human skeleton 300,000 years old, now on display in the Natural History Museum of Ulaanbaatar, was found there, along with axes and other tools.

In the early 1950s, a huge **iron cauldron** was found in **Gurvansaikhan sum** and brought to the museum in Ulaanbaatar in 1952. Local people had worshipped it for centuries and called it "Chinggis' cauldron". In the latter part of 2001 the sum authorities demanded that the giant pot be returned; alleging that the disastrous *zud* (severe winter) that had hit the province over the past three years was caused because the pot was no longer there to protect the local populace. Authorities in Ulaanbaatar have not yet determined the cauldron's fate, and it remains under close guard inside the Central Museum.

## SHAAZAN KHOT (PORCELAIN TOWN)

This site corresponds to the ruins of an important town, about two kilometres west of the Ongiin River, in Saikhan Ovoo sum (in the western part of the province). Its name refers to the numerous pieces of broken porcelain discovered there. Pieces of money inscribed in Chinese and in a square script have also been found, some dating to the 11th century. The Mongol archaeologist Kh. Perlee has suggested that the town dates to the Mongol Yuan period (1270–1368) and that blacksmiths, ceramists and craftsmen lived here. The earthen walls are almost three metres thick.

## UNSTIIN KHIID (TSAGAAN OVOO MONASTERY)

This monastic complex, dating from 1915, was one of the last religious edifices built in Mongolia before the communist take-over. Located in Erdendalai sum, five kilometres from the Tsagaan Ovoo brigade, it had 320 monks. Of the eight temple halls that used to stand here, only two remain: the Tsogchin, or congregation hall, and the *datsan* of Lamriin-Maidar, to the west of the Tsogchin. There are also a few buildings used by the monks as living quarters. In 1958, the monastery buildings were taken over by coal miners.

# Dornogov

This province of 110,000 square kilometres, located in the south-east of the country and bordering on China, is part of the Gobi desert belt. Its climate is arid, and its relief little varied. Drought and sand storms are frequent, and in the summer, temperatures reach over 40°C. The highest mountains, the **Khulag Uul**, are located in Khatanbulag and Khövsgöl sums and reach 1,436 metres. Sand dunes, at Bürden Gashuun, Tsagaan Els, and Tavan Tolgoi, stretch along the borders of the aimag, but actually represent less than five per cent of its territory. Dornogov (Eastern Gobi) has mineral springs, such as those at **Khalzan Uul**, near Choir. The fauna of the Dalai-Bumbat Gobi includes *argali*, ibex, wild ass, black-tailed gazelle, white gazelle, and lynx.

Dornogov has a population of over 50,000 inhabitants. Most make their living by livestock breeding and the sale of raw materials such as wool and cashmere. The recent harsh winters, known as *zud*, did not seriously affect the province, but it received another threat in 2000 when the deadly hoof and mouth disease struck. Entire sums were quarantined and the army was deployed to ensure that no people or livestock entered or left the affected areas.

The second big industry in Dornogov—still in its development stages—is oil. The first oil wells were drilled in the early 1950s by the Soviets. The Russians have left, but Australian and American companies have replaced them. Most of the prospecting occurs in Zuunbayan sum.

Certainly Dornogov's greatest economic asset is the Trans-Mongolian railway, which passes through Choir, Sainshand and the border town Zamyn Uud. It was the laying of these tracks in the 1930s that disrupted the great gazelle migrations that passed from the Gobi to the eastern grasslands, drastically reducing their numbers.

## SAINSHAND

This town of 20,000 souls, located at 952 metres above sea level, and 456 kilometres from Ulaanbaatar, is on the Trans-Mongolian railway line, 10 hours from the capital. It is divided into two districts: a residential area near the train station and the main town a couple of kilometres to the south. West of these districts, and hidden in a depression, is an **old Soviet military base**. After 1990 it was stripped down for parts and now stands in seemingly post-Armageddon ruins. On the hill overlooking the main town, with its turret pointed in the direction of China, is a large **tank monument**.

The facilities needed for the traveller are centred on an attractive main square and garden. The blocks of stones set at the entrance to the **Government House** were formerly part of the main monastery in the area, which was destroyed in the 1930s. The Telecom office has an **Internet** Café, although the connection tends to be slow.

The **Saran Khokhoo Theatre** is named after a play written by the local bard Danzan Ravjaa. The **market and jeep stop** is located next to the gymnasium (behind the theatre).

There are two reliable **hotels** in Sainshand, and both are usually full of train travellers. The Ikh Goviin Naran Hotel has decent private rooms and a good restaurant; it is

*Saran Khokhoo Theatre*

located just north of the Square. The Od Hotel is in the same building as the Government House, and the entrance is in the back. The rooms are dormitory style and the bathroom is communal. There are several restaurants around town—the Ergeliin Zoo, behind the Government House, is a local favourite.

## THE PROVINCIAL MUSEUM
West of the post office, this museum underwent significant renovation in 2000, and offers a clean, well-displayed selection of the local flora and fauna (first floor) and history (second floor). There is also a decent display of fossils and dinosaur bones. One section is dedicated to **Manzav**, the 'brave hero of the Gobi', who fought in the 1921 Revolution. There are also exhibits for **Damba**, who took part in the repression of the 'counter-revolutionary' uprising of 1932, and **Dambadarjaa**, who crossed the Mongol frontier in a terrible snowstorm in the winter of 1944, after having stolen 70,000 horses.

## THE MUSEUM OF DANZAN RAVJAA
Opposite the post office, this museum is dedicated to Danzan Ravjaa, the great 19th century artist-prince, and author of *The Life Story of the Moon Cuckoo*, a great classic of Mongol literature. Some of his paintings and his collection of medicinal herbs are on display. A wax figure of the saint dominates the centre of the room, and visitors are asked to leave a donation on the box in front of it (in place of an admission fee). After Danzan Ravjaa's death in 1856, his personal assistant Balchinchoijoo swore an oath to protect the works of art and manuscripts his saint had left behind. This duty fell to his descendants, and the current 'curator', Altangerel, is the fifth generation.

*The poet monk Danzan Ravjaa.*

## DASHCHOILIIN MONASTERY

Before communism, there were some 80 monasteries in Dornogov. None were left standing after Choibalsan's storm troopers sent them to ruin in the 1930s. A new monastery was opened in Sainshand in 1991; it is located in the *ger* districts to the north of the town square.

## AROUND SAINSHAND

Khamariin Khiid monastery, 38 kilometres south of Sainshand, was founded in 1820 by the poet-monk Danzan Ravjaa. He allegedly liked the spot because of a hunting bunker nearby that could be used to protect the temple from bandits. In its day, the complex included temples, a library, a functioning museum (believed to be the first in Mongolia) and a three-story drama theatre. You can still see traces of the foundations of these buildings. The site now includes two new working **temples** serviced by eight monks. There is a large stupa and a special hut that encloses the spring. A couple of kilometres away are the **caves** where Danzan Ravjaa and his disciples meditated. There are some interesting *ovoos* (sacred rock cairns) nearby. A large *ovoo* called 'Shambala' is where locals come to 'speak with Danzan Ravjaa.' And the symbolic twin *ovoos* on another hill (known as 'breast *ovoo*') are dedicated to women. Dinosaur bones and fossils have also been found in the area.

*A lama outside Khamariin Khiid, a monastery founded in 1820.*

*A ger and Lenin, side by side in Choir.*

Altangerel, the curator at the Danzan Ravjaa museum, leads tours to Khamariin Khiid. There is a very basic wood cabin reserved for guests. In the evening, the friendly monks will bring by food, water and candles. Altangerel also operates the **Tavan Tohoi** *ger* **camp**, 18 km from Sainshand. Camel trekking can be organised from here.

Danzan Ravjaa was the fifth incarnate of the seven Gobi *hutagts* (saints). Different sites around Dornogov are attributed to the other *hutagts*. One such place is the **mountain temple of the third** *hutagt*, a small brick temple re-built in the mid-1990s. The history of the third *hutagt* is confused, as locals proclaim him as a devout Buddhist and loved individual. At least one historical text, however, wrote that he had been a desert pirate, adept only at robbing caravans that passed his monastery. Nevertheless, the mountain dedicated to him is a holy site and only men are allowed to climb to the peak (women can go as far as the temple). Wishes made from this mountain are likely to come true, locals attest.

## ZAMYN UUD

Zamyn Uud is Mongolia's sand-filled southern gateway to China. Desertification of the surrounding steppes is so bad that the sand forms small dunes in the streets. The Japanese 'Green Hat' foundation is sponsoring a project to plant one million poplar trees in this sum over the next ten years. Despite this, Zamyn Uud is by far the most developed sum in the country, and the only one that contributes money to the national budget. It makes its money off import taxes and small trade with China—the Chinese town Erlian is right across the border.

Zamyn Uud has **mobile phone service, Internet** access, and a branch of the Trade and Development bank (on the second floor of the train station). There are three functioning hotels in town: the Tsagaan Shovoo, the Bayangol and the Jintin. The latter is a modern facility with excellent clean rooms and billiards.

There is little reason to stop in Zamyn Uud, unless you are waiting for onward transport. It is possible to take a local (overnight) train to Zamyn Uud from Ulaanbaatar; and catch a van across the border. The van ride costs Tg8,000 and includes departure tax. You must already have a visa for China.

## GOBI SUMBER AND CHOIR

Like Darkhan, Erdenet and Ulaanbaatar, **Gobi Sumber** is a self-contained aimag—with its own governor, Parliament representative, and government allowance. Unlike the other municipalities, however, Gobi Sumber is poor and has little prospects for development, despite being named a 'Free Trade Zone'.

It is located in the north-west corner of Dornogov, on the site of what was once the largest **Soviet military base** in Mongolia. There is a huge airfield located in **Lun Bag**, which is 10 kilometres north of **Choir**, the main town in the province. The massive tarmac is off-limits to visitors, but you can wander about the surrounding barracks, now in ruins. One interesting sight is a banged up MiG fighter jet model, tilted towards the sky.

The central part of Choir (like Sainshand), is located in a depression two kilometres east of the main train station. All around the area are the ruins of old Soviet sculptures, and buildings emblazoned with Socialist slogans. The apartments here, now mostly skeletons, once housed thousands of Russian soldiers.

Choir makes a suitable base to explore **Choir Mountain** to the east, or **Halzan Mountain and springs**, to the south. The **Choir monument**, near Choir town, includes rock inscriptions dating to 688–691, the beginning of the second Turkish khanate. This is the oldest dated monument in the runic script in the region.

Choir lies halfway between Ulaanbaatar and Sainshand on the Trans-Mongolia trainline (about five hours from each). There are two very scruffy hotels in town; one next to the train station and the second about a five minute walk east of the station. There is no main market but several shops offer basic supplies.

## KHATANBULAG SUM

At **Bichigt Khad**, in Khatanbulag sum, are interesting motifs of saddled horses, both standing and galloping, identical to drawings of horses of the Huns discovered in the Dunhuang caves in Gansu (China). Most of the rock carvings found in the Eastern Gobi date to the Bronze Age, but some are younger and belong to the Xiongnu or even Kirghiz periods (second half of the ninth century-early 10th century), as may be the case here. Apart from its rock carvings, Khatanbulag is interesting for its rocks and cliffs, 240 kilometres from Sainshand. Despite the remoteness of this area, a tourist camp sometimes opens here in summer.

## MANDAKH SUM

Western Dornogov Aimag is not frequently visited, but has a few sights. The most significant are the ruins of Olgii Khiid, once one of the most important monasteries in southern Mongolia. The remains are located at Bayan Uul, near the mountain massif of Ölgii, in the southern tip of Mandakh sum. The streets are orientated east-west and a large central avenue, along which ritual processions were held, runs north-south.

Just 12 kilometres west of Olgii Khiid is the Petrified forest of Suikhent. Formed in the Mesozoic era, these are the petrified fallen trunks of giant trees. There are unique rock formations here and the area is inhabited by herds of black-tailed gazelle. Another petrified forest is at Tsagaan Tsav, near Mount Ganzag.

To the south is Ergeliin Zoo Nature Reserve, founded in 1996 to protect the fossils of the giant dinosaurs of the Mesozoic era. This reserve extends over some 60,900 hectares. At the western edge of the sum is the Zagiin Us Nature Reserve, created in 1996 to protect a series of great granite cliffs, including Ashig Khorgoo Chuluu. This reserve covers 273,000 ha over three provinces: Dornogov, Dundgov, and Omnogov.

# Other sites in Dornogov Aimag

To the north of the aimag is Senjit Khad, a beautiful site with a natural stone arch, 95 kilometres from Sainshand. East of here are the Tsonjiin Chuluu hexagonal basalt columns. They lie 160 kilometres north-east of Sainshand in Delgerekh sum.

About 100 kilometres south-east of Sainshand are the sand dunes of Burden Bulag and Argalant Ulaan Els, among the largest dunes in the Gobi Desert. Dalai Els is a wide band of sand, about 30 kilometres south-west of the Erdene sum centre (south-east of Sainshand).

Senjiin Khudag, a rock inscription discovered in Örgön sum, east of Sainshand, reads "1884. Pr. J". This marks the passage here of the famous Russian explorer Nikolai Przevalski who crossed Central Asia several times, and made remarkable observations on the fauna and flora of the Gobi. He gave his name to the wild horse (takhi), which survived—until 1967—in the vast expanses of the Gobi and is now being reintroduced to Mongolia.

# Ömnögov

Although its surface area (165,400 square kilometres) represents over a tenth of Mongolia, this is the least densely populated aimag (46,000 inhabitants). The reason is that Ömnögov (South Gobi) is also one of the hottest, most remote and most arid regions in Mongolia. The mountains that cross the west and centre are extensions of the Altai, with the vast expanses of the Gobi stretching out at their feet. Travellers are interested in the area not only for its spectacular scenery and camel treks, but for its trove of dinosaur fossils.

Compared to other desert regions, the **flora** of the Gobi is extremely rich. More than 250 types of plants have been identified here, including many medicinal plants, and endemic ones such as the golden karagana, or Gobi feathergrass (*Stipa gobica*) and the saxaul (*Haloxylon ammodendron*). Two-thirds of the 86 varieties of Mongol plant defined as endemic grow in the Gobi. The **fauna** is similar to that of the Gobi-Altai, with many rare species, particularly in the Züün Saikhan Mountains. Hunting and poaching have spelled the decline of some wild animals, but you might still see wild ass, fox, *argali*, ibex, Saiga antelope, black-tailed gazelle, bearded vulture, eagles, martens, and jerboa. Snow leopards and the Gobi bear are more rare.

The South Gobi has thousands of reptile and mammal fossils. In the **Bayan Zag** area, the first fossils and dinosaur eggs were discovered in the 1920s. At **Tögrögiin Shiree**, two dinosaurs (*Protoceratops* and *Velociraptor*) were found, frozen in a combat position. At **Nemegt**, is the largest cemetery of Eurasian dinosaurs.

Camel breeding is still an important component to the local economy and Ömnögov has a fifth of all Mongolia's camels. The camel provides high quality wool and milk with a high fat content. As the 'ship of the desert' it can go for days without food or water. In recent years, however, goats have become more popular as the price for cashmere has increased.

Minerals are abundant in this province: coal, tungsten, molybdenum, iron, copper, gold, fluorite, oil, as well as semi-precious stones such as chalcedony, jasper, and agate. The area around **Dalanzadgad** has huge reserves of anthracite estimated at three billion tonnes. Surprisingly, there is also a small agricultural sector; irrigation and the drilling of wells have allowed the cultivation of apples and fodder.

A US funded project to jump-start the economy in the Gobi areas is particularly strong in Ömnögov. The project puts out a newspaper called the *Gobi Business News* (printed in English and Mongolian), and seeks to educate nomads on the complexities of capitalism.

*Previous Pages: Two-humped Bactrian camels gather on the Gobi sands.*

GOBI AIMAGS

## DALANZADGAD

The main town of the province of South Gobi, Dalanzadgad is located on the eastern side of the Gurvansaikhan Mountains, at an altitude of 1,406 metres, and 553 kilometres from Ulaanbaatar (1.5 hours by plane).

The **museum** is interesting for its presentation of the flora, fauna, and history of the Gobi. There are two hotels in town, near the post office. However, most travellers prefer to stay at the **Gurvansaikhan** tourist camp, about 30 kilometres from Dalanzadgad, from where excursions are organised. A second camp is located 160 kilometres from Gurvansaikhan, at **Duut Mankhan** (singing sands).

Thirty-five kilometres from Dalanzadgad is **Mani Khiid**, a monastery razed to the ground in 1937. There used to be 45 monastic complexes in the province, and this was the first *ger*-monastery to be founded again after 1990. On one side of the tent hangs a portrait of Chinggis Khaan.

## GURVANTES SUM

It is at **Nemegt**, in Gurvantes sum, that the largest Eurasian dinosaur cemetery was uncovered. During a joint Italian, French, and Mongol palaeontological mission in July 1991, several remains of *Tarbosaurus* were identified in this valley, including a large skeleton with its bones still perfectly connected. In the sediment surrounding the skeleton, the skin print of the Tarbosaurus was perfectly clear thanks to excellent fossilisation conditions. Be forewarned it is strictly prohibited to pick up dinosaur bones, to buy them, or to export them without government authorisation.

**Khermen Tsav,** west of the valley of Gurvantes, is a range of mountains of strange shapes, in rosy-red colours, the most famous of which is rather phallic.

If you are travelling to Gurvantes from Dalanzadgad, and have the time, make a stop in Bayandalai sum to see the **monument of Maan't**, written in the Uighur-Mongol script. Further west, one reaches **Noyon sum**, where locals can show you rock carvings at localities called **Zavssar Uul** and **Arabjakh.**

## NOMGON SUM

At **Bayanbulag** in Nomgon sum (south-east of Dalanzadgad) are remains that the Mongol archaeologist Perlee believes to be those of a **Gobi fortified town** dating to the beginning of the Hun period. Arrowheads used 3,000 years ago and tools of the same type as those used by the Xiongnu 2,000 years ago have been found there. Soldiers, artisans, and agriculturists lived in and around this town.

Also in Nomgon sum are the remains of **Shar Tolgoin Kherem**, a ruined town, to the north of the Shiveet Mountains. It had a square plan and was surrounded by earthen walls 1.5 metres tall and six metres wide. It is not known when or by whom it was built. At a site called **Bichigt Khudag**, researchers have located **rock carvings**. In the southern part of the sum, look for the 13th-century inscription at Dalan Uul.

In the southern reaches of the aimag, intrepid travellers will find the remains of the **Chinggisiin Dalan**, extensive walls similar to those found in northern Khentii and Dornod aimags.

# Protected Areas

## THE GURVANSAIKHAN MOUNTAIN NATIONAL PARK

This park, with a surface area of 4,100 square kilometres, stretches over 100 kilometres and includes the strictly protected zone of Yoliin Am. The Gurvansaikhan Mountains (the Three Beauties) are three rocky hills, the highest of which is 2,815 metres. They belong to a mountain system dating to the Palaeozoic area and are inhabited by large numbers of *argali* sheep and ibex. The flora here is varied, and includes aromatic juniper, wild onion, rhubarb, wild thyme, gentian, willow, elder and dog rose. From the summit of **Mount Erdentsogt**, one can see the Ikh and Bag Bogd mountains, as well as Mount Delgerkhangai, 200 kilometres away.

*Left: A Khalkh Mongol stands near the glacier of Yoliin Am.*
*Above: A team of paleontologists takes a drive across the Gobi Desert.*

The **Yoliin Am** (Vulture Valley), a protected site in 1965, is 62 kilometres north-west of Dalanzadgad. Very wide at the entrance, it narrows gradually into a remarkable gorge. A spring two or three kilometres long winds its way through the defile and in July, freezing into a thick **corridor of ice** that stretches along a considerable distance. In earlier times, the blocks of ice rarely melted, being protected from the vicious sunlight by the canyon walls. This, however, has changed in recent years, partially because of the multitudes of tourists that walk on the ice (a barrier is now set up at the height of summer). One can still see ice here in July but it is almost completely melted by August. Following the canyon to the very end, one emerges into a beautiful wide valley. The surrounding mountains are home to *argali*, ibex, and many birds of prey, as well as numerous small rodents particular to the Gobi. A small **museum** marks the entrance to the protected zone and provides information on the petrified trees, fauna, and flora of the Gobi. The walk along the canyon must be done on foot. The **Dungenee Gorge** is a pretty valley and gorge, near Yoliin Am.

South of Yoliin Am is **Khurren Sum**. Here travellers can find the remains of **Godil Khuree**, a town once surrounded by thick walls of adobe, attributed by the locals to **khaan Togoon-Tomor** (1333–1368), the last khaan of the Mongol Yuan dynasty. Scholars, however, consider this hypothesis unlikely.

The **Khalzangiin Els**, 'dunes of Khalzan', are a wide band of sand in the southern part of Mandal Ovoo sum. The excursion here can be organised from the tourist camp at Yoliin Am.

The **sands of Khongor** are north of the Baruunsaikhan Mountains, and in the northern part of the Sevrei and Zöölön Mountains, about 200 kilometres west of Dalanzadgad in Sevrei sum. They extend for 185 kilometres and include dunes that can reach 20 metres in height. The sound produced by the masses of moving sand can be heard from afar, and when it occurs, it is said that it can be mistaken for the sound of an aeroplane! Hence their name 'singing sands', or 'musical sands'. Near Khongor Gol, at the northern edge of the dunes, is an oasis.

# Palaeontological and archaeological sites

## PALAEOLITHIC SITE OF OTSON MAAN'T

This site is located south-east of Dalanzadgad, 54 kilometres south-east of Khanbogd sum, on the Bayan-Ovoo road, not far from the Chinese border. In ancient times, this was the location of one of the richest oases of Central Asia. Occupied for several tens of thousands of years, it was probably abandoned because of climatic changes that brought drought. Its last inhabitants, in the Neolithic period, left it about 4,000 years ago, and since then the area has been deserted. The inventory of the stones found here testifies to Neanderthal-style work.

The discovery of **Otson Maan't** has shown that the appearance of humans in the desert areas of Central Asia dates back at least to 125,000 years ago. About 10 kilometres north of the site, on a plateau in a narrow gorge, is a large rock with **engravings** on it, representing horses as well as a large number of ducks in flight followed by an eagle. In the same area is a **cave**, in one of the tallest mountains around, at the edge of the sandy desert and the mountain. At the summit of a neighbouring mountain, one can see a stone *kurgan*. Further traces of Palaeolithic habitation have been found in the Gurvansaikhan region.

If you visit the area, you will surely see the **Galbaa Gobi**—200 kilometres of *gobi* located east of the Khörkh Mountains. In its northern part are ruins of three 17th-century monasteries.

## BAYAN ZAG (*RICH SAXAUL*)

This is a Neolithic site where the large dinosaur skeletons on show in the Ulaanbaatar Natural History Museum were found. In the West it is better known as the **Flaming Cliffs**, so named by explorer **Roy Chapman Andrews**. In the same area he also discovered petrified forests, remains of mammals, and in particular the skeleton of a hornless rhinoceros, the largest known mammal in the world. Bayan Zag is in **Bulgan** sum, 70 kilometres from the Gurvansaikhan tourist camp, in a desert zone that, as its name suggests, is strewn with saxaul bushes. Huge forests once covered the region but only the *zag*, the saxaul, is left today. There are several sites to visit in the Bayanzag area. **Tögrögiin Shiree** is another place to look for dinosaur fossils, the **Moltzog Els** is an area of excellent sand dunes, and further north, travellers will find the saltwater **Lake Ulaan**, the largest lake in the province.

## THE UIGHUR STELE OF SEVREI SUM

This stele is located six kilometres south-east of Sevrei sum, in a plain opening out in the south onto the wide delta of the Edzin Gol. It is a marble stele with runic inscriptions in Sogdian on both sides. This is the only monument with runic characters to have been found in the Gobi. Until its discovery in 1948, it was thought that the area of distribution of runic monuments was limited to the north of the country. It is thought to date to the eighth or ninth century, and is located on the southern frontier of the Uighur Empire, on the direct route taken by the Turkish and Uighur campaigns towards China. It is most likely a triumphal stele erected on the khaan's orders after the victorious return of Uighur warriors from a military campaign in China. The use of Sogdian for the inscription is not surprising since after the conversion of the Uighurs to Manichaeism in 763, under the influence of Sogdian missionaries, Sogdian became the second state language of the empire.

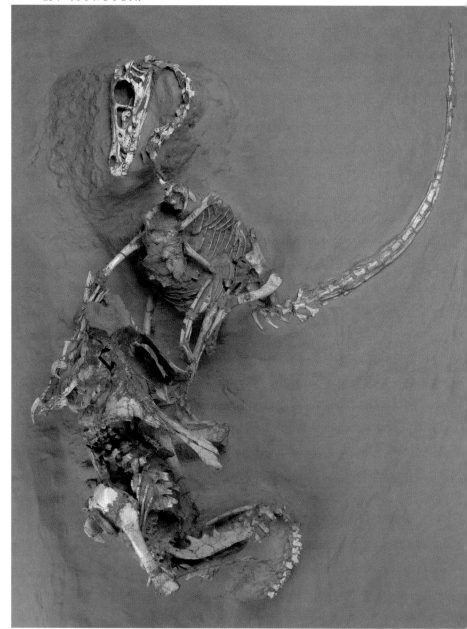

*'Fighting dinosaurs' specimen.*

# A BONE TO PICK

There are a few great places in the world to look for dinosaur fossils. One of them is Mongolia. Here I am in the aimag of Omnogov in southern Mongolia, I am leading the 12th instalment of American Museum expeditions that began in 1990. Working closely with colleagues from the Mongolian Academy of Sciences we have collected an impressive array of fossil bones—dinosaurs, mammals, turtles, and lizards. These specimens are now part of the collection of the Mongolian Academy of Sciences and are part of the pantheon of great discoveries made in Mongolia by successive groups of palaeontologists.

If anyone ever thought the life of an international dinosaur collector was a romantic, thrilling endeavour they should be right here, right now. It is hot, body temp + 10, haven't bathed in weeks, I am filthy. Empty beer cans (great source of liquid and carbohydrates—especially when heated to ambient temperature) and broken glass obstruct every elevation of the clutch; every gear change is a surprise. I am exhausted and hungry as I muscle a heavy Unimog full of gasoline barrels that last few kilometres toward our base camp,

*The American Museum Expedition excavates at Ukhaa Tolgod.*

GOBI AIMAGS

*The desert camp of Roy Chapman Andrews*

our little city filled with my stinking companions and the place on the desert floor I call my bed.

The history of dinosaur discovery in Mongolia has to be old. People have been out in the Gobi for a long time. In places, we come across Neolithic stone tools, Bronze Age remnants, Turkic burial platforms, Chinggis Khaan era pottery and coins, and the latest in discarded Chinese plastic kitchenware. In some areas dinosaur bones are so obvious that you cannot miss them. Eighty million year old fossils can be so well preserved, so white, so pristine that they look like any other bones—like the smashed sheep, camel, horse and yak carcasses that litter the desert floor. The locals must have seen this stuff for millennia. Adriene Mayer, in her book *The First Fossil Hunters: Palaeontology in Greek and Roman Times*, has even speculated that dinosaur bones from the Gobi Desert may have been the root cause for mythological monsters. Perhaps, as the caravans moved across the Gobi, their stories about unusual animal bones with beaks, bumps and big teeth metamorphosed into stories of dragons and gryphons. It is also almost certain that some of these fossils ended up in powder form as '*longgu*' (a traditional Chinese sedative and tranquilliser also used for the treatment of palpitation, insomnia and bad dreams), in the dimly lit pharmacies to the south.

The modern era of dinosaur paleontology began in the 1920s when the American Museum of Natural History conducted a series of expeditions to Mongolia and other parts of Asia. Termed the Central Asiatic Expeditions, the goal of these expeditions was to find the ancestry of humankind. In this aspect they were unsuccessful—but along the way they collected spectacular remains of dinosaurs and other fossil animals and demonstrated that Mongolia was a treasure trove of fossils.

Roy Chapman Andrews led the expeditions. Andrews was by most accounts a brilliant expedition leader

*Desert drive in the Unimog*

and a vigorous self-promoter. The excellent biography by Charles Gallenkamp (*Dragon Hunter*, 2001) portrays him as a complex person, confidant in the Gobi Desert as well as New York social circles. These desert expeditions were

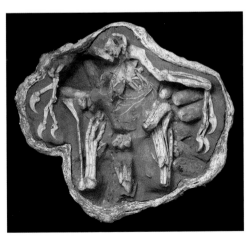

*An Oviraptor nest*

some of the largest and most expensive ever developed. From the field quarters in an old Ming Dynasty palace near Tianamen Square in Beijing, the expeditions were planned. Camel caravans were sent out in advance carrying supplies and fuel. The armed party (chaperoned out of China by military guard) traversed the Gobi Desert

GOBI AIMAGS

in open touring cars. Andrews was able to convince some of the wealthiest men of his time to shell out huge sums of money to finance his ventures. Although he was not much of a scientist (yet, he did hold a Ph.D. from Columbia University), the success of these expeditions was due to Andrew's leadership and planning. After retiring from the Museum, he was able to turn the exaggerated accounts of his exploits into a money stream that supported him for the rest of his long life.

Fossils were found early on in the Central Asiatic Expedition, but the most famous locality was discovered in 1922, on the last day of the field season. Andrews notes record that they were lost on an old caravan road on their way back to Beijing. While Andrews went to get directions at a small garrison, Walter Granger, second in charge and the chief palaeontologist, accompanied by the expedition photographer William Schackelford, went the other direction to look at a few small hills of red rock. When they approached, a vast bright red cliff, invisible to the north, lay exposed before them. Immediately fossils were found. Because of the late date, they only collected a few specimens, and the caravan continued toward Beijing. This locality became popularly known as the Flaming Cliffs, because of the bright orange colour of the rocks and the "way they burned deeply in the sun in the afternoon". The Mongolian name for the area is Bayan Zag, which in characteristic Mongol fashion is a simple

*RC Andrews and his team pack fossils into crates.*

descriptor meaning "many zag trees". The fossils that were found included a small skull of a dinosaur and the remains of a single egg—thought at the time to be that of a bird.

The next year, in 1923, the expedition headed straight for Bayan Zag. It was here that they found the first unequivocal dinosaur nests. During the 1923 season alone they collected three of the most important theropod (the meat eating dinosaurs that are closely related to modern birds) dinosaur specimens ever discovered—*Oviraptor, Velociraptor* and *Saurornithoides*. These were reported on in a seminal paper simply titled "Three new Theropoda, *Protoceratops* zone, central Mongolia". In addition to describing these animals, this paper spun the account how the *Oviraptor* died while raiding the nest of the plant eater *Protoceratops*. The *Oviraptor* specimen had been found lying on top of a dinosaur nest. At the time the nest was thought to be the nest of the small plant eater Protoceratops. It was not until our own expeditions, 70 years, later that conclusive proof was found that these were not the eggs of a Protoceratops being devoured by a marauding Oviraptor. Instead it is the nest of Oviraptor itself, which died while sitting atop, probably brooding its yet to be hatched eggs—just like modern birds.

Today tourists often visit Bayan Zag with the idea of following in Andrew's footsteps. It is close to several tourist camps and the airport at Dalanzadgad. A few years ago an entrepreneurial nomad even opened a camel riding concession where tourists could be led around on a camel and have their picture taken with the cliffs as a backdrop (and I am sure pick the fleas off themselves on the bus back to the tourist camp). Yet, important specimens are still to be found there, and our expedition has collected several. Although the area looks much the same as Andrews described it, it has suffered from the depredations of modern tourism. Trash litters the valley, roads are cut on every cliff rim and traverse the valley floor, and human shit lies mixed with that of ibex, goat and sheep in every area protected by the red cliff face.

By the end of the 1920s a changing political climate caused cessation of AMNH activities in Mongolia until our involvement began anew in 1990. The storm of political purges of the 1930s ensured that no outsiders, particularly American scientists, would be allowed to explore and map Mongolia. It was not until after WWII that the large-scale paleontology expeditions were reinitiated in Mongolia. This time it was the Soviets, using a variety of military equipment, were able to extend operations far outside of

*Following pages: the dinosaur hunters fling up some Gobi sand as they inspect a fossil site.*

GOBI AIMAGS

the relatively pacific areas explored by Andrews. In one of these areas, in the Nemegt Basin they found some of the greatest dinosaur localities ever discovered. Places with names like Altan Ulaa, Kheerman Tsav, and Tomb of the Dragons produced spectacular dinosaurs like the *Tyrannosaurus* relative *Tarbosaurus*, the armoured *Talarurus*, and the duck-billed *Saurolophus*.

Following the Russians were the Poles, who conducted a series of expeditions through the 1960s and 1970s called the 'Polish-Mongolian expeditions'. Under the leadership of Zofia Kielan Jaworska, these expeditions collected many new kinds of dinosaurs and their mammalian and lizard contemporaries. They also discovered significant new localities. Research on these materials is still ongoing—led by many of the scientists who took part in the expeditions.

Undoubtedly their most famous discovery was the 'Fighting Dinosaurs' found in the white sands of Tugrugeen Shireeh, near Bayan Zag, in 1971. This specimen represents an adult Protoceratops locked in a death struggle with a Velociraptor. The Protoceratops is crouched, the Velociraptor is lying on its right side. The talons of the Velociraptor's right hind limb are embedded in the neck of its prey, while its hands are raked across the skull—the right arm caught between the powerful jaws of the Protoceratops. Caught in a sudden dune collapse, this fossil is a snapshot of a battle that raged between these two animals about 80 million years ago. This treasure of dinosaur paleontology is on display in the Natural History Museum in Ulaanbaatar along with other fossils collected by Soviet, Mongolian and Polish palaeontologists.

For over a decade my colleagues and I have been patrolling much of the same terrain in search of dinosaurs and other fossil animals. Much of our effort is concentrated at Ukhaa Tolgod, which we discovered in 1993. One would like to think that careful planning and perseverance were needed to make such discoveries, but Ukhaa, like the Flaming Cliffs was discovered as much by happenstance as it was by skill. In fact we had driven by the place on a number of occasions, when one day in 1993, with our caravan mired in the sand, we decided to take a short look. After only a few minutes we knew it was he best place we had ever seen. This locality has become one of the greatest localities for dinosaur remains in the world, in one of the greatest areas to find dinosaurs on the planet. So far we have found remains of hundreds of dinosaurs and as importantly thousands of specimens of mammals and lizards that lived with them.

At Ukhaa Tolgod we have discovered the remains of an animal we named

Citipati—a close relative to *Oviraptor* (Citipati is the Tibetan protector of the funeral pyre). In addition to beautiful Citipati specimens, we have found animals sitting atop nests brooding them, and even embryos. What does this tell us? A few things—one, because the animals were sitting atop their nests in the same fashion as birds we can determine that the behaviour of nesting that we see in today's birds has a history that extends well into the dinosaurian ancestors of our fluffy friends.

What accounts for this great preservation? Usually when an animal dies or has been killed, the carcass is scavenged and the skeletons disarticulated. It is a rare occurrence for such fossils to be buried quickly—usually in a stream or river—and preserved. At some Mongolian sites something else happened that suggests that the animals were buried alive. Geological evidence tells us that Ukhaa Tolgod, the Flaming Cliffs and perhaps Tugrugeen Shireeh the landscape of 80 million years ago was one of large, sparsely vegetated, sand dunes occasionally dissected by ephemeral ponds and rivers. The sand that made up these dunes had a peculiar quality so that it soaked up water, and the sediment that the dunes lay on was not porous. If enough rain fell the dunes became saturated, and just like sand castles built too close to the water— the dunes catastrophically liquefied, running out as a large debris flow. This flow captured all in its wake—burying animals on their nests, fighting, in their burrows and perhaps even in social groups.

The history of dinosaur excavation in Mongolia is a not even a century old. Compared to most other continental areas, only a handful of expeditions have been active. The locality of Ukhaa Tolgod was a great discovery, yet we are still out here looking for the next place. Each year we follow a familiar route—out from Ulaanbaatar, across the steppe and into the desert. The places to look are expansive and palaeontologists have just scratched the surface. There is much to do. Undoubtedly the next hundred years will completely change our contemporary view.

By Mark Norell (far right), *Chairperson of the Division of Palaeontology at the American Museum of Natural History in New York. Photographs by Mick Ellison.*

GOBI AIMAGS

# Bayankhongor

The province of Bayankhongor, east of the Gobi-Altai, borders onto China in the south. This is the second largest aimag Mongolia with a surface area of 116,000 square kilometres and a population of 90,000 inhabitants. Locally known as the 'Land of three belts', it is a plateau crossed by three mountain chains. The **Gobi-Altai chain**, in the centre of the province, includes the Ikh Bogd Mountains, which reach 3,957 metres. In the north lies the **Khangai chain**, which is crossed by many rivers including the **Baidrag Gol**. The **Tsagaan Bogd Mountains** lie in the south, these reach 2,480 metres. The province has a surprising number of lakes, given the arid climate. The largest is **Böön Tsagaan**, in the depression that separates the Khangai and the Gobi-Altai.

Part of the **Great Gobi Reserve** belongs to Bayankhongor Aimag. The fauna here is varied; the mountains are the home of ibex, *argali*, snow leopards, lynx, musk deer, wild boar, beavers, and birds of prey. The plains are the domain of the white gazelle, the black-tailed gazelle, the steppe fox, and very rare species such as the wild ass, the wild camel, and the Gobi bear. Marmots and rabbits are omnipresent. Bayankhongor is one of the largest providers of fur in the country, in particular marmot skins.

Bayankhongor has significant mineral deposits, including gold, which was first exploited in the 1940s by the Soviets. Mining operations are currently active in Bayan Ovoo sum, north-east of the aimag capital. Mineralogists report that the aimag is also rich in copper, iron, tungsten, molybdenum, precious and semi-precious stones such as turquoise, lapis-lazuli, and marble. In 1990, platinum, iridium, and osmium were discovered.

Bayankhongor was hit hard by the series of brutal winters that began in 1999. The three sums of Gurvanbulag, Jargalant and Zag suffered huge losses of livestock after deep snows blanketed pastureland. During the first winter, scores of herders, the strongest of each family, were forced to leave home with their animals, and trek north to the safe valleys in Arkhangai Aimag. Witnesses to the mass migration reported seeing thousands of dead animals en route. The aimag is slowly recovering, but the fate of hundreds of herding families, bankrupted by their losses, is still precarious.

## BAYANKHONGOR CITY

Located at 1,845 metres above sea level, 620 kilometres south-west of Ulaanbaatar, Bayankhongor was founded in 1942 on the **Tuin River**. Its large park has a huge statue dedicated to the glory of the worker heroes in the purest tradition of Soviet Realism. The Naadam Stadium includes the **Provincial Museum**, which is usually closed unless a foreigner requests a visit. If you need basic supplies, a small market is held along the main avenue. The **airport** is two kilometres south of town and the requisite **hotel** is 200 metres south of the Square.

The *ger*-shaped monastery of **Lamiin Gegeenii Khuree**, built in 1991, is at the end of the main avenue. It took the name of an older monastic complex destroyed in 1937, which was located 20 kilometres further east.

South of the capital, the ruins of the 16th century **Tuin Khiid** (monastery) are located at the point where the Tuin and Shargaliuut rivers merge, near a small artificial lake.

## ERDENESOGT SUM

**Mount Dösh Tolgoi**, an extinct volcano in Erdenetsogt sum (north of the aimag capital), has a crater 150 metres wide, and lava flows covering more than 11 kilometres. Dozens of deer stele have been identified in Erdenetsogt sum, at a place known as Shatar Chuluu. Stone figures of various periods, *kereksür*, and a stone lion can also be seen in this area.

The **Shargaljuur hot springs** (altitude: 1,492 m) are located 16 kilometres north-east of the town of Bayankhongor, in a narrow gorge on the west bank of the Shargaljuut River (in Erdenetsogt sum). These boiling hot springs (90°C) are used in a spa (there are about 300 springs here).

**Khachin Lamin Lavran** is a ruined monastic complex located in Erdenetsogt sum, 45 kilometres from the town of Bayankhongor, in the Tuin River basin. In

*Travelling across the Gobi Desert requires sturdy horses.*

winter, one can reach it directly by following the river, which saves 17 kilometres. In 1961, a directive from the Party turned one of the temples into a **Museum of Religion**. The name of the monastery means 'Labrang of the purifying monks'. *Khachin* was the name given to the monks who carried out the daily purifications intended to protect the purity of the Bogd Gegeen.

## GALUUT SUM

The magnificent **Galuutiin Khavtsal** (Goose Gorge) is located in Galuut sum, northeast of the aimag capital. Thirty-eight kilometres north-west of the sum centre is a **stele** with deer and a snake carved on it. In the mountains of this sum are several sites of **rock carvings**.

Not far from the Galuut gorge, in very pleasant surrounds, is a small lake inhabited by swans. **Duut Nuur** means the 'Resounding Lake'. Many lakes in Mongolia have this very old name because, it is said, of the deafening fracas which comes up from them when the ice melts. A popular legend says that the noise is due to the mooing of a horned animal of a particular type, a 'black water cow', which is thought to live in the lake. From time to time, it emerges from the waters to follow a domestic cow and mate with it, thus increasing and enriching the herds.

## JARGALANT AND GURVANBULAG SUMS

In the northwest part of this sum is the **Egiin Davaa** pass, which marks the border between Arkhangai and Bayankhongor. In summer it can be crossed by vehicle, but deep snows make it impassable most of the time. The scenery here is spectacular, with good views of peaks that reach over 3,000 metres. The tallest, **Büren-Khairkhan**, is 3,877 metres. Jargalant is also home to a fine **deer stele** on Kirgiz-Khüren hill.

West of Jargalant, on a high plateau, is Gurvanbulag sum. In the north-west of this county is **Khökh Nuur**, a moraine lake with good **hiking trails** surrounding it.

## BOGD SUM

The province of Bayankhongor includes some of the highest summits in the Gobi-Altai chain, among them **Mounts Ikh Bogd** (3,957 m) and **Bag Bogd** (3,590 m), both located in the seismicly active **Bogd Sum**. In 1957, a huge earthquake shook the region, creating a fault several hundred kilometres long, and giving birth to new lakes, gorges, and waterfalls.

A **glacier** three to five kilometres wide slides down from Ikh Bogd and spreads out along 20 kilometres towards the Arsat and Jargalant valleys. Snow and ice form an astonishing contrast with the sand dunes next to them. More than 100 kilometres north of Ikh Bogd, west of the Gashuun River, are several volcanic craters: Khüren-Aarg, Shovon, and Süüder.

GOBI AIMAGS

Smaller than Böön-Tsagaan Nuur (see below), but no less scenic, the **Orog Nuur** salt water lake is at 1,198 metres above sea level, at the foot of the Ikh Bogd Mountain. It is 110 kilometres south Bayankhongor City, and although it is a full 28 kilometres long, its depth does not exceed five metres. The ice that freezes it from November to April can reach two metres thick. Its waters are muddy, and sand dunes, reeds, and small saline groves surround its banks. The lake is full of fish and frequented by migratory birds. Around the lake are three distinct zones of sand, one of which, to the east, stretches for over 40 kilometres.

## BAYANLIG SUM

In the south-east of the aimag, in Bayanlig sum, **stone implements** dating to the Palaeolithic have been found in grottoes. In the same sum is an important series of rock carvings at **Bichigtiin Am** (Valley of the Writings). One of these represents cavaliers riding caparisoned horses, and is thought to date to the Iron Age. Recently, a joint Mongol and American archaeological expedition discovered, in the same sum, the oldest remains ever found in Mongolia, dating back to the earliest part of the Stone Age.

# Natural Sites

## THE BAIDRAG RIVER

The Baidrag River, which comes down from the Khangai Mountains, flows through a magnificent network of gorges and canyons, such as **Galutiin Khavtsal**. The Baidrag military fort, built by the Manchus in 1719 and inhabited by artisans and potters, once existed on its banks. The river flows into **Lake Böön Tsagaan**, a great saltwater lake in the Gobi Desert.

## BÖÖN-TSAGAAN NUUR

This large desert lake of 240 square kilometres is located at 1,336 metres above sea level in Baatsagaan sum. The sand on the bank, blown by the wind, has formed here a veritable promontory in the middle of it. The lake, inhabited by geese and swans, increased in size significantly after an earthquake in 1957.

## BAYANGOV, NARIIN KHÖKH, AND TSENKHER GORGE GOBIS

There are good sand dunes scattered across the province. One place to investigate is the **Tsenkher gorge**, between Mounts Jinst and Edren, in Bayan-Öndör sum. This narrow band of sand stretches for 40 kilometres. Another area is the **Nariin Khökh Gobi** (or Khökh Nar), which belongs to the great Gobi of Tsenkher Nomin (west of the Tsenkher gorge), and the **Bayangov Gobi**, both located in Jinst sum.

# From Shin-Jinst to Ekhiin Gol (crossing a *gobi*)

This long distance jeep journey to the remote south crosses vast desert steppes cut by chains of mountains. It is the domain of gazelles, wild asses and wild camels, and its vegetation is scattered with saxaul shrubs and thin grasses. One of the first sights on this journey is **Tsagaan Khaalganii Rashaan Us**, the 'spring water of the white door'. A rocky gorge, to the south-east of Shin-Jinst, belongs to the Gobi-Altai chain. Next comes **Zuun Modnii Rashaan**, the 'spring of a hundred trees', midway between Shin-Jinst and Ekhiin Gol. One can see the giant tree of the Gobi, the *toroi*, which has the peculiarity of possessing leaves from several different species. In summertime there may be a tourist camp set here. Further south is the 1,160 metre tall **Mt Dösh**.

The traveller finally reaches **Ekhiin Gol**, the name of a river as well as an oasis 17 kilometres long and five kilometres wide. It is located at the edge of the Great Gobi where fruit, vegetables, and seeds are grown. This is one of the hottest places in Mongolia and also the home of a science station. A **water reservoir** has been built here, fed by mineral springs, to irrigate the plantations of poplar and saxaul.

*Sand dunes sculpted by the wind in the Gobi.*

# Gobi-Altai

A huge province of wind-swept plains and high mountains, Gobi-Altai (142,000 square kilometres) is located in the south-west part of the country, with a significant part of its south bound by China. As its name suggests, it is here that the Gobi steppes join the Altai Mountain chain. The landscape is typically one of Central Asian desert and semi-desert. The north-east is the most irrigated and most favourable for habitation, thanks to the snow melt from the Khangai Mountains. Stony plains crossed by dry riverbeds are characteristic of the landscapes of the Gobi-Altai.

The Altai range cuts through the central part of the province; its highest peak, **Tsast Bogd**, stands at 4,090 metres and is permanently snow-capped. Between this range and the mountains to the north are wide bands of desert such as the great **Sharga**, **Biger**, and **Khuis** gobis. The second highest summit, the **Khüren-Tavan** (3,802 m) is located in the south-west of the aimag.

The north-west of the Gobi-Altai is cut by a wide band of sand dunes called **Mongol Els**, and bordered by the Zavkhan River. The sands of Mongol Els continue for some 600 kilometres, joining the sands of Bor Khiar in Zavkhan Aimag. Gobi-Altai has about 20 saltwater lakes. The largest lake, **Sangiin Dalai**, is in the north, near the sands of Mongol Els. There are several oases in the south.

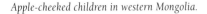

*Apple-cheeked children in western Mongolia.*

The majority of its 74,000 inhabitants live in the north-east of the aimag and livestock breeding dominates economic activity. The herders in the trans-Altai Gobi consider that wormwood and wild onion, which grow in the stony ground, are essential components of good quality fodder, as they contain high levels of protein, fat, and vitamins A and C. These factors, herders say, make mares' milk and the sheeps' meat particularly tasty and nutritious. Cross-breeding between *argali* (wild sheep) and *yangir* (wild goat, ibex) has been carried out in Khaliun sum.

Gobi-Altai has small scale agriculture. Among the crops that have been grown are cotton, apples and grapes. Further economic production is expected following the completion in 2005 of a US$39 million **hydro-electric project** that is underway in Taishar, north of the provincial capital.

## ALTAI CITY

Set dramatically on a dry plain, with high snow-capped peaks in the distance, is the provincial capital Altai, located 1,005 kilometres west of Ulaanbaatar. Before 1960, it was known as Yösön Bulag (the 'nine springs'). This town of 15,000 people sits at 2,160 metres above sea level, making it the highest city in the country.

Altai is one of the windiest towns in Mongolia, and dust frequently blows down the usually empty streets. There are two **hotels** in town, the better one being the Altai Hotel on the main street, close to the museum. If you need supplies, there is a fairly good market in the centre of town, the jeep stop is also here for those seeking onward transport. The airport is two kilometres north-west of town.

On a hill overlooking Altai is a Soviet-era monument depicting a sailing ship, an odd sight given the desert surrounds and distance from the ocean. The local monastery, built in 1990, is called **Dashpeljilin Khiid**. It is open for services most mornings and the monks allow photography on the grounds.

## NORTH OF ALTAI CITY

**Khunkher Zulsan spa**, 50 kilometres north of the town of Altai, relies on the springs in the Khassagt Khairkhan Mountains. The waters are known for their curative properties and locals come here for health treatment. The nearby **gorges of Khunkher** are superb. About seventy kilometres north of Khunkher Zulsan is **Eree Nuur**, a pretty lake set like a jewel among the sand dunes. Climb on to the highest dune for a great view.

Along the trail which links Altai to Uliastai, not far from the Taishir sum centre, are a series of hexagonal basalt organ pipes several metres tall called **Tsagaan Olom**. They are one kilometre from the bridge. Close by is the proposed site of a multi-million dollar hydro-electric dam.

## BIGER SUM

This sum, south-east of the aimag capital, is home to a **vineyard**, one of the few in Mongolia. Another oddity is that the doors on *gers* in this area are oriented to the north, rather than the south as is the dominant practice. This arid and stony region is cut, in the south, by a chain of high peaks with an average altitude of 3,400 metres; **Burkhan Buudai** reaches 3,741 metres. Also in Biger are the **rock carvings of Bichigt Khad.** Biger makes a good stopover if you are travelling between Altai and Boon Tsagaan Nuur in Bayankhongor Aimag, or if you are making the long haul south to the Great Gobi Strictly Protected Area.

# Protected and natural sites

## THE GREAT GOBI RESERVE

Created in 1975, this is the largest protected zone in Mongolia and one of the five largest in the world. In 1991, it was designated by the United Nations as a **world biosphere reserve.** Many of the plants and animals of the Gobi are endemic and certain species here are still unknown to science.

The park is a land of climatic extremes, mountainous massifs and rare oases. It is a haven for some of the most rare animals of Central Asia, including the wild camel and the Gobi bear—the only desert bear—which grows no larger than a normal year-old bear cub. Among the other threatened species living in the reserve are the Asian wild ass, snow leopard, ibex, *argali*, Saiga antelope, and black-tailed gazelle.

The reserve is divided into two sections. Section A, is the larger of the two, and takes up the southern parts of Gobi-Altai and Bayankhongor. Section B straddles the Gobi Altai-Khovd border, south of the Altai range. In the trans-Altai Gobi, the vegetation includes 200 of the 860 varieties of plant that grow in the Gobi. Plants (and their seeds) in this region are used by locals as supplement to a mostly meat diet. Rhubarb roots, for example, rich in starch, can be ground into flour for making cakes. **Saxaul** and *karagana*, or 'steppe acacia' (Gobi feathergrass), are typical of the local vegetation. Within the reserve, an institute for the study of the flora and fauna of the region is carrying out scientific research on the habitats and life style of the Gobi wildlife.

## KHASSAGT-KHAIRKHAN STRICTLY PROTECTED AREA

This protected zone is named after the **Khassagt-Khairkhan Mountains**, a range that marks the central point of the reserve. The highest peak is Mount Khassagt Bogd (3,578 m), surrounded to the west and south-west by the **Khuis** and **Sharga** Gobi, and to the north-east by the basin of the Zavkhan River.

This reserve of steppe, mountain and gobi includes summits over 3,000 metres

*Summer ger camp in Khovd Aimag. In winter, many families move their homes to the sum centres.*

next to *gobi* at 900 metres. Its geographic diversity brings together in a single mountain zone a varied combination of animals and plants. Of all the reserves of Mongolia, this one offers the widest variety of protected species. Fauna here includes *argali*, ibex, snow leopard, marten, Altai pheasant, bearded vulture, and other rare species.

## THE SHARGA GOBI AND ALAG KHAIRKHAN

Ninety kilometres wide and 120 kilometres long, the **Sharga Gobi** begins 90 kilometres west of the town of Altai. In its centre, is **Shargiin Tsagaan Nuur** (lake), surrounded by saxaul bushes. South-west of the Sharga, the **Alag Khairkhan Nature Reserve** (36.4 ha) takes in the mountain of the same name, as well as the gorges around it, including the **Bugat Khavtsal gorge**. It lies on the road to Bugat sum.

## EEJ KHAIRKHAN MOUNTAIN NATURE RESERVE

This reserve, created in 1992, stretches over 22,500 hectares and is located in Tsogt sum, west of the oasis of Zakhuin Bayan Burd. Eej Khairkhan (Dear Mother) has a strange shape and is reminiscent of a petrified dinosaur. The 2,275 metre high mountain lies 150 kilometres from Altai, a bit north of section A of the Great Gobi Reserve. It has nine caves, though none are deeper than four metres. **Stone figures** have been found around the mountain. Basic **accommodation** in little cabins is available in summer.

## SENJIT KHAD

The rocky mountains of Baitag Bogd are located in a wide *gobi*, which stretches between the Altai chain and the Tenger mountains. On their southern slope, south of the Olon Bulag, is a strange mountain pierced by a large hole known as the **Senjit Khad** of Baitag Bogd. Several thousands of years of erosion by the fierce Gobi winds have drilled this hole, five to six metres wide, 3.5 metres high, and 15 to 16 metres long, through which several horsemen could pass side by side. This summit, at over 3,000 metres, is so flat that the local inhabitants organise horse races on it. Nearby are sheer cliffs and several precipices. North of these cliffs, the larch forests are reputed locally for the high quality of the plants that grow there, and are visited regularly by the inhabitants from Bulgan and Altai sums in neighbouring Khovd Aimag. Near Baitag Bogd are remains of fossilised animals.

## Archaeological sites

Rock carvings can be found in several areas, including **drawings of chariots** in Dariv sum, and **carvings of deer** in Chandman sum, perhaps Palaeolithic in date. **An engraving of a cart** drawn by horses and transporting a *ger*, can be seen at the winter camp (*Övöljöö*) of Ulaan Chuluu in Khaliun sum, probably dating to the Bronze Age.

Bronze age **Drawings of domestic animals**, are located in Tseel sum, near its border with Naran sum, about 85 kilometres south Altai, near the Tsagaan River. A **Painted rock**, dated to between 3000 and 1000 BC, is located at Iamaat Uusni Bulag in Altai sum.

*Mongolian elder using the traditional 'fire starter kit'*

# Zavkhan

This aimag, shaped like a jigsaw puzzle piece, is in the western part of Mongolia. With 106,000 people and 82,200 square kilometres it has the highest population density in the country (of the 18 large aimags). The northern part of the province is one of the coldest areas of Mongolia: the average temperature in January is –32°C, and at Tosontsengel, temperatures as low as –50°C have been recorded.

The eastern part of the province is covered in thick forests and dominated by snow-covered peaks; among which is the magnificent sacred mountain **Otgontenger Uul**, the highest point of the Khangai chain (4,031 m). The western part is a striking contrast: there are vast stretches of semi-desert, salt lakes, and sand dunes, including one of the largest in Mongolia, the **Bor Khiariin Els**. The north of the aimag is cut by a gigantic fault, 400 kilometres long and 20 metres wide. Starting in the Khan Khöökhii Mountains (Uvs), it passes north of the Oigon and Bust-Khar lakes and continues as far as Lake Sangiin Dalai. This fault last stirred in 1905 when the area was struck by a quake that probably would have measure 8 on the Richter scale.

Zavkhan has over forty mineral springs, the most famous of which is at Otgontenger Uul; which now has an on-site spa. Zavkhan has another distinction; the two presidents that have served Mongolia since the political changes in 1990 both came from this province.

## ULIASTAI

The mountains that surround this city make it one of the more attractive provincial capitals in the country. And unlike other capitals, this one has more than just Soviet history. The town dates back to 1733 when it served as a garrison for Manchu soldiers (and the home of the Manchu commander-in-chief). Little of the original architecture, however, stood up to Soviet town planning.

This city, with an altitude of 1,745 metres, is 1,115 kilometres from Ulaanbaatar, 388 kilometres from Mörön, and 195 kilometres north-east of Altai. Because of its location at the edge of the Khangai Mountains, traffic comes here via Tosontsengel. In comparison, very few cars go to Gobi-Altai from here.

Uliastai has pleasant streets lined with poplars that were planted when the Manchus were here. It is set in a narrow basin through which flow the Bogd and Chinggistei rivers.

Uliastai is divided into two main districts. The central district is located on the west bank of the Chinggistei River. The town square, government buildings, museums, shops, and hotels are located here. The **provincial museum** holds exhibits on flora, fauna and aimag history. One section is dedicated to Manchu torture devices and chains that were used at the Uliastai garrison in the 19th century. The second museum shows off famous people of Zavkhan, including the former and current presidents Ochirbat and Bagabandi.

The industrial district is located on the south-east bank of the Chinggistei and was built up in the 1950s. Behind the stadium starts a zone of dachas (modest wooden houses that serve as holiday houses for the city dwellers).

The hill of Javkhlant Tolgoi, north of the main street, allows a good view over Uliastai. Deshindarjaa Khiid, opened in 1990 and is located 3.5 kilometres north of the centre. The monks here are welcoming and allow photography on the grounds.

Of the 48 monastic complexes that once existed in this aimag, the nearest to Uliastai was the important monastery of Iaruugiin Khuree, of which a few ruins remain. It can be found near the Iaruu River, north of the nearby town of Aldarkhaan.

The gateway to Uliastai is the impressive Zagastai Pass, which can be covered in snow even in summer. The springs of Ulaan Khalga are nearby.

## TOSONTSENGEL AND SURROUNDINGS

Located 181 kilometres north-east of Uliastai, this town has a certain charm to it with its unpaved streets and Wild-West atmosphere. The industrial centre here developed around the wood-processing complex, the evidence of this shows in the many log buildings around town. If you are looking for something to do, the surrounding hills offer excellent hiking opportunities. Otherwise, you could visit the small monastery north of town.

There are two small hotels in the centre, both of similar quality and price. Tosontsengel is also a hub for MIAT aeroplanes that fly to the western aimags of Bayan-Ölgii and Khovd. If you have just come through Arkhangai—and its horrendous roads—a flight further west may be a welcome relief.

Lake Telmen is a large saltwater lake (198 sq. km) located in the basin of a wide steppe to the south-west of the Bulnai Mountains, about 60 kilometres west of Tosontsengel. Once fed by the Ider River, the Khooloi River now drains into it. The lakeshore is sandy and muddy. Lake Kholboo is a pretty alpine lake, at an altitude of 1,940 metres, in Nömrog sum, north of Lake Telmen. It is accessible by a difficult trail from Khödrög. To the east of Lakes Kholboo and Khunt, nearly at the border with Khövsgöl, is Lake Büst, with a small hilly island in the centre of it.

# Natural sites

## THE SOLONGOT PASS

This pass, at over 2,000 metres above sea level, is on the border of Zavkhan and Arkhangai aimags, between the towns of Tosontsengel and Tariat. Nearby is a small lake, a favourite nesting site for migratory birds. Just after the pass, the road goes down to the old brigade centre of **Tsetsukh**, and just before reaching a wide valley, several **funerary tumuli** can be seen. Slightly off the road, a curious line of low, slender standing stones ends in a stele set on the back of a stone tortoise, itself badly damaged, which must post-date the stone alignment itself.

## OTGONTENGER UUL STRICTLY PROTECTED AREA

Mount Otgontenger (4,031 m) was first climbed by a Mongol expedition in 1955, and is the highest peak in the western part of the Khangai chain. It is located in Otgon sum, on the border with Aldarkhaan. Between the sum centre and Mt. Otgontenger is a little temple, built in 1994. There is another monastery at Otgon as well as several old tombs.

The mountain is approached across a stony area, which opens up to a scenic glacial lake. Climbers will need to be prepared with proper equipment, including crampons and an ice axe. After hiking around the area, the hot springs on the northern slopes make for a welcome visit. National Park fees of must be paid when entering the area.

In the 1960s, an aeroplane slammed into the side of this mountain, killing all 42 people on board. Volunteers finally cleared the wreckage in the summer of 2000, prompted by a recent clean up of Mt. Everest. Most of the lighter material was hauled away and the heavy parts were pushed into a crevice. While the team was working, the high lama of Zavkhan Aimag went to the mountain to pray for rain to help the drought stricken province. The clean-up team demanded that he wait until their work was done, and the monk agreed to give them three days. Sure enough, on the third day, the skies clouded over and the team was caught in a snowstorm.

Travellers usually camp in this area, although there is a hotel and spa nearby. It's worth asking about ceremonies to honour the mountain, which are occasionally organised here. Few cars travel to Otgontenger; those looking for a lift should ask around the jeep station in Uliastai. Otherwise, you could charter a jeep for about Tg300 per kilometre.

## DAYAN

About 40 kilometres west of Otgontenger and 60 kilometres east of Uliastai is the mountain site of Dayan, in Aldarkhaan sum. Tourist facilities have been set up here close to a pioneer children's camp.

## OIGON NUUR

This 18 kilometre long salt lake, at an elevation of 1,644 metres, is located to the west of the Bulnai Mountains, in Tudevtei sum, in the tectonic basin of the Khan Khökhii Mountains.

## BAYAN NUUR AND KHAR NUUR

At the edge of the Bor Khar sands is **Bayan Nuur**, a large salt lake in the west of the aimag, in Santmargats sum (25 kilometres south-west of the sum centre). According to an Atlantis-type legend, the town that used to stand here was submerged under its waters. **Khar Nuur**, 14 kilometres long and 50 metres deep in places, extends along the south of the Margats mountain range, at the northern edge of the Bor Khar sands. Travellers should be aware of deep sand that can ground jeeps to halt.

## MONGOL ELS

This vast expanse of sand offers good dunes along the Zavkhan River. **Mongol Els** continues for some 330 kilometres in the Khiargas depression, joining the sands of **Bor Khar**. More dunes, called **Galuutiin Els**, are located in Tsetsen Uul sum.

# Archaeological and cultural sites

## STONE FIGURES, ROCK CARVINGS AND DEER STELE

In Zavkhan, the 'man stones' and other stone figures are mainly found at funerary sites. In Santmargats sum at **Khöshöö** there are four statues surrounded by a succession of 16 *balbal* stones.

The **statue of Tsorghiin Ekh**, in Nömrög sum includes three ibex carved on a stone around the tomb that accompanies the statue. About 300 metres from the stone figure is a complex of fifty *balbal*.

There are two statues in the **Iaruu valley**, without heads. Not far from the first statue is a tomb, east of which are 14 balbal stones. Another tomb can also be seen near the second tomb.

A statue of a woman, 1.6 metres tall, is located in **Zagastai** area of the Khatavch valley, Ider sum. Nearby is another, much smaller statue.

**Rock carvings** have been identified in Tsagaan Khairkhan sum, in the north-east of Bulnai sum, in Ikh Uul sum, near the Ider River, and in Iaruu sum. **Deer stele** can be found in Telmen and of Aldarkhaan sums.

# Uvs

Dominated by lakes, deserts and huge mountains, Uvs Aimag offers some of the most forbidding terrain in the country. This aimag of 102,000 inhabitants, in the north-west of Mongolia, lies at the junction of the Altai and Khangai mountain chains, and borders onto the Republic of Tuva in Russia.

With a surface area of 69,600 square kilometres this province is characterised by great ethnic diversity and a remarkable variety of natural scenery over a relatively small area. The majority of the population is Dörvöt (40 per cent) and Bayat (35 per cent), two groups belonging to the Oirat branch of the Western Mongols. But there are also Khalkh (16 per cent), Khoton (6 per cent), and Kazakh (1 per cent), the remaining inhabitants being Torguut and Uriankhai.

The Dörvöt and the Bayat form part of the ancient tribes that lived in what is presently Mongolia long before the creation of the empire by Chinggis Khaan. They have a tradition and a culture all their own. Belonging to the Oirat branch, they were sometimes allied, sometimes enemies of the Khalkh, and more often in open rebellion against the Manchus. Their specificity vis-à-vis the Khalkh was accentuated by the Manchu policy of administering the Khalkh and the Oirat separately. The Oirat, whose name means 'people of the forest', form about 10 per cent of the population of Mongolia. (In most census' they are lumped together with the Khalkh).

The climate here is extremely continental, with average summer and winter temperatures fluctuating between +30°C and −42°C, sometimes going down as far as −50°C.

Like its neighbouring provinces, Uvs has many thermal springs. Several mountain peaks reach over 4,000 metres, including Kharkhiraa Uul (4,116 m), Turgen Uul (4,245 m), and Tsagaan Degli Uul (4,215 m). Uvs is also known as the 'Great Lakes Depression'. It includes the country's largest salt lake, **Uvs Nuur**, at 743 metres above sea level, the lowest point in the whole of Western Mongolia. It is five times more saline than the ocean and although fed by 200 rivers and streams, it has no outlet. The second largest salt lake is Khiargas Nuur.

The north-east of the province is a vast sandy zone: the **Böörögiin Els** are the largest in the country with a surface area of 4,000 square kilometres They stretch east of Uvs Nuur as far as the Zavkhan Aimag border.

Various cereal crops are grown in the east, mainly wheat. Traditionally, the Oirat always invested heavily into agriculture or crafts, more than the Khalkh. Locals also grow a fruit called Sea-Buckthorn berry, which they ferment into a bitter tasting wine.

The region has important mineral reserves: coal, copper, iron, and molybdenum. Access to the Russian frontier means that petrol and food stuffs can be imported directly, paid for by the Mongols in furs, leather, cashmere, and wool.

Despite the trading, all is not well with the Russians. Cross border cattle rustling is a part of life in this region, and border guards on both sides have failed to stem of the tide of thievery. Every year a few people are shot and some killed in defending or stealing livestock. In 1999, nearly 80 per cent of the prisoners in the local jail had been charged with cattle rustling or illegal border crossing. Travellers should check with authorities about permits as the problem with cattle rustlers sometimes limits travel in border areas.

Another problem in Uvs has been a series of winter storms called 'zud', which plagued the territory in recent years. Along with Bayankhongor and Dundgobi, Uvs Aimag has been a hard-hit province, with losses of livestock in the hundreds of thousands.

## ULAANGOM

This sleepy town of about 30,000 inhabitants is located only 70 kilometres from the Russian frontier and 1,340 kilometres from Ulaanbaatar. It sits in the Uvs Nuur depression at 939 metres above sea level, and sees extreme climatic changes through the seasons. The town is not as eye-pleasing as the other provincial capitals of western Mongolia, but serves as a convenient base while exploring the nearby lakes and mountains.

The bust of Tsedenbal, the communist leader who ran the country from 1952 to 1984, dominates the town square. Nearby is the statue of Givaan, a Mongolian hero killed in 1948 during a frontier skirmish with Kuomintang troops. A large part of the exhibits on show in the **Museum** are devoted to the birds that live in huge

## REMARKS ON LOCAL ETHNOGRAPHY

The Dörvöt and the Bayat not only speak dialects that differ from the Khalkh, but have maintained distinctive cultural traits. A particular form of dance, still very popular, is the *bielgee*, or 'dance of the body'. This ancient rite is performed in the *ger*, either in a crouching position or seated on the heels. The lower part of the body stays still and the dancer limits his movements to the upper part—head, shoulders, and hands—imitating the movement of animals or representing scenes of the everyday life of the herders (i.e. milking, herding, hunting). The 'dance of the cups' is another distinctive trait of the Western Mongols. The Dörvöt place the full cups on their head, the Bayat on their knees, and they have to dance without spilling a drop. The style of hat worn by the Dörvöt and the Bayat is a survival of the duulakh, a hat used by all Mongol tribes in the 13th century.

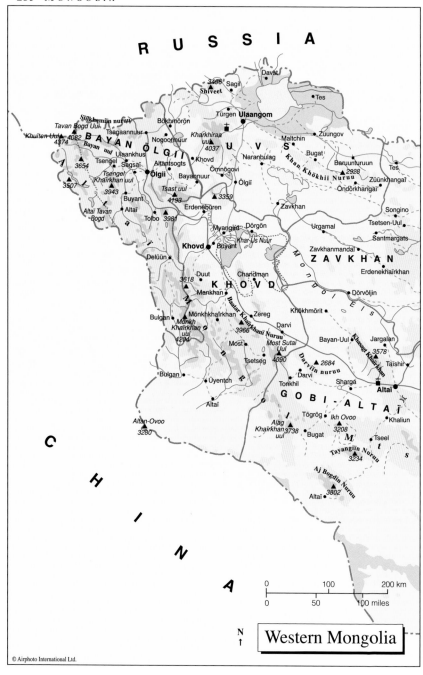

Western Mongolia

colonies around the lakes. An old inscription from the Turkish period can also be seen. The temple of **Dechinravjaalin** was built on the site of the original monastery, founded in 1757. The old complex had seven temples and 2,000 resident monks. There used to be fourteen monastic complexes in Uvs Aimag. To the north-west of Ulaangom, near the Buural River, in Turgen sum, are the ruins of the large monastery of Dashchoilin. There are a couple of **hotels** in town; the Kharkhiraa Hotel and the Bayalag Od Hotel. The latter has a decent restaurant.

## MALCHIN SUM
On January 14, 2001, an MI-8 helicopter carrying politicians, journalists and aid workers crashed here, killing nine passengers (five foreign and four Mongolian). The group were on a mission to review humanitarian aid distribution and relief efforts to herders suffering the difficult winter. A 2.5 metre tall **monument** dedicated to those who perished has been laid at the crash site.

Also in Malchin, near the Jajaa pass, are two **stone statues near tombs**. In front of the first, 18 *balbal* stones are orientated south-east. There are another 47 in front of the second.

*Two climbers head for the high peaks of the Mongol Altai.*
*Mongolia's tallest mountain soars to 4,374 metres.*

# Natural sites

## THE GREAT LAKES

Large numbers of gulls and migratory birds live at **Uvs Nuur** in summer. This immense lake (80 km wide and 80 km long) is located 28 kilometres north-east of Ulaangom. Although at a relatively low altitude, it is one of the coldest places in the whole country in winter. The **basin of Uvs Nuur** is characterised by remarkable ecological diversity—desert, marsh, dunes, semi-desert, steppe, *taiga*, tundra, and glaciers—in a relatively compact zone. For this reason, it is now among the ten world sites chosen for an international research programme on biospheres. Since 1993, the basin has acquired four strictly protected zones. The zones include Uvs Nuur, Mount Tsagaan Shuvuut, Mount Türgen and Altan Els. All the mountain valleys in the basin are rich in funerary sites. More than 2,000 belong to various periods (Scythian, Xiongnu, Turkish, Mongol).

The large saltwater **Khiargas Nuur**, with sandy shores, is located 90 kilometres south-east of Ulaangom, at 1,426 metres above sea level. It is fed by water from the Khankhökhi Mountains and is linked in the south to **Airag Nuur**, a small freshwater lake. It then flows into the Zavkhan River, of which an affluent in turn flows into Lake Har (on the border between Khovd and Zavkhan aimags).

**Achit Nuur**, located at the edge of Bayan Ölgii Aimag, at an elevation of 1,464 metres, is the largest fresh water lake in the province and also the largest lake in the Mongol Altai. Its waters join those of the Khovd River.

The saltwater lake **Üüreg Nuur** (1,426 m), alongside the Ölgii-Ulaangom road, is located among superb scenery, surrounded on all sides by the high summits of the Altai. The fishing and hiking opportunities are good here and it makes a perfect camping area. **Rock paintings**, representing animals, can be seen in the gorge of the Tsagaan River; which is a western affluent of Üüreg Nuur.

Somewhat modest in size, the **Khar Us Nuur** saltwater lake is located south-east of the Kharkhiraa Mountains in Ömnögov sum. The lake, sometimes called Ölgii Nuur, extends along the road from Khovd to Ulaangom.

## KHARKHIRAA VALLEY

This is a pretty site equipped for tourists, with small chalet-hotel and *gers*, all unfortunately in a bad state. It is located 32 kilometres south-west of Ulaangom, near the Tarialan sum centre. From here, hikers can start treks to Mount Kharkhiraa.

## THE KHANKHÖKHI CHAIN

The **Khankhökhi Mountains** form a vast chain that stretches for almost 180 kilometres. They are located north of Khiargas Nuur and the highest peak, **Duulga**

Uul, is nearly 3000 metres high. In 1905, a violent earthquake shook the region, centred on a 400 kilometre long and 20 metres wide fault line. The fault extends from north of Lakes Oigon and Büst-Khar, and crosses the whole aimag from Zavkhan to Lake Sangiin Dalai.

East of the Khankhökhi, at a place known as Khar Us, used to stand the monastery of Zorigt van Navaantserengiin Khuree, which was destroyed in the earthquake. In Öndörkhangai sum, on the south slopes of the mountains called the '33 Khankhökhi', a ritual of veneration called the 'White Standard' (*Tsagaan Süld*) used to be carried out each autumn. The ceremony included a great *naadam* (sports festival) and honoured the khaan Jagatai (Tsagaadai), son of Chinggis Khaan.

## THE KHARKHIRAA MOUNTAINS

Mongolian and international climbers have been drawn to this range of permanently snow-capped peaks. The highest, Kharkhiraa, stands at 4,037 metres above sea level. Close by is the equally impressive Turgen Uul (3,965 m). The area is reached from the Kharkhiraa valley in Tarialan sum, 34 kilometres from Ulaangom. Hikers should come provisioned with all supplies and climbing gear.

## THE SANDS OF BÖÖRÖGIIN ELS

Located north of the Khankhökhi Mountains, this is the largest expanse of sand in all of Mongolia. Geographers note that these are also the world's northernmost sand dunes. They reach 40 to 45 kilometres in width and some of the dunes are 30 metres in height. The eastern part of these sands, Altan Els (Golden Sands) is a protected area.

# Archaeological and cultural sites

About fifty tombs have been identified near Ulaangom, in the Chandmani Mountains. Deer stele are located near Airag Nuur in Zavkhan sum. Rock carvings can be seen at Bugat, in Khiargas sum (east of Ulaangom), an inscription in old Mongolian has been found in Naranbulag sum (south-east of Ulaangom).

In Tarialan sum (south of Ulaangom) is a stone figure, under a metre in height; no tomb has been located nearby, and it may have been moved from its original location. A stone figure in the Boh Moron sum centre is located behind the school. Locals say it was brought here from a nearby mountain.

*Following pages: the mountainous backdrop of Üüreg Nuur*

# Khovd

The ethnically mixed Khovd province was an important frontier outpost for the Manchus. Today it is the economic centre of western Mongolia and a popular destination for travellers. This province is bordered to the south and south-west by China and to the west by Bayan-Ölgii Aimag. It has a surface area of 76,100 square kilometres and a population of 90,000.

The scenery in this province is varied, with snow-covered mountains, deserts, large lakes, and zones of green pastureland. In the Altai, Möngkh-Khairkhan Mountain reaches 4,362 metres, making it the second highest point in Mongolia. The north-east corresponds to the depression of the Great Lakes, the largest of which are the fresh water lakes of Khar Us and Khar, and the salt water lake of Dörgön.

The south of the province is part of the trans-Altai Gobi, with great desert steppes, the habitat of rare species such as wild camel, Gobi bear, wild ass, *argali*, and the steppe gazelle. Khovd is a popular province with foreign hunters, who are mainly interested in the Altai *argali*, larger than the Gobi *argali*.

The population of Khovd is ethnically and linguistically mixed, belonging principally to the Oirat branch: Dörvöt, Torgut, Bayat, Uriankhai, Zakhchin, Miangat, and Ööld. The Torgut live mainly in Bulgan sum and the Zakhchin live in Altai, Uyench, and Mankhan sums. The Kazakh occupy Khovd sum, while the Miangat live (not surprisingly) in Miangat sum.

The main economic activity here is livestock breeding, although agriculture remains important, particularly in the river valleys and lake depressions. Khovd is known throughout the country for its watermelons; potatoes, fruits, and fodder are also grown. Khovd's mineral deposits are rather unglamorous, comprising mainly of coal, lignite, and rock salt.

## KHOVD CITY

Khovd City, built up by the Manchus, was the seat of power for western Mongolia during the reign of the Qing dynasty. It was built on the foundations of a Manchu military fortress, which was first established in 1718 on the banks of the Khovd River, and then transferred in 1762 to the banks of the Buyant River. The fact that a Chinese community once lived here explains the irrigation canals, parts of which can still be seen. The cultivation of rice was a traditional occupation of the immigrants. A Turkish-speaking Uighur population, which had come from Xinjiang, also lived in the city. Khovd City is located in a pretty valley in the northern foothills of the Altai, at an elevation of 1,405 metres. It is 1,425 kilometres from Ulaanbaatar— about four hours by plane or five gruelling days by jeep.

THE OLD TOWN: SANGIIN KHEREM
There is little left today of the old **fortress of Sangiin Kherem** other than a few ruins. The site, north of the present town, was built in the 18th century. It had a square plan, and walls five metres tall and two metres thick. Around the walls were the commercial and living districts. Within them were temples, a Chinese cemetery, and the residence of the Manchu governor: a drawing of the fort inside the provincial museum shows in detail how grand it once was.

THE MODERN TOWN OF KHOVD
Continuing from its 19th century legacy, Khovd is still the most important economic and cultural centre in western Mongolia. The central square is named after Ayush, a figure famous in Mongolia for resisting Manchu power and for the part he played in the 1921 Revolution. Near the century-old poplar trees of the square are the theatre, Government House and the **Provincial Museum**. A unique exhibit in the museum is a reconstruction of the paintings in the Palaeolithic grotto of Tsenkheriin Agui.

There are two **hotels** in the centre of town. The Buyant Hotel is geared towards tour groups and maintains high, non-negotiable prices for average rooms. A very noisy generator is used here during blackouts (frequent in summer). A better option is the friendly Khovd Hotel, which lacks the generator, but has running water and spacious rooms overlooking the town square.

To the south of town are the stadium and a zone of wooded parks, with irrigation canals. A daily market is held a block south of the main square. In the east is the industrial zone with its brick, cement, and food factories. The northern edge of town is bordered by rocky hills that offer good views of the surrounding desert. The airport is located five kilometres to the south.

**Tureemel Amarjuulagai Khiid**, the main temple in Khovd, was originally called the Shar Sum (Yellow temple). It was first built in 1770, 10 kilometres from the modern town, destroyed in 1937 and rebuilt on the same spot in 1990. By the end of the 1990s the monks decided to move into town, and built a new monastery (with a new name) on the main street. Before the communist purge, Khovd had 19 monastic complexes with some 50 temples.

## AROUND KHOVD CITY
**Khar Us Nuur**, a huge lake 30 kilometres east of Khovd, is not the most scenic lake in Mongolia, but is a real draw for birdwatchers. It is the second largest freshwater lake in the country: its length spanning 72 kilometres and its width at 23 kilometres. The lake runs into the **Chono Kharaikh River**, which itself flows into another great fresh water lake, the Khar. **Khar Nuur** then flows into the saltwater lake of Dörgön; these two lakes border onto Zavkhan Aimag and run alongside the huge zone of

sandy desert called **Mongol Els**. The **Khovd River** flows into Khar Us Nuur, forming a wide marshy delta, a favourite habitat for geese, partridges, ducks, and gulls. In the middle of the lake is an island called Ak-Bash, 'white head' in Kazakh. Visitors will need an experienced guide and driver to navigate around the marshy shores and creeks. The national park office in Khovd City can lend assistance, as well as details about the best spots to observe wildlife.

To the west of Khovd, the **Khokh Serkhii Strictly Protected Area** is a mountain range belonging to the Altai chain. It serves to protect rare fauna including *argali*, lynx, snow leopard, ibex, Altai pheasant, and the bearded vulture. The highest summit in the range, **Mount Takhilt**, is over 4,000 metres tall.

## UYENCH AND ALTAI SUMS

The far southern part of Khovd Aimag is a remote area of rocky desert, canyons and semi-permanent saltwater lakes. The **Great Gobi Strictly Protected Area** fills out its bottom half (see p. 271). The approach to the region is through the **Ulaan Davaa pass** (2,845 metres). The region is also home to the **Ovoo of Kharuul**, a huge cairn with a diametre of 50 metres and height of 25 metres. It was one of the 13 large *ovoo* built by the Torguut.

In the **Iaman Us gorge**, in Uyench sum, are the **rocks of Mount Khaniin Khad**. A caravan trail used to pass through this canyon, and the rocks along it were covered in **engravings**. They belong to several periods, from the Bronze Age to the Xiongnu and the Turkish period. The Bronze Age drawings show chariots and battles, with bows and axes of the Karasuk type. The Xiongnu period drawings feature animals, *tamga*, and processions of chariots. These are vaguely reminiscent of the processions that can be seen on the funerary monuments of illustrious khaans. The drawings of the Turkish period are almost always grouped on the left part of the rock, low down. It is possible that during an earlier period, this part was covered as the older drawings are all located higher up on the rock face, between two and nine metres up. Beside several series of *tamga* of various shapes is another type of drawing, notably a rider carrying a quiver. There are also two inscriptions in runic characters. More engravings can be seen in Buyant sum (at Baatar-Khairkhan), and in Bulgan, Tsetseg, Möngkh-Khairkhan, Duut, and Möst sums.

# Natural and protected sites

## THE BULGAN RIVER

This river comes from the eternal snows of the Altai and flows through Bulgan sum in the southern part of the aimag. It has been decreed a protected zone along 25 kilometres of its course, in an area known for its rare river beavers. The silver beaver, the black sable, and the marten also live here. The protected zone nudges right into China, so take care not to stray too far if you are walking here. The area also happens to be plagued by flies and clouds of mosquitoes—come prepared with extra bug repellent.

## THE SHARGA MANKHAN STEPPE NATURE RESERVE

The Mankhan steppe is located in the valley of Khar Us Nuur (Mankhan, Darvi, and Zereg sums), 70 kilometres from the town of Khovd. It is one of the last places where the Saiga antelope still lives. The **sands of Mankhan** stretch over 280 square kilometres between Khar Us Nuur and Mankhan sum.

## MÖNGKH-KHAIRKHAN

These beautiful mountains, crowned by **glaciers** over a surface area of 200 square kilometres, belong to the Mongol Altai. They reach 4,362 metres, and are located in the sum of the same name, on the border of Bayan-Ölgii Aimag. The climb to the highest peak is a walk-up, but hikers should bring crampons for walking the last section. The **deer stele** found in Möngkh-Khairkhan sum show deer, horses, bows and arrows. Other stele have been located in Altai sum and near Khovd city.

## THE SUTAI MOUNTAINS

The highest peak here, **Mount Tsast Bogd** (4,090 m), is in Darvi sum, in the eastern part of the aimag. It lies on the border of Gobi-Altai Aimag, near the saltwater lake of **Tsetseg Nuur**.

## BULGAN SUM: CULTURAL CROSSROADS

Khovd is one of the most diverse aimags in terms of ethnicity. Bulgan sum, in the south-west of the aimag, is one of the most varied districts of western Mongolia. It is located in the Mongol Altai and belongs geographically and historically to the valley of Dzungaria, an area that stretches into Chinese Xinjiang. Of the 7,000 people here, the Torgut, a sub-branch of the Oirat, are in the majority, followed by the Khoshuut, who came from Xinjiang two centuries ago, and the Kazakh. There are also a few Zakhchin and Uriankhai, who emigrated from neighbouring areas. Another interesting figure to have passed through here was the French friar William of Robruck, who stayed in Bulgan on his journey to Karakorum in the 13th century. The 'French connection' was recently expanded when, in 1999, a delegation from Bulgan travelled to Robruck's hometown in French Flanders.

WESTERN AIMAGS

## TSAMBAGARAV UUL

This mountain (4,202 m) is covered in snow year round, and is located at the edge of Khovd Aimag (Erdenbüren sum) and Bayan-Ölgii (Bayannuur sum). Its name means 'sacred white'. To the south-east, at **Salkhitiin Shuudain Zost** (Erdenbüren sum) some remarkable engravings have been found on a large rock, representing Xiongnu warriors riding caparisoned horses. On the same rock, are other riders, hunting scenes, ibex, and *argali*. Apart from the Xiongnu warriors, most of the carvings are thought to belong to the Bronze Age. The mountain offers some good hiking, horse trails and camping spots. The snowy peak is also accessible to climbers with crampons.

# Archaeological and cultural sites

## PALAEOLITHIC ERA: THE CAVES OF KHOIT-TSENKHER

These two caves are located 25 kilometres south-west of Mankhan sum, along the Khoit-Tsenker River. They were explored in 1967 by a joint Mongol and Soviet archaeological expedition. Inside are some of the most remarkable examples of Stone Age wall paintings in Mongolia. They are thought to date to the Upper Palaeolithic period (20,000 to 15,000 BC). They have unfortunately been damaged by graffiti, but one can still see bulls, ibex, *argali*, gazelles, camels, elephants, ostriches, snakes, and trees. The animals are painted red, against a yellow-white background.

One of the caves measures 40 metres in length, and the second, which has two rooms, 130 metres. The discovery of these caves was of great importance: it confirmed the hypothesis that the mountainous part of Western Mongolia, along the Mongol Altai and the Great Lakes, had been inhabited by Stone Age hunters. It also showed that wall painting was not confined to Western Europe, but occurred in Asia as well.

## STONE FIGURES

About 70 kilometres south-west of the **Tsetseg sum** centre is a stone figure near a square tomb. The face is damaged and he holds a ritual cup in his right hand. Other figures have been found in Miangat, Erdenbüren, Mankhan, Buyant, Zereg, and Möngkh-Khairkhan sums.

# Bayan-Ölgii

The Kazakh dominated province of Bayan-Ölgii lies in the western corner of the country, touching both China and Russia. This relatively small province of 46,000 square kilometres has 100,000 inhabitants and is dominated geographically by the Mongol Altai mountain range. It was created on July 25, 1940 from the western parts of Khovd and Uvs aimags, and given special recognition as a 'Kazakh Aimag'. The highest peaks reach over 4,000 metres and are permanently covered in snow and ice. Among them are Möst, Tsengel-Khairkhan and the Tavan Bogd range, the latter covering the Mongol and the Russian Altai. The lowest areas of the aimag are formed of rocky desert hills.

The population is composed of 78 per cent Kazakh, Uriankhai (17 per cent), and a small percentage of Dörvöt, Torgut, and Khalkh. In the old Tuvan district (from Tuva, a Turkish minority) of Tsengel there now live about 1,500 Tuvans, who form the second Turkish-speaking minority of Mongolia after the Kazakh. The Kazakh, although a majority in this province, represent less than five per cent of the country's total population. They have their own culture and their language belongs to the Turkish Qipqak family.

The central and northern parts of the aimag have quite a few lakes, the largest of which are Tolboo and Dayan. **Springs** are also abundant. The most popular ones are those of **Ak-su** and **Chikhertinn Rashaan**.

Like the Mongols, the Kazakhs are nomadic livestock breeders and live in *gers*. The mountainous and arid landscape is almost completely devoid of trees and therefore not favourable for agriculture, although wheat and fodder are grown near the rivers.

Bayan-Ölgii is located away from the large industrial centres of the country but it nevertheless has some small private businesses (leather, Kazakh embroidery), as well as a few brick and wood processing factories. Its mineral riches are quite important as it has deposits of tungsten, copper, and silver.

Because of its location, the province plays an important role in economic exchanges with China and Russia. Commercial agreements have also been made with Kazakhstan. Mongolia imports flour, onions, tobacco, oil and spare parts from Kazakhstan, and exports tungsten, copper, carpets, and leather. In the early 1990s, when the economic situation was at its worst, people here fled in large numbers to Kazakhstan. Although some have returned, thousands of Mongol-Kazakhs are still in Kazakhstan. A once a week Kazakh airline that connects Ölgii and Almaty has been suspended, but travellers may want to check if this service has resumed.

Aside from the **Naadam festival** held in July, Bayan-Ölgii is home to two unique festivals. In March, the locals here celebrate **Nauryz**, a traditional Kazakh holiday

*A lone horseman trods across a sunlit valley in Khovd.*

that celebrates the coming of spring. Like the Mongol Tsagaan Sar, it features feasting, gift giving and sport competitions. In the first week of October, 'eagle hunters' gather in the aimag capital for the **Golden Eagle Festival**. Competitions are held for the best-trained eagle, while women participate in a competition for the best *tuskiigiiz* (wall hangings). The festivals show the strength of Kazakh tradition in this area, reputed to be stronger than anywhere in the country of Kazakhstan.

## ÖLGII CITY

The main town of the province (1,710 m) is located on the Khovd River, four hours by plane, and 1,636 kilometres from Ulaanbaatar. This is a relatively new town, founded in 1921, with a predominantly Kazakh population.

The Altai Mountains cast their shadow across the town, which is centred on a square dominated by a **monument to the heroes of the 1921 revolution**. At first glance it appears like many other provincial capitals, with its classical style Government House, blocky apartments and *ger* districts. But there are also elements of the Kazakh culture; including signs in the Kazakh language, a mosque, and a large number of stray cats (Mongols are not fond of cats and don't keep them as pets, thus they are not found in Mongol towns).

The **museum** on the square is three stories high; the first floor with flora and fauna exhibits, the second floor with historical artefacts and the third with Kazakh clothing and cultural items. There are helpful signs in English. Around the corner (in the MPRP building) is the **Mongol Altai Nuruu Special Protected Area office**.

*Right: A Kazakh woman sets to work on a tuskiigiiz (wall hanging).*

This is a good place to visit before heading to the countryside, as the English speaking staff can help arrange permits and give advice on **hiking trails** and popular attractions. Atai, the director of the office, is an experienced mountaineer and can give tips on which peaks to tackle.

The **market** in Ölgii is the most interesting in the countryside, with crowded and colourful stalls, a livestock stable, and the occasional busker. A few sellers offer traditional Kazakh skullcaps, but if you are interested in buying a wall hanging or carpet you will need to contact a local family who sells them. The market is also a good place to hire a jeep; bear in mind that most of the public jeeps don't leave until the late afternoon.

Ölgii has no Buddhist temple, but there is a **mosque**; the sounds of the call to prayer may give you a dose of culture shock if you have been travelling around other parts of Mongolia. The mosque has contacts with Islamic countries, particularly Turkey, and some locals have taken part in the hajj to Mecca in recent years. Islam, however, is not a major force in Ölgii, and is just starting to be studied again after the communist religious purge.

Those with time might want to hike up the Khovd River—west of town—to some quiet fishing spots. Alternatively, you could visit the Mondosh Mountains in nearby Bugat sum, where researchers have found rock carvings of *argali* sheep, horses, and figures with bows and arrows.

There are three **hotels** in town; the best is the Tavanbogd, located opposite the Kazakh National Theatre. Don't expect too much luxury; power and water shortages are frequent. The restaurant in this hotel is good, but the adventurous may want to

---

## THE STONE MEN OF BAYAN-ÖLGII

Around 20 anthropomorphic statues have been identified in Bayan-Ölgii. They have traits in common with those from other areas of Mongolia, but differ from the latter by their belts, made of an assemblage of small square plaques. In their right hand they hold a ceremonial cup, with an unusually long neck. Their date has not been clearly established, but they probably belong to the Turkish period. For centuries, the Mongols have interpreted these figures in their own way, venerating those that the shamans called *uushkai* (from the Sanskrit upâsaka, 'one who has entered into the Buddha's religion'); there were both 'white uushkai' and 'black uushkai'. This veneration was continued and integrated by the lamas who spread the custom in Mongolia.

---

try the little wagon/restaurants around the market. A local dish (which you must special order) is *shashlyk*, Kazakh fried meat.

The airport is located five kilometres north of town. If possible, don't check your bags. The flights are usually overloaded which means bags are delayed for a couple of days. The Post Office, on the main square, has an **Internet Café**.

## TOLBOO SUM

This town, 76 kilometres from Ölgii, has an interesting Kazakh cemetery and a mosque with dry brick towers in an architectural style very unusual for Mongolia. West of the sum centre is Tolboo Nuur, a large saltwater lake of 185 square kilometres (18 km long), located at 2,080 metres above sea level. It is just off the Ölgii-Khovd road. This was the site of a memorable battle in 1921: after intense clashes which lasted 42 days, the joint units of the regular Mongol army and the Soviet Red Army overpowered the detachments of the White Guards and drove them out of the country. The event is commemorated by a monument south of the lake, near the town of Tolboo. Close to Tolboo Nuur is an area called **Bayan Enger**, where researchers have found a number of **rock carvings**.

*Kadal, an eagle hunter of Tsengel sum.*

## DELUUN SUM

South-east from Tolboo is the sum of Deluun, and its superb mountain lake,

**Döröö Nuur.** The slopes around the lake contain many old tombs, suggesting that this was once an important funerary site. This is an ideal region for **walking and hiking.** Continuing south from here you will reach Delüün sum centre, a good place to meet skilled eagle hunters. Fifty kilometres west of this sum centre is the **Chikhertiin Rashaan Springs,** at 2,480 metres above sea level. East of Delüün is the **Khokh Serkhii Strictly Protected Area** (see the Khovd Aimag section).

## ULAANKHUS SUM

Bayan-Ölgii is justifiably famous for its rock carvings, but as with the rest of the country, they are difficult to find without a knowledgeable guide. One of the main sites is in Ulaankhus sum, at **Tsagaan Salaa** and **Baga Oigor.** Here about 10,000 drawings on the rocks are scattered over a 15 square kilometre area. They date to the Neolithic period and the Bronze Age. Among them are numerous hunting scenes, and representations of wild and domestic animals, sometimes grouped together into herds of hundreds of beasts. These drawings are among the most interesting in Central Asia and are far more numerous than at any other site in this part of the world. The Ulaankhus sum centre, west of Olgii, is on the road to Tsengel sum.

Also in Ulaankhus sum is the mighty **Tsengel Khairkhan mountain,** a snow-covered peak of 3,967 metres. The mountain, which can also be reached from Tsengel sum, gives birth to the Khovd and Sagsai rivers.

## TSENGEL SUM

As the gateway to the Altai Tavan Bogd National Park, Tsengel sum is one of the most frequently visited towns in the province. Despite this, the main town offers nothing in the way of tourist services, and most visitors only stop for petrol. If you are looking for transportation, ask around at the tiny outdoor market.

Apart from the impressive alpine scenery, this region also offers a significant number of archaeological sites. Near the Tsagaan Gol (river), at **Tsagaan Denjiin Ulaan Üzüürt,** are two deer stele. They are quite different from the ones usually seen in the rest of the country; one is carved with an anthropomorphic face and the other has a deer's head. An area called **Shar Teel** has **deer stele** and **rock carvings,** here one can find horse, deer, and ibex motifs carved on a flat stone.

There are several 'man stones' in Tsengel sum, notably the group at **Kharangatin Bilcher.** One of them holds a cup in his right hand, with a purse attached to a belt of square plaques. The use of this type of belt, worn by warriors and made of small square plaques of silver, has continued until this day in some regions of Khövsgöl and Bayan-Ölgii aimags. Another statue nearby is decapitated, and behind it is a *kurgan.* There are several more statues as **Tsagaan Khudag.** Behind one of them is a square *kurgan.* The other represents a figure with earrings, a thick moustache, and a small bag hanging from his belt. Anthropomorphic statues can also be found at a

# WINGED WEAPONS

It's a chilly morning, 15 degrees Celsius below zero, and a slight breeze is blowing from the north. But the sky is clear and the great blue dome above cups the rugged horizon in all directions. From here, at the top of Kizilguduk Mountain, seventy-year old Taikhun and his eagle Khana (*right photo*) have a perfect view of the terrain below. Khana's hood has been peeled off her head and she instinctively scours the ground for movement: a fox, a rabbit, or a wolf. Her eyesight is eight times better than a human's and she will spot any living creature within a 500-metre radius.

There is nothing, and Taikhun slips the leather hood over the head of his Golden eagle. Taikhun looks back to the valley below. We can barely make out his adobe home in the distance, little puffs of smoke rising from its chimney. The walls inside the home, adorned with the skins of recently captured animals, attest to Khana's skill as a hunter. Across the valley we can see Jantimeer, one of Taikhun's eleven children, and the flock of sheep he is pasturing on the hillside.

Taikhun pulls his black corduroy jacket close to his body and gently strokes Khana's feathers. Then he grabs the reigns of his shaggy black horse, and nudges it forward with a few quick jabs to the ribs. The horse clambers along the ridge until we reach a precipice, where Taikhun dismounts, Khana still clinging to his gloved arm.

Holding the seven-kilogram bird aloft, Taikhun inches toward the edge, peers over the valley and sees something below. A fox. He whips the hood off his bird and shouts. She is off at once, huge brown wings rising from her body and pumping into the air. Her full wingspan, two metres, casts a shadow below that is rapidly approaching the earthbound animal.

At the last second her yellow talons arch forward, and the fox sees its own image reflected in the eagle's glossy eye.

*By Michael Kohn*

place known as **Sargalin-Kulbai** near the Mogoit region. (Not far from the Tsengel wood processing factory). One of the statues here is surrounded by an enclosure of stone slabs and about fifty *balbal*. The term *balbal* refers to an old Turkish custom that consisted in placing standing or uncut stones (*balbal*) on top of tombs. The stones represent the enemies killed by the deceased.

# Natural sites

## ALTAI TAVAN BOGD NATIONAL PARK

This National Park extends over 636,200 ha, including Tsengel, Ulaan Khus, Sagsai, and Altai sums. The **Tavan Bogd** (Five Saints) chain includes the highest peak in Mongolia, **Khuiten Uul** (4,353 m), which overlooks the frontiers with China and Russia. It is a spectacular summit, covered in vast glaciers, and the home of the snow leopard. Climbed for the first time in 1956, it is one of the hardest of all ascents for alpinists in Mongolia. The climb begins after a 40-kilometre approach route and a 120 kilometre drive from Ölgii.

Attempting this climb requires proper equipment, some mountaineering experience and good guide. Contact one of the adventure-geared travel agencies for details. Another place to seek assistance is the National Park office in Ölgii. You will need to bring all your own equipment. Since the range is close to China and Russia, a special **border permit** is needed, which can be obtained in Ölgii or Ulaanbaatar. Some travellers have been fined and sent back for not having the required papers. National Park fees also apply.

There are around 35 **glaciers** in Tavan Bogd, including the 20 kilometre long Potanii Glacier. West of Tavan Bogd is the 12 kilometre long **Przevalski Glacier**.

South of Tavan Bogd are a group of pretty alpine lakes. **Khurgan Nuur**, doted with islands, is 22 kilometres long and 28 metres deep in places. It is located north of the Möst Mountains, at an altitude of 2,073 metres. Six rivers feed it, and the Khovd Gol flows from its eastern end. **Khoton Nuur**, only three kilometres north-west of Khurgan Nuur, is fed by a dozen rivers. A number of moraines, which are the result of earlier glaciation, have accumulated around these two lakes. Both offer good fishing and camping opportunities.

South of Khurgan Nuur, **Dayan Nuur** is a moraine lake 18 kilometres long and fed by small rivers and snow melt. Near its shore stands a very popular stone statue known as 'Dayan the Pious', and behind it are the remains of the foundations of three square tombs. West of Dayan Nuur and south of Khurgan Nuur is the Möst Mountain range, which reaches 3,934 metres and borders on China.

Note that since these lakes are close to the Chinese border, permits must be purchased from the border office in Ölgii.

## TSAST MOUNTAIN

On the border with Khovd Aimag, in Bayannuur sum, **Tsast** mountain reaches 4,193 metres in height and is more easily accessible than Tavan Bogd. This has become a popular walking and horse trekking area for travellers. Tsast and nearby **Tsambagarav** Mountains (see the Khovd section) are usually reached from the south, as they are just off the main route between Ölgii and Khovd.

## TSAGAAN NUUR

This small lake, at an altitude of 2,173 metres, is in the Siikhem chain, north of the aimag capital. Slightly to the north-west of the lake is the small town of Tsagaannuur. This old Russian base, with several ruined buildings, serves as a depot for oil imported from Russia. Mongol lorry drivers come here to get petrol, which they take back to Ölgii, Khovd and other towns in the west.

# Kazakh history and culture

The Kazakh—a Turkish word meaning 'free man', 'adventurer', 'separated from the herd'—originally belonged to a confederation of Uzbek tribes from which they separated to form a political unit in north-east Turkestan. The Mongol Kazakh are thought to come from the Kereit and Naiman tribes, who are mentioned in the Mongol chronicle, the *Secret History of the Mongols*. At the end of the 1860s, part of the Kereit settled down on the northern slope of the Altai, and nomadised along an affluent of the Khovd River, in the present Bayan-Ölgii Aimag. After the 1921 Revolution and the agreement over the establishment of frontiers between China, Mongolia, and Russia, the Kazakh herders continued to travel from one country to another, ignoring these new demarcations, until the creation in 1940 of a territory intended specifically for them.

The Kazakh have retained their language and culture, although a certain number of mixed marriages have occurred with members of other tribes. Until the 1921 Revolution, the Kazakh of Bayan-Ölgii used the Arabic script; in the 1930s and 1940s, they continued to use it, along with the Latin alphabet. From 1942 onwards, Cyrillic became obligatory. Today, there is a tendency to go back to the traditional Arab alphabet. Many newspapers and books in this script are imported from neighbouring Kazakhstan, and the language is taught in schools.

The Kazakh are Hanafite Sunnis, and Islam has played a role as a cultural bond among them. In the 1930s, all their mosques were destroyed and the pilgrimage to Mecca forbidden, the last one having taken place in 1926. In 1992, a new mosque was built at Ölgii, and the first official *Hajj* (pilgrimage to Mecca) was carried out, after an interruption of 66 years, with financial help from the World Muslim League and the Saudi Hajj Ministry.

The Kazakh are the heirs to the old traditions of Turko-Mongol falconry, and they have maintained their traditional crafts. For centuries, they have made felt carpets decorated with geometric, zoomorphic, or cosmogonic motifs, the most popular of which are the "ram's horns". The Kazakh felt carpet is similar in technique and decoration to those that have been discovered in the Pazyryk *kurgan* (Altai). Today, there are many small family businesses in Bayan-Ölgii producing Kazakh leather and embroidery.

## HUNTING WITH EAGLES

The tradition of hunting with eagles has existed for 2000 years and is still going strong among the Mongol Kazakh.

When a Kazakh has managed to capture an eagle, a special celebration is held during which the elders, or Aksakal, recite poems of praise while the older women cover the wings of the bird in owl feathers; the owl is considered a sacred bird because of its sharp vision and its hunting skills, and is a symbol of strength and bravery to the Kazakh. Its feathers are believed to bring good fortune; thus the hats of unmarried girls are decorated with owl feathers in hopes of attracting a suitor.

Training an eagle is a long and serious business. The bird must first of all learn to stay perched on a piece of wood, its head covered by a hood that prevents it from seeing. Then, it must learn to fly and to return to its master when called. It is taught to catch small animal skins (fox or rabbit). Next it is swung on a rope for hours on end to get it used to the horse's gallop. Only the female birds—stronger and more aggressive than the males—are used for hunting.

She will live in her owners' home like a pet, but is somehow regarded as a part of the family, as she brings luck. A good eagle will catch up to 50 animals in one season. During communism the Kazakhs had to turn nearly all their scoop over to the authorities, nowadays they can keep the skins or sell them for profit. In this way, there has been a sort of revitalization of the sport since 1990. At the age of about eight or ten, the eagle is returned to the wild so that she can find a mate.

## MUSIC

*"When you are born, the sound of music opens the door to the world; when you die, music will accompany you to your tomb."* Kazakh saying

For the Kazakh, music was as important as horse breeding. They have their own epic tradition—the Kazakh or Kirghiz epic cycle of Er-Töshtük—and specific musical instruments, the most popular of which is the *dombra*, a two-stringed instrument made of pinewood, in the shape of a large soup ladle. Singers of ballads, the **aken**, are both poets and musicians, and played an important role in society; in the old days, the aken even had the power to arbitrate in inter-tribal disputes by singing and playing the **dombra**. All the large festive gatherings generally end with a **dombra** performance, played in solo and then followed by the singers, both men and women.

## FOOD

The Kazakh eat a variety of meat dishes, either dried or smoked horse and sheep. Their national dish is the **besparmak**, boiled horse or sheep served with large noodles and eaten with the fingers. Besparmak means 'five fingers' in Kazakh. *Baoursak* is a dish of small pieces of noodle fried in lard.

## THE NAURYZ FESTIVAL

Nauryz had been banned for forty years, so it was with great joy when the officials in Ulaanbaatar allowed the Kazakhs to reclaim this great festival. Nauryz (the Persian *Noruz*) marks the first month of the New Year in the lunar calendar and is held in March with feasts and sporting events.

*For the Kazakhs, hunting with eagles is a family affair.*
*This is how the traditions have been passed on through the generations.*

# Recommended Reading

## Art

Bartholomew Terese and Berger Patricia, *Mongolia: the Legacy of Chinggis Khan*, exhibition catalogue, Asian Art Museum, San Francisco 1995
Kessler A. and Kellser A., *Empires Beyond the Great Wall: The Heritage of Genghis Khan*, University of Washington Press 1997

## Guides

Mayhew Bradley, *Mongolia*, Lonely Planet 2001
Shagdar Sh. *Fifty Routes Through Mongolia.*

## History & Culture

Beall Cynthia and Goldstein Melvyn, *The Changing World of Mongolia's Nomads*, University of California Press 1994
Chambers James, *Genghis Khan*, Sutton Publishing 1999
Christian David, *A History of Russia, Central Asia and Mongolia: Inner Eurasia from Prehistory to the Mongol Empire* (History of the World , Vol 1), Blackwell Pub, 1999
Gallenkamp, Charles, *Dragon Hunter: Roy Chapman Andrews and the Central Asiatic Expeditions*, Viking Press, 2001
Grousset René, *The Empire of the Steppes: A History of Central Asia*, Rutgers Univ Press 1999
Kahn Paul, *Secret History of the Mongols: The Origin of Chingis Khan*, Cheng & Tsui Company; 1999
Kotkin S and Elleman B eds., *Mongolia in the Twentieth Century: Landlocked Cosmopolitan*, M.E. Sharpe 1999
Morgan David, *The Mongols* (Peoples of Europe), Blackwell Pub, 1990
Nicolle David, *Attila and the Nomad Hordes: Warfare on the Eurasian Steppes 4th-12th Centuries*, (Elite Series, No. 30), Osprey Pub Co 1998
Ratchnevsky Paul, *Genghis Khan: His Life and Legacy*, Blackwell Pub 1993
Rossabi Morris, *Khubilai Khan*: His Life and Times, California Univ Press 1990
Thompson E. and Heather Peter, *The Huns* (Peoples of Europe Series), Blackwell Pub, 1999

# Travel

Allen Benedict, *Edge of Blue Heaven: A Journey Through Mongolia*, Robson Book Ltd 1999

Becker Jasper, *The Lost Country: Mongolia Revealed*, Sceptre 1999

Croner Don, *Travels in Northern Mongolia*, Polar Star Publications 1999

Da Pian del Carpino, *The Story of the Mongols whom we call the Tartars: Friar Giovanni Di Plano Carpini's Account of his Travels*, Caso A. ed., Branden Publishing Co 1996

Defrancis John, *In the Footsteps of Genghis Khan*, Univ of Hawaii Press 1993

Huc René-Evariste, *Travels in Tartary, Tibet and China* (1884-1846), 2 vols, South Asia Books 1988

Lawless Jill, *Wild East: The New Mongolia*, ECW Press 2000

Man John, *Gobi: Tracking the Desert*, Yale UP 1999

# Literature

Metternich Hilary ed., *Mongolian Folktales*, Avery Press 1996

Yep Laurence, *The Khan's Daughter: A Mongolian Folktale*, Scholastic Trade 1997

# Religion

Balzer Marjorie, *Shamanic Worlds: Rituals and Lore of Siberia and Central Asia*, M.E. Sharpe 1997

Bokar Rinpoche, *Tara The Feminine Divine*, ClearPoint Press 1999

Foltz Richard, *Religions of the Silk Road: Overland Trade and Cultural Exchange from Antiquity to the Fifteenth Century*, St Martin's Press 1999

Heissig Walter, *The Religions of Mongolia*, Kegan Paul 2000

Powers John, *Introduction to Tibetan Buddhism*, Snow Lion 1995

Stewart J., *Riding Windhorses: A Journey into the Heart of Mongolian Shamanism*, Destiny Books 2000

Tucci Giuseppe, *The Religions of Tibet*, California Univ Press 1988

# Natural history

Novacek Michael, *Dinosaurs of the Flaming Cliffs*, Anchor 1997

Steinhauer-Burkart Bernd, *Gobi Gurvansaikhan National Park*, Selbstverlag Dr. Bernd Steinhauer-Burkart 1999

# Language

Bat-Ireediu J. and Sanders A., *Mongolian Phrasebook* (Lonely Planet Language Survival Kit), Lonely Planet 1995

# Photography books

Dehau Etienne, *Terre mongole*, éditions Amez, 1994
Sermier Claire and Dehau Etienne, *La Vallée du Grand Ciel*, Vents de Sable, 2000

*A mother and daughter tightly wrapped in traditional dels.*

# News

For daily on-line news briefs, check the Montsame Daily News page at: www.montsame.mn. The Email Daily News (for US$10 per month) provides excellent coverage of local affairs, contact: ganbold@magicnet.mn
Ulaanbaatar has three English-language weekly papers, available on many newsstands and the Post Office: *The Mongol Messenger* (PO Box 1514, Ulaanbaatar, www.mongolnet.mn/mglmsg/index). *The UB Post* (Ikh Toiruu 20, Ulaanbaatar, www.theubpost.mn) and *Mongolia This Week* (www.mongoliathisweek.mn)

# Internet Sites

The **Mongolian Tourism Association** (www.travelmongolia.org) operates a site with travel, hotel and tour operator information. The **Free University of Berlin** (http://userpage.fu-berlin.de/~corff/infomong.html) provides a collection of articles, maps, and legal documents on Mongolia. Also useful is the **United Nations Mongolia page** (www.un-mongolia.mn), which includes in-depth articles written by local journalists. **Mongolia Today** (www.mongoliatoday.com) is a well-made on-line magazine touching on current events and culture. **Rural Business News** (www.rbn.mn) offers substantial business tips for Gobi nomads. For good links, try the **Virtual Library** (www.indiana.edu/~mongsoc). Virtual travelers will want to visit **Roger Gruys'** quirky page at www.bluepeak.net. Other sites to try for weather and practical information include www.mongoliaguide.com and www.ulaanbaatar.net.

# Maps

Maps in Cyrillic and English are widely available in Ulaanbaatar. The 'Tourist Map of Mongolia' features Mongolia (1:2,500,000) on one side and Ulaanbaatar (1:10,000) on the other. Also good is the 'Road Map of Mongolia' (1:2,500,000), which offers kilometres between cities and towns.
Maps of each aimag (1:1,000,000), and more expensive topographical maps (1:500,000), are also available. Both are useful if you are using a GPS. Check hotel and museum gift shops, the first floor of the State Department Store, or the Map Shop (on the Big Ring Road, south of Gandan Monastery). China maps, available in western countries, often include Mongolia. Try the Periplus China map (1:8,000,000) or Cartographia China map (1:6,000,000).

# Glossary

| | |
|---|---|
| u | ou as in 'source' |
| ü | ew as in 'new' |
| ö | o as in 'money' |
| o | o as in 'knot, jot' |
| e | as in 'let, get' |
| aa | a as in 'jar' |
| ee | ei as in 'reign, feign' |
| ii | ee as in 'teem' |
| oo | o as in 'born' |
| öö | o as in 'blown, alone' |
| üü | oo as in 'moon' |
| ai | a-i, as in 'dive, I' |
| ei | ay as in 'say' |
| iu | 'you' |
| oi | oy as in 'toy' |
| z | dz |
| kh | like a Scottish 'ch', as in 'loch' |

VARIOUS EXPRESSIONS

| | |
|---|---|
| I do not understand: | *Bi oil(g)okhgui* |
| It is not possible: | *Bolokhgui* |
| It is possible: | *Bolno* |
| Thank you: | *Bairl(a)la* |
| Not at all ('no problem!'): | *Zügeer* |
| Goodbye: | *Bairte* |
| What is this?: | *En iu ve?* |
| Good/bad: | *Sain/muu* |
| Excuse me: | *Uuchlare* |
| How much does it cost?: | *Iiamar ünte?* |
| What does this word mean?: | |
| *Iu gesen ük ve?* | |
| I do not know: | *Medekhgui* |
| I do not know any Mongolian: | |
| *Mongol khel medekhgui* | |
| There is none/ he is not here: | *Baikhgui* |
| There is some: | *Baina* |
| Large/small: | *Ikh/bag* |
| To your health!: | *Erüül mend* |
| It is delicious: | *Ikh amt-te bain* |

GREETINGS

| | |
|---|---|
| Hello (singular form): | *Sain Bain uu?* (are you well?) |
| (plural form): | *Sain baitsgaan uu?* |
| I am fine, how are you?: | *Sain, sain bain uu?* |
| What's the news?: | *Sonin saikhan yute bain?* |
| Not much, I am fine (in peace): | *Iumgui, taivan saikhan* |
| How is your health?: | *Tani bie sain uu?* |
| Have a good trip, good journey: | *Sain iavare!* (or) *Ayan zamda sain iavare!* |
| *Note: When taking leave from people and they wish you a good trip, one should answer:* | *Sain suuj baigarai (keep well!)* |
| *Greetings in the steppe tend to have a seasonal character; in summer, one would say:* | |
| Are you spending the summer well?: | *Saikhan zusalj bain uu?* |
| Are the cattle fattening well?: | *Ükher mal targalj bain uu?* |
| Are you watching the sheep well?: | *Khon sain khariulj yavn uu?* |

I'm not hungry any
more/I've had enough: *Bi tsatsan/bolloo*
I can't eat that: *Bi enig iddeggui*

AROUND TOWN
Post office: *shuudan*
Shop: *delgüür*
Hotel: *zochid buudal*
Hospital: *emnelgiin gazar*
Toilets: *joorlon*, or *bie*
Monastery: *süm or khiid*

TRAVELLING
Road, track: *zam, khar zam*
(metalled)
Straight ahead: *chigere*
Right: *baruun tishe*
Left: *zuun tishe*
Stop!: *zogs!*
I'm getting down: *buna or boui*
Far: *khol*
Near: *oirkhon*
Airport: *nisekh ongotsni buudal*
Airplane: *(nisekh) ongot*
I need help:
*nadad tuslamj kheregte bain*
I need a doctor: *nadad emch kheregte*
The car is stuck: *mashin suusan*
There is no more petrol: *benzin duusan*
There is no electricity: *toog baikhgui*
Prolong a visa: *viz sungulakh*
Permit, authorisation: *zövshööröl*
Fine: *torguul*

TIME
Today: *önödöör*
Tomorrow: *margash*
Yesterday: *öchigdör*
Now: *odoo*

QUESTIONS
Why?: *yaagad*
When?: *kheze*
Where? (no movement): *khan*
Where? (with movement): *khashaa?*

HOTEL/ MONEY/ RESTAURANT
Money changer: *valiut solikh tovchoo*
Single room: *neg khüni ööröö*
Double room: *khoir khüni ööröö*
How much is a room for one night?:
*Neg khonogt ööröö iamar ünte ve?*
Key: *tülkhür*
Local restaurant: *guanz*
Cafe: *cafe*
Large/upscale restaurant: *restauran*
The bill: *totsoo*
Money, change: *zadge möngk*

COUNTRYSIDE
Mountain: *uul*
Mountain range: *nuuru*
Lake: *nuur*
River: *gol*
Col: *dawaa*
Sand: *els*
It's raining: *boroo orj bain*
Is it going to rain?: *boroo orokh uu?*
Horse: *mor'*
Saddle: *emeel*

If you want to try riding, ask for a:
calm horse: *nomkhon mor'*
European-style saddle:
*tsergiin emeel* (military saddle)

NUMBERS
1: *neg*
2: *khoir*
3: *guruv*

| | |
|---|---|
| 4: | döröv |
| 5: | tav |
| 6: | zurga |
| 7: | doloo |
| 8: | naim |
| 9: | yeus |
| 10: | aruv |
| 11: | arvan neg |
| 12: | arvan khoyor |
| 20: | khorin |
| 21: | khorin neg |
| 30: | gooch |
| 31: | goochin neg |
| 40: | dooch |
| 50: | taiv |
| 60: | jar |
| 70: | dal |
| 80: | nai |
| 90: | yir |
| 100: | zuu |
| 101: | zuu neg |
| 111: | zuu arvan neg |
| 200: | khoyor zuu |
| 1000: | miang |
| 2000: | khoyor miang |
| one million: | sai |

DAYS OF THE WEEK

In general, to designate the days of the week from Monday to Friday, the Mongols say the 'first day', 'second day', etc. Saturday is the 'half-good day', and Sunday the 'completely good day'. (Until the late 1990s the work week included a half day on Saturday)

| | |
|---|---|
| Monday: | neg dekh ödör, |
| shortened to: | negdkhödör |
| Tuesday: | khoirdkhödör |
| Wednesday: | guruvdkhödör |
| Thursday: | dörövdkhödör |
| Friday: | tavdkhödör |
| Saturday: | khagas sain ödör |
| Sunday: | buten sain ödör |

FOOD AND DRINK

| | |
|---|---|
| Hot water: | khaluun üs |
| Cold water: | khuiten üs |
| Boiled water: | butsalsan üs |
| Tea: | tsai |
| Mongolian tea (salted, with milk): | sütai tsai |
| Black tea: | khar tsai |
| Fermented mare's milk: | airag |
| Alcohol: | arkhi |
| Vodka: | tsagaan arkhi |
| Cow's milk alcohol: | shimin arkhi |
| Milk: | süü |
| Fizzy drinks: | undaa |
| Wine: | dars |
| Mineral water: | borjon |
| Beer: | piv |
| Salt : | davs |
| Brochette: | shorlog |
| Soup: | shöl |
| Yoghurt: | tarag |
| Vegetables: | nogoo |
| Tomatoes: | ulaan lol |
| Cabbage: | baitsaa |
| Onions: | songin |
| Vegetable soup: | nogoote shöl |
| Meat soup: | makhte shöl |
| Meal: | khol |
| Meat: | makh |
| Vegetable dish: | nogoote khol |
| Meat dish: | makhte khol |
| Egg: | öndög |
| mutton: | khoini makh |
| Beef: | ükhrin makh |
| Chicken: | takhiani makh |

Marmot meat: *tarvagni makh*
Pork: *gakhain makh*
Meat-filled dumplings: *buuz*
Meat pasties: *khuushuur*
Sugar: *elsen chikhe*
Sweets: *chikher*
Rice: *tsagaan buuda*
Potatoes: *tomis*
Bread: *talkh*

A FEW MONGOLIAN SPECIALITIES
**Shimin arkhi** (or *zaal'te üs* 'clever water'):
an alcohol made from fermented cow's
milk and distilled several times.

MILK PRODUCTS
*Ööröm*: a cream of boiled milk; the
boiled milk is stirred with a ladle until a
thick skin forms on it, which is removed,
cooled and dried. It can be kept through
the winter.
**Shar tos**: 'yellow butter', produced
from melted *ööröm* and used for
making cakes and biscuits.
**Aaruul**: curds that are dried in the sun.
**Arts**: sour soft white cheese.

MEAT-BASED PRODUCTS
**Buuz**: large dumplings filled with
mutton and bits of onion.

**Baansh**: small mutton dumplings
cooked in stock.
**Boodog**: a Mongolian speciality made
from goat or marmot. Preparation starts
by pulling the innards out from the neck,
after which, various spices, vegetables,
and white-hot stones are stuffed into the
cavity. The neck is sewn up and the
carcass is placed on an open fire to cook
for several hours. When the meat is fully
cooked, the animal is carved open and
the hot rocks removed. Each guest is
obliged to juggle one of the rocks
between their hands, an activity said to
be good for your health. The entrails of
the animal are cleaned, stuffed with fat
and blood, and seasoned with garlic, salt,
onions, and other spices before being
boiled and eaten as a form of black
pudding.
**Khorkhog**: another classic Mongolian
cooking method, this involves placing
strips of meat, vegetables, spices, water
and hot rocks inside a large metal
canister. While the hot rocks and water
steam the contents from the inside, the
sealed metal jug is placed over an open
fire.

# INDEX

Compiled by Don Brech
Records Management International Ltd.

Claire Sermier studied philosophy at the Sorbonne in Paris and taught briefly in Central Africa. She has travelled widely in South America, and from 1981 to 1984 was given a research grant to work in Mongolia. She has been working for several years as a tourist guide throughout the world, and more specifically in Mongolia.

Etienne Dehau has published many articles on Asia and Latin America, and has been travelling to Mongolia for fifteen years as a photographer and tourist guide. In 1994, he published *Terre mongole*, and in 2000 *Mongolie, la Vallée du Grand Ciel*, in collaboration with Claire Sermier.

Helen Loveday has a BA in Chinese and a PhD in Chinese archaeology from Oxford University. She has contributed to several Odyssey projects, including the authoring of the guide to Iran.

Michael Kohn studied literature at UC Santa Barbara and spent three years working as the English editor of *the Mongol Messenger*. He has freelanced for a variety of media organisations including the Associated Press, *South China Morning Post*, Rough Guides and BBC radio.

The publishers thank the following people for their contributions to this book. First and foremost: Claire Sermier and Etienne Dehau for their original material. The staff at *the Mongol Messenger*, Graham Taylor at Karakorum Expeditions, Ts. Tsendsuren, B. Baigalmaa and B. Baagii, for important research in Ulaanbaatar. N. Bat-Erdene provided the illustrations and Tom Le Bas put the maps together. Au Yeung Chui Kwai created the cover. Michael Coe, Mark Norell and Mick Ellison provided material for the special topics. Helen Northey and Don Brech provided proofing and indexing assistance. Credit is also due to the many Russian and Mongolian researchers and archaeologists, who spent years studying the historical sites mentioned within.

This first edition Odyssey guide was originally published in French by Guides Olizane. While every effort has been made to provide new information, rapid changes in Mongolia mean that some details will be out of date by the time of publishing. We encourage our readers to provide feedback to be included in our second edition. Please write to:

Airphoto International Ltd, 1401 Chung Ying Building
20-20A Connaught Road West, Sheung Wan, Hong Kong
Email: odysseyb@netvigator.com

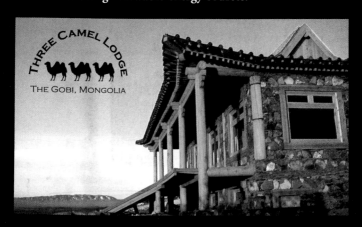

THE ASSOCIATION
OF INDEPENDENT
TOUR OPERATORS

R

*Holi*

**Contac**

e

ailway

dia

l itinerary

6

co.uk

Speciali
and sma
all the c
and Irar
Georgia

S t

a st

es East Limited
Street, Cirencester
tershire GL7 1QD
ne: 01285 651010
Fax: 01285 885888
steppeseast.co.uk
www.steppeseast.co.uk